Strategic Curriculum Change

The curriculum is a live issue in universities across the world. Many stakeholders – governments, employers, professional and disciplinary groups and parents – express strong and often conflicting views about what higher education should achieve for its students.

Many universities are reviewing their curricula at an institutional level, aware that they are in a competitive climate in which league tables encourage students to see themselves as consumers and the university as a product, or even a 'brand'. The move has prompted renewed concern for some central educational questions, about both what is learnt and how.

Strategic Curriculum Change explores the ways in which major universities across the world are reviewing their approaches to teaching and learning. It unites institution-level strategy with the underlying educational issues. The book is grounded in a major study of curriculum change in over twenty internationally focused, research-intensive universities in the UK, US, Australia, The Netherlands, South Africa and Hong Kong. Chapters include:

- Achieving curriculum coherence: curriculum design and delivery as social practice
- Assessment in curriculum change
- The whole-of-institution curriculum renewal undertaken by the University of Melbourne, 2005–2011
- The physical and virtual environment for learning
- People and change: academic work and leadership

This book presents a theorised and contextualised approach to the study of the curriculum, and carries on much-needed research on the curriculum in higher education. It is an essential for the collection of all academics at university level, and those involved in policy making, quality assurance and enhancement.

Professor Paul Blackmore is Professor of Higher Education and Director of King's Learning Institute, King's College London, UK.

Dr Camille B. Kandiko is Research Fellow at The King's Learning Institute, King's College London, UK.

The Society for Research into Higher Education (SRHE) is an independent and financially self-supporting international learned Society. It is concerned to advance understanding of higher education, especially through the insights, perspectives and knowledge offered by systematic research and scholarship.

The Society's primary role is to improve the quality of higher education through facilitating knowledge exchange, discourse and publication of research. SRHE members are worldwide and the Society is an NGO in operational relations with UNESCO.

The Society has a wide set of aims and objectives. Amongst its many activities the Society:

● is a specialist publisher of higher education research, journals and books, amongst them Studies in Higher Education, Higher Education Quarterly, Research into Higher Education Abstracts and a long running monograph book series.

The Society also publishes a number of in-house guides and produces a specialist series "Issues in Postgraduate Education".

● funds and supports a large number of special interest networks for researchers and practitioners working in higher education from every discipline. These networks are open to all and offer a range of topical seminars, workshops and other events throughout the year ensuring the Society is in touch with all current research knowledge.

● runs the largest annual UK-based higher education research conference and parallel conference for postgraduate and newer researchers. This is attended by researchers from over 35 countries and showcases current research across every aspect of higher education.

SRHE

Society for Research into Higher Education
Advancing knowledge Informing policy Enhancing practice

73 Collier Street
London N1 9BE
United Kingdom

T   +44 (0)20 7427 2350
F   +44 (0)20 7278 1135
E   srheoffice@srhe.ac.uk

www.srhe.ac.uk

Director: Helen Perkins
Registered Charity No.313850
Company No. 00868820
Limited by Guarantee
Registered office as above

Society for Research into Higher Education (SRHE) series

Series Editors: Lynn McAlpine, Oxford Learning Institute
Jeroen Huisman, University of Bath

Published titles:
Intellectual Leadership in Higher Education: Renewing the role of the university professor
Bruce Macfarlane

Forthcoming titles:
Everything for Sale? The Marketisation of UK Higher Education
Roger Brown

Reconstructing Identities in Higher Education: The Rise of 'Third Space' Professionals
Celia Whitchurch

The University in Dissent: Scholarship in the Corporate University
Gary Rolfe

Strategic Curriculum Change

Global trends in universities

Paul Blackmore and Camille B. Kandiko

Routledge
Taylor & Francis Group

LONDON AND NEW YORK

First published 2012
by Routledge
2 Park Square, Milton Park, Abingdon, Oxon OX14 4RN

Simultaneously published in the USA and Canada
by Routledge
711 Third Avenue, New York, NY 10017 together with the Society for
Research into Higher Education (SRHE)
73 Collier Street
London, N1 9BE
UK

Routledge is an imprint of the Taylor & Francis Group, an informa business

British Library Cataloguing in Publication Data
A catalogue record for this book is available from the British Library

Library of Congress Cataloging in Publication Data
Blackmore, Paul, 1954-
Strategic curriculum change : global trends in universities / edited by Paul Blackmore and
Camille Kandiko.
p. cm. – (Research into higher education)
1. Education, Higher – Curricula – Cross-cultural studies. 2. Curriculum planning – Cross-cultural
studies. I. Kandiko, Camille. II. Title.
LB2361.S8195 2012
378.1'99–dc23
2011052742

ISBN: 978–0–415–80932–0 (hbk)
ISBN: 978–0–415–80934–4 (pbk)
ISBN: 978–0–203–11162–8 (ebk)

Typeset in Galliard
by Swales & Willis Ltd, Exeter, Devon

Printed and bound in the United States of America
by Edwards Brothers Malloy

Contents

Contributors

Katherine Bergeron is Dean of the College and Professor of Music at Brown University, USA

Paul Blackmore is Director of the King's Learning Institute at King's College London, UK

Richard James is Chair of Higher Education, Pro-Vice-Chancellor (Participation and Engagement) and Director of the Centre for the Study of Higher Education at the the University of Melbourne, Australia

Camille B. Kandiko is Research Fellow at the King's Learning Institute at King's College London, UK

Peter McPhee is Professorial Fellow of the University, Emeritus Centre for the Study of Higher Education at The University of Melbourne, Australia

Emma Medland is Lecturer in Higher Education at the King's Learning Institute, King's College London, UK

Ian Scott is Deputy Dean and Professor and Director of Academic Development at the Centre for Higher Education Development, University of Cape Town, South Africa

Amy B. M. Tsui is Pro-Vice-Chancellor and Vice-President (Teaching and Learning) and Chair Professor (Chair of Language and Education) at The University of Hong Kong, China

Saranne Weller is Assistant Director of King's Learning Institute and Senior Lecturer in Higher Education at King's Learning Institute, King's College London, UK

Series editors' introduction

This series, co-published by the Society for Research into Higher Education and Routledge Books, aims to provide, in an accessible manner, cutting-edge scholarly thinking and inquiry that reflects the rapidly changing world of higher education, examined in a global context.

Encompassing topics of wide international relevance, the series includes every aspect of the international higher education research agenda, from strategic policy formulation and impact to pragmatic advice on best practice in the field. Each book in the series aims to meet at least one of the principal aims of the Society: to advance knowledge; to enhance practice; to inform policy.

Curriculum and curriculum change are highly contested and sensitive topics. Paul Blackmore's and Camille Kandiko's book examines how research-intensive institutions undertake curriculum change. They view curriculum change as including the unstructured and spontaneous learning that takes place within and outside the formal environment. Thus, they use network theory as a theoretical framework, arguing that successful curriculum change requires an organisational perspective attending to how universities function and are structured.

Lynn McAlpine
Jeroen Huisman

Preface

Our work on strategic curriculum change springs from a wish to see how research-intensive, internationally focused universities are responding to the changing environment for higher education. We were aware that a number of institutions had decided to look carefully at what they were offering their students and that, in some cases, really quite major changes were being made. Parallel discussions on curriculum review have been taking place worldwide, often covering similar ground. Discussions included fundamental ideas about higher education, but they were also grounded in the practicalities of delivering a curriculum in a real institution, with inevitable staffing and resource constraints. It seemed to us that there was a huge amount to be learnt from the experiences of the various institutions; we wanted to write not only about the idea of curriculum, but how it actually happens in real universities and how those institutions have set about making changes. This book draws on several years of research and other activity in the higher education curriculum field and, in particular, on a major project.

In 2009, King's College London (KCL) began an initiative to explore curriculum distinctiveness in research-intensive institutions. Collaborating with the University of Warwick, King's Learning Institute at KCL led on a Higher Education Funding Council for England (HEFCE)-funded project on curriculum reform, titled The King's-Warwick Project (KWP). This included background research, a web-based global survey of institutions engaging in curriculum reform, and international site visits to over twenty institutions in five countries. Institutions visited included Utrecht University, Maastricht University, University of Cape Town, University of the Witwatersrand, Stellenbosch University, University of Chicago, University of Wisconsin-Madison, Harvard University, Brown University, University of Pennsylvania, Temple University, University of Melbourne, University of Sydney, University of Western Australia, University of Hong Kong, Chinese University of Hong Kong, Hong Kong University of Science and Technology, University of Aberdeen, University of Southampton, The London School of Economics and Political Science, Imperial College and University of Manchester.

Many members of King's College and the University of Warwick were involved in review discussions, in a number of capacities. Working groups met on each of the five major curriculum characteristic themes: Research-Rich Environments;

Academic Literacy; Interdisciplinarity; Global Connectedness; and Community Engagement. There were also additional working groups on Graduate Attributes and Employability; Assessment; Leadership Development and Support Services. Details of these groups' membership and findings can be found in the project reports. A brief report and the full project report are available for download at http://www.kcl.ac.uk/study/learningteaching/kwp.aspx

Following the report, work continued in two main areas. Both KCL and Warwick have used findings and recommendations from the report to review and assess their curriculum, and propose changes to enhance the student experience in each institution. There has also been continued academic research on curriculum change, resulting in a number of publications, including this volume.

Strategic Curriculum Change: Global Trends in Universities draws on the findings of the King's Warwick Project, the global site visits, and the authors' own research in teaching, learning and higher education. Leads on working groups for the KWP were asked if they were interested in further contribution, and were fortunate to receive chapters from two area experts in this volume, with Saranne Weller writing on social practices and notions of transformation in the curriculum and Emma Medland writing about assessment.

Further contributions in the volume include four international case studies of institutions leading on different aspects of curricular reform. These chapters, all by senior institutional leaders and academics, provide unique insight into the 'lived experience' of curriculum reform in diverse settings. We have case studies from: Katherine Bergeron at Brown University; Amy Tsui at the University of Hong Kong; Richard James and Peter McPhee at the University of Melbourne and Ian Scott at the University of Cape Town.

The authors are very grateful for all of the contributions to the KWP, the final report, and continued curriculum research. We hope this volume presents a theorised and contextualised approach to the study of the curriculum, and carries on much-needed research on the curriculum in higher education.

Part I

Curriculum coherence

Knowledge, relationships and networks

Chapter 1

The networked curriculum

Camille B. Kandiko and Paul Blackmore

Research-intensive universities around the world are reviewing what and how they teach. The curriculum, a long neglected field in higher education, has become a live area for debate. This book reflects the new focus on curriculum and also on curriculum change in universities. We explore how institutions have used curriculum changes strategically to achieve their institutional goals and aims. Although we take a very broad view of curricula, we have focused on how research-intensive institutions use the curriculum to provide a distinctive experience for their students. In this context, the curriculum can become central to all of the work of the university, linking researchers, academics and students and their mutual learning and development.

The curriculum has been defined 'as a set of purposeful, intended experiences' (Knight 2001: 369), focusing attention on what is formally taught. However, like many others, we view the curriculum more broadly, and include the unstructured and spontaneous learning that takes place within and outside the formal academic environment. The curriculum offers a useful lens to view higher education, and sharpens the focus on students and their education, notions that are often lost in the study of universities. The curriculum has received surprisingly little attention in research on higher education. It has not traditionally featured much in literature in Europe (Squires 1987) and in the UK (Barnett and Coate 2005) and still faces definitional issues in the US (Lattuca and Stark 2009). The curriculum continues to be conceptualised in various and often conflicting ways, in different contexts and across a range of disciplinary and epistemological domains (Fraser and Bosanquet 2006).

In this chapter we first briefly review some of the major international trends in higher education that set the context for curriculum review, situating the discussion in current forces acting upon higher education and how these changes play out. Then we outline a number of ways of studying the curriculum. Following this we consider the ways in which universities are organised to deliver and support the curriculum, drawing out how network forms of organisation can facilitate change in institutions. Using network theory as a theoretical framework, we advocate a social practice approach to understanding curriculum change. This leads to a discussion of the methodology of the book. The chapter concludes with an overview of the chapters and case studies in the book.

The context for curriculum review

While we focus in this book on university-wide curriculum change, we bear in mind that there are several levels at which higher education can be viewed. Many universities are global enterprises, with research-intensive institutions competing across borders for staff, students, research funding and prestige. All universities are, to some extent, part of a national system. However, national-level discussions about what the curriculum should achieve and the attributes graduates should attain often appear abstract and idealised, and far removed from organisational and institutional realities. Regional and reputational groupings provide another organisational layer. Changes at any one of these levels have consequences across systems, often beyond those that are intended. However, reform at a variety of levels can provide an opportunity to review the organisation of institutions that have evolved as organic systems, and for the goals of the curriculum to be made explicit and linked with the broader mission and practices of the institution. It can also be a time to analyse the relationships between sectors and institutions.

As higher education becomes an increasingly global activity, curriculum changes are now happening throughout the world, but the effect on higher education systems, academic staff and students varies immensely. The advent of mass higher education in many countries means that a small-scale, *laissez faire* approach to curriculum provision has in many places given way to the more systematic support of much larger numbers of students (Trow 1974, 2000). Overseas students are recruited with enthusiasm, particularly in countries where there is considerable incentive to attract high-fee entrants, such as in the US and Australia, and until recently, the UK. As other European countries teach increasingly in English, including at an undergraduate level, and states such as Qatar, Singapore and Hong Kong invest to become regional hubs, competition for overseas students is becoming more intense. A consequence of the increased international flow of students is that many staff teach significant numbers of overseas students, with some programmes enrolling more overseas than home students. This raises complex questions around the world about how curricula can respond to increased demands and increased diversity, often in the face of declining state-funded resources, themes discussed throughout the book.

Throughout society globalisation is leading both to convergence, with many social and cultural practices becoming more alike, and to divergence, with localised responses to global changes (Vaira 2004). In curricula, we can see a great deal of the former, as universities across the world adopt similar curriculum processes; at the same time, some curricula are becoming more diverse, as distinctive approaches are taken in response to local conditions and needs. Globally and supra-nationally there are trends towards standardisation through structural reforms, including the adoption of modular provision and credit systems (Mason *et al.* 2001). The Bologna

Process is one example of a 'unified system that facilitates mobility, transparency and recognition of qualification' (Karseth 2006:255). Such changes lead to the standardisation of educational structures, processes and outcomes. This can be contrasted with competition at global, national and regional levels driving institutions to specialise and show distinctiveness, often through unique curricular offerings. This can result in greater institutional differentiation, that has either evolved, as in the US, or been created through government policy to encourage competition, as has happened recently in the UK. Some trends are both convergent and divergent, such as when initiatives promoting more flexibility in the curriculum and increased student choice are tightly bound by university requirements.

Despite forces of convergence, higher education has always had multiple purposes. Functions of the university broadly include providing a general education for all students; the education of specialists (in disciplinary and professional fields); the education of researchers; and the education of educators, the disciplinary and professional experts who provide the knowledge for the aforementioned functions (Short 2002). Universities also process information, creating, teaching, disseminating, storing and accrediting it (Gumport 2000; van Alstyne 1998). Globally there has been a shift in universities from an internal orientation, including the development of future academics and research for the academic community, towards an increasingly external orientation. This focus on public and private 'impact' has thoroughly permeated higher education. For example, increased cooperation and cross-fertilisation across disciplines has led to innovations in solving societal problems and longer-term developments in fundamental ways of understanding (Hansson 1999). The applied and interdisciplinary nature of such activity can potentially have a dramatic impact upon the curriculum. However, this is not yet the norm in research-intensive institutions, where traditional, department-based structures for teaching and learning activities remain strong, especially at the undergraduate level.

In a number of countries there is a developing trend towards privatisation of government and state-wide public systems of higher education, and consequent increased student fees and tuition (Lyall 2011). It has been argued that the role of higher education is shifting from that of a social institution to an industry, with consequential developments in academic managerialism, academic consumerism and academic stratification (Gumport 2000). Examples include the increased business ethos of universities, discourses of 'students as customers' and the prioritising of science and mathematics fields at the expense of social sciences and humanities. The greater economic focus on higher education and the more business-like approach in universities are reflected in policy discourses around the world that are dominated by issues of access and completion. In many countries the principal focus is on getting students into and out of higher education, with less attention being paid to what happens in the 'black box' of the curriculum. Such trends are also reflected in curriculum changes, with many institutions requiring business plans for new courses, including market research and enrolment targets.

The discourse of 'student choice' emphasises that higher education is increasingly seen as a market, reflected in greater competition within and across departments, schools, universities and sectors beyond. Certainly the metaphor of the student as customer has gained in strength. In the UK, national league tables repeatedly draw attention to the success or otherwise of universities in providing an efficient service to their students, one that is frequently measured by students' own views. Rankings now drive many institutional decisions in the US, Asia, Australia and elsewhere. This shift has major consequences for academic work. More demanding fee-paying students challenge the dominance of research, even in research-intensive institutions. The provision of a uniformly high standard of student experience is bound to test the relatively informal ways of working that many academic staff retain. As service provision becomes more complex, increasing numbers of curriculum-related tasks that were previously seen to be the responsibility of academic staff are performed by professional support staff.

In addition to institutional structures becoming more commodified, there is a parallel trend towards some forms of knowledge being valued more highly than others, with a premium on entrepreneurial and 'useful' knowledge (Clark 1998; Kerr 2001). Universities have increasingly assumed a responsibility for promoting economic growth, especially by providing 'job-ready' graduates. Employability of graduates is a central government priority in many countries, and many curricular initiatives seek to make students more employable by helping them to develop and evidence a range of skills. Some staff in universities question whether employability should be a concern of universities, because they believe either that universities exist for the disinterested pursuit of knowledge or that, in successful universities, graduates are likely to be highly employable anyway. Proposals for curriculum change have to contend with perceptions that change is driven by an ideology that is in tension with many faculty members' sense of their own professional identity.

At the same time as teaching and learning have increased in importance as academic activities, research demands are also growing. In many countries research is more selective and funding increasingly hard to obtain. When academic standing, recognition and reward are principally based on research achievement, as is usually the case in research-intensive institutions, there may be little incentive for staff to engage in teaching and learning beyond the required minimum. This does little to help the cause of curriculum change. However, the presence of research, both in terms of outcomes and of the skills of researchers, can provide excellent support for the development of research-intensive curricula.

The curriculum

The curriculum and curriculum change are highly contested and sensitive topics. The curriculum functions as 'a locus and transmitter of values' (Rudolph 1977: 3) within an institution and across higher education systems. Control of the curriculum is a source of power in universities and has vast financial implications.

Curriculum innovation often attempts integration of both people and subjects in universities where staff highly value autonomy. All of these aspects also present complex challenges for studying and researching the curriculum.

It has been suggested that the curriculum can be viewed through four lenses (Bernstein 1975, 2000). The planned or intended curriculum features in course documentation. The created or delivered curriculum reflects the planned curriculum translated into practice. The received or understood curriculum refers to the intended learning experience and the way it is understood by students. The hidden or tacit curriculum contains those parts that are not formally a part of the curriculum, but that are nevertheless conveyed through educational content and processes and by the organisational culture. Often the first two receive most of the attention, with very little acknowledgement or analysis of the last category. This highlights the complexity of the curriculum, and its dynamic nature.

Discussions of curriculum often deal with educational goals, aims and values on one side and the practical concerns of managing provision on the other, with little connection between them. The study of curriculum traditionally covers four areas: subject content, the 'what' of curriculum; process (or organisation); pedagogy, encompassing methods of teaching and learning; and assessment. A fifth area, namely learning outcomes (often expressed as graduate attributes or skills), has emerged in both policy and academic spheres in recent years.

Content is often the most visible aspect for students, the control of which is frequently devolved to individual academics, who sometimes receive little or no training in curriculum design and planning. Notions of content are often synonymous with curriculum structure at the unit (module) or programme level. Content, the essential 'what' in learning, is often taken for granted and is sometimes not considered in policy discourses that focus on the 'who' and 'how' of curriculum (Maton 2009). Yet it can drive the curriculum, as can be seen when content-based courses constitute the curriculum structure and teaching staff are allocated to teach modules that do not reflect their expertise or interest.

There are continuing debates about the relative merits of theory-based academic or disciplinary knowledge in contrast to practical or mission-oriented knowledge (Short 2002). The latter is often found in more professionally oriented subjects, such as Engineering and Law. The organisation of content varies dramatically in these two orientations, and this difference is a key inhibitor of university-wide curriculum change, as the inherent tension is played out by staff who may take strong positions on what they value. There is a developing critical literature around the curriculum that analyses 'our understanding of how and why certain kinds of knowledge and knower identities become privileged' (Shay 2011:327) and the individual and societal repercussions of this privilege, which are highlighted throughout the case studies in the book. This provokes questions about not only what is taught, but also how this affects those who are being taught. Taking a critical stance of this kind may lead to consideration of how more diverse pedagogical approaches could support the learning of larger groups of students. Such a stance contrasts with research that focuses on curricula in terms of disciplines and research areas, and which may prioritise the outward-facing entrepreneurial activities of faculty (Clark 1998) over issues of teaching and learning.

Notions of process in the curriculum are often conceptualised as encompassing the interactions of teaching and learning. However, the process varies considerably, and is highly influenced by particular teachers and learners. Reflecting this variability, the teaching profession has been characterised as 'relational, developmental, dialogic and non-replicable' (Parker 2003:535). This builds on communities of practice research, where learning is seen as largely drawn from reflections on individual practice (Wenger 1998). Such a conception of teaching and learning highlights the sharing of practice through inducting students into the models of knowledge development in the disciplines as the primary process for students accessing and understanding content. This relational view of the curriculum is further explored in Chapter 2. An advantage of focusing on process is that it offers a way in which students can be encouraged to take more responsibility for their learning. Education is situated as requiring the engagement and effort of students, rather than positioning them as passive Platonic 'empty vessels' waiting to be filled by their teachers. Thus students claim and earn an education rather than receive or, worse, buy one.

Tensions between a focus on content versus process often surface as arguments between depth and breadth. It can be argued that paying attention to learning processes enables students to learn about learning itself, and also to make connections among disciplines. However, students may find it difficult to make sense of the connections across broad sets of introductory courses. Increasingly, interdisciplinary courses are seen as a way to bridge gaps in coherence across such courses. This approach requires the integration of content from different disciplines in a structured format. Process-focused models of curriculum development support students by combining the organisation of content with pedagogical practices, which focus on scaffolding the curriculum at the beginning and slowly, but deliberately, removing the support structure over time (Knight 2001).

In the sciences, new and inherently interdisciplinary fields such as Bioinformatics have grown significantly. Indeed many of the most active areas for research transcend traditional disciplinary boundaries. There has been a broadening of social sciences and humanities disciplines to be more inclusive of newer fields of study, embracing Women's Studies, gender and inequality studies and area and cultural studies. Such efforts have not merely 'patched' knowledge onto existing knowledge fields, but asserted that they could offer new perspectives on knowledge, as in the case of Women's Studies, which 'rests on the premise that knowledge in the traditional academic disciplines is partial, incomplete, and distorted because it has excluded women' (Andersen 1987:224). The integration of such disciplinary shifts into larger university curriculum change projects has been continuing for more than thirty years (Howe 1984). The content-based debates and changes of the 1980s have shifted to more organisationally based changes, with current trends towards more interdisciplinary study, first-year initiatives and final-year capstone integrative projects.

Interdisciplinarity has been more common in the US, in part because of the use of general education requirements in the major and minor system, contrasting with the more 'purist' disciplinary approach taken by most institutions in the UK and traditionally in several Commonwealth countries. There are a developing number of programmes where students can build their own degree, focusing on a particular theme, such as sustainability, and bringing together the necessary disciplinary approaches required for the project. Globally, the greatest changes are in Medicine and the health sciences and a great deal of literature focuses on innovative change within these curricula; however, this trend has not been as widely adopted beyond these fields.

A curriculum can be viewed as a 'recipe', as one of many ways that knowledge can be organised, structured and made meaningful by students. The curriculum is the result of a continual interaction between the 'product' of learning, such as students' knowledge development, skills and attributes, and the 'process' of learning through reflection and related pedagogical practices. The curriculum can also be seen as a social construction and as a site for socio-political and cultural decision-making processes (Karseth 2006), as a consequence of which the curriculum is in constant contestation, development and reform.

We argue here for a process-oriented curriculum that positions learning as developmental and transformational, rather than always working towards pre-specified goals. A student-centred, transformational curriculum encourages learners to develop cycles of engagement and critical reflection (Parker 2003). In many countries there is a strong trend towards education that is focused on skills and outcomes, with the aim of satisfying external stakeholders, such as governments, business and industry. Governments seeking an economic return from their investment in universities often focus on training and skills development. Curriculum change is a product of these interrelated changes and can only be understood by reference to them, as can the changing nature of academic work, the roles of staff and students, and the purposes and products of universities.

The questions of who the curriculum is for, what should be taught, by whom, and how, are related to societal forces affecting higher education that are broadening the range of forms of knowledge with which the university deals, and extending its purpose. Such an approach profoundly affects the research, teaching, outreach and service missions of an institution. This is all embodied in the organisation of the institution. The next section explores how university structures and processes can be strategically aligned, leading to a discussion of how conceptualising universities as networks can create an environment that supports the aims and goals of the curriculum.

Strategic views of university organisation

Successful curriculum change requires an understanding of how universities function, how they are organised and how they are structured. Often changes take place through formal strategic planning processes. As we point out later, this has a long tradition in higher education (Keller 1983). Strategic planning can take several forms: it can be rational, using methodical approaches to develop clear goals; it can adopt natural approaches that take advantage of the current environment; or it can have an open orientation (Scott 2003). However, it could be argued that catalysts for action, such as responding to competition, differentiation or comparative advantage, have been rare in higher education, owing to a lack of a clear market (Cooke and Lang 2009). Despite decades of planning, universities may still seem to be places of 'organised anarchy' (Cohen and March 1986) or 'loosely coupled systems' (Weick 1976). Universities are very complex organisations and we argue that some of the more conventional ways of viewing organisations may be counterproductive when attempting to encourage change. We explore this further below, and then argue that taking a network view of an organisation is likely to lead to more effective curriculum change.

A strategic approach to curriculum change has to take account of two traditional perspectives on the higher education curriculum. A discipline-based view tends to be more internally focused and usually works within vertical structures containing strong departments. A vocational/professional model is more external in its orientation and often operates across disciplines and fields of study (Karseth 2006). These categorisations echo divisions noted on page 45 about theoretical and practical knowledge. However, from the early development of universities, there has always been a mixture of such approaches (Evans 2010a, b). A strategic approach works to combine the best of both theoretical and practical approaches.

Many traditional structures and other aspects of higher education are rooted in disciplinary and academic practices that have successfully evolved over many years. Drawing from a sociological perspective, Meyer *et al.* (2007) argue for viewing 'higher education as deeply affected by – indeed, something of an enactment of – structures whose nature and meaning have been institutionalized over many centuries and now apply throughout the world' (187). These traditional aspects are not necessarily improved upon by many new and 'emergent' features (Parker 2003) that may not take full account of the local context, and that may attempt to impose a change that does not fit the culture. We suggest that strategic change is by definition not change for change's sake, but one with a clear end goal in mind. Further, the means must be appropriate to the ends if it is to be genuinely strategic.

That so many institutions undertake fundamental curriculum reviews is evidence that universities are not strategically self-adjusting, because the curriculum is perceived to have fallen out of alignment with what is needed. Short (2002) argues that the gap between the rationale of curriculum plans and the actuality of curriculum goals 'lies with the assumption that the organization of the curriculum of higher education should be done in the same manner that the university organizes to do its research and knowledge production' (139). If universities are to thrive in a more complex and fast-moving environment, they may need to be able to work much more flexibly in terms of teaching and research. As Meyer *et al.* (2007) have suggested, universities need to create structures that allow for continuous processes of change at an incremental rate rather than needing regular major overhauls.

Many institutions have taken strategic approaches to change, focusing on the student experience, while not ignoring the wider environment of higher education. Universities can strategically align their unique resources, such as their institutional mission, their physical setting and through linking strong research areas. There are lessons to be learnt across institutions and countries, even though local context is an important factor (Sporn 1999). Many universities have worked strategically to create structures, processes and physical environments that encourage research and entrepreneurship (Krücken 2003), and which can also be used in curriculum restructuring. Some of the most strategic changes have been based in a view of the organisation that recognises the complex reality of higher education. We suggest that research on network forms of organisation has a great deal to offer research on curriculum change. An appreciation of how notions of networks have developed in organisational theory is therefore necessary.

Network forms of organisation

Organisations have often been categorised as either hierarchies or as markets. A hierarchical view emphasises structure, but a highly structured organisation may become rigid and slow to respond to changing conditions. A market-oriented view of the organisation stresses the need for flexibility to help it more strategically manage complexity than a hierarchical firm. Developments in principal-agent theory and transaction cost economics in the 1980s positioned these two notions at opposite ends of a continuum (Podolny and Page 1998). However, the two views did not adequately describe a number of organisational structures and features.

In 1990, Powell advanced the idea of network forms of organisation, which are typified by reciprocal patterns of communication and exchange. This notion was applied to a variety of industries, including artisanal and high-technology trades, and has since been widely adopted as a useful view of organisational structure. Network forms of organisation bridge the theoretical and the practical gap between hierarchical and market views, seeing the broader, more societal context of the organisation and viewing economic exchange as embedded in a social–structural context (Powell).

There are three primary features of network-like arrangements. First there are lateral and horizontal patterns of exchange, which are not confined within hierarchical chains of command. Second, interdependent flows of resources create trust-based relationships between actors. Finally, there are reciprocal lines of communication, not only commands from above. We argue that this approach to the analysis of organisational behaviour can provide a unique lens for studying curriculum change in universities. An advantage of this approach is that it can apply at many levels, allowing for analysis of higher education as a global enterprise, as national systems and regional groupings, and at individual institutional and within-institution levels.

Networks can exist in a variety of forms. They can be structural forms (Powell 1990), as seen in much of the biotechnology industry. They can operate as forms of governance (Podolny and Page 1998), particularly when there is loose organisation and little hierarchy. Gaining recent prominence through Facebook and Twitter, networks can also exist as socio-cultural forms of interaction (Granovetter 1995). Organisational network research has broadened to cover many areas, including social capital exchange; embeddedness, exploring how established patterns of interaction are within an organisation; network organisations; and knowledge management and social cognition (Borgatti and Foster 2003). This research is based on actors (persons, organisations, concepts) and ties (links between actors), and has been applied in business settings (Uzzi and Gillespie 2002); across communities of practice (Lave and Wenger 1991); inter-organisational learning cycles in biotechnology (Powell *et al.* 1996); and leadership (Pastor *et al.* 2002), amongst a wide variety of settings. There are also developments in how organisations function in neural network patterns (Wong *et al.* 2000), drawing on neuroscience and systems research.

Network forms of organisation in higher education

As with many organisations noted on page 11, various aspects of higher education do not fit comfortably within traditional economic theories based on hierarchies and markets. These include the role of universities in knowledge production and dissemination and the lack of a clear 'bottom line'. Markets are based on prices, and prices are 'unsuccessful at capturing the intricacies of idiosyncratic, complex, and dynamic exchange. As a result, markets are a poor device for learning and the transfer of technological know-how' (Powell 1990: 302–3). They are also based on an assumption of free, widely available information and ease of finding alternative buyers and sellers. None of the market-based features easily apply to higher education, a point which is further made by the extensive government regulation of higher education. The other view, of hierarchies with 'clear departmental boundaries, clean lines of authority, detailed reporting mechanisms, and formal decision making procedures – is particularly well-suited for mass production and distribution' (ibid. 303). However, hierarchies are poor at adapting to change and working across boundaries, both of which are essential aspects of higher education.

Network theory is relevant to many of the features of higher education, such as status hierarchies and reputational concerns, non-easily measured exchange, long-term relations and interdependent relationships (ibid.). Networks highlight the relationships between different units, shared benefits and burdens, and flexible notions of reciprocity. However, networks also have disadvantages; they can become closed over time and lead to a loss of freedom of individual entities. In higher education, this restriction is seen in exclusive university groupings, such as the Ivy League in the US, the Russell Group in the UK and the Group of Eight in Australia. Further disadvantages are seen in the challenges of creating interdisciplinary-based institutions, research centres and programmes.

Network conceptions of organisation have several features which make them particularly well-suited for exploring organisational change in higher education. It is through networking that cooperation and collaboration take place, and the building of relationships to sustain such activities over time. The flexibility that networks bring to organisations makes them adaptable to changing environments and uncertain resource provision. The open structure of networks also facilitates innovation and the sharing of tacit knowledge and expertise. Possibly most useful for higher education, networks can promote learning and the sharing of knowledge. Network forms of organisation can 'foster learning, represent a mechanism for the attainment of status or legitimacy, provide a variety of economic benefits, facilitate the management of resource dependencies, and provide considerable autonomy for employees' (Podolny and Page 1998:57). In this book we take ideas from network theory, drawing on many disciplines and decades of research, and apply it to how the curriculum functions in higher education.

The value of a networked approach has been found across many fields. Research developments in the field of dynamic network analysis, with notions of multiple networks occurring simultaneously (Carley 2003) offer further insights for higher education, including the ways in which inter- and intra-institutional networks in teaching, research and practice can enhance one another. Such networks can create 'learning nodes' centred on new programme development and the sharing of practice. Using an artificial neural network approach, Tang *et al.* (2006) found that 'scale-free' or egalitarian network structures were more effective in knowledge transfer than hierarchical networks. In academia, it is often the case that junior researchers have unique ideas to contribute, which can be lost in a complex bureaucratic hierarchy. Network paradigms are particularly useful in facilitating interdisciplinary initiatives in institutions, as they offer an organisational focus on 'relational, contextual and systemic understandings' (Borgatti and Foster 2003:991).

Network structures allow new ways to consider how to keep the benefits of disciplinary structures but take advantage of opportunities of interdisciplinary working, sharing ideas across disciplines and situating disciplines in relation to one another. For what is 'educative about the curriculum is the area of overlap, that is to say simultaneous engagement and interaction, between the domains of knowledge, activity and self' (Parker 2003:542). This promotion of the relational aspects of the curriculum, and how they can be used to enhance the student experience and the student learning environment, are explored in the following chapter. Much of the interest in interdisciplinary teaching begins with research, such as when faculty form cross-disciplinary or interdisciplinary research collaborations across the institution, which then filter down to teaching interests. Flexible administrative structures can facilitate interdisciplinary collaborations in both research and teaching.

Another way network connections can be made is through joint appointments in which faculty are appointed to two departments, fostering links between the departments and making research and teaching connections. Such initiatives provide a set of possibilities to consider in restructuring curricula to offer or require interdisciplinarity. In research-intensive institutions, research centres often form as a result of research collaborations, which are not necessarily funded by large grants. Some institutions include teaching programmes in the remit for such centres. Questions that arise regarding the policies, purposes, processes and outcomes of such interdisciplinary endeavours are detailed further on pages 76–81. Although the structures provide the opportunity for interdisciplinarity, it is academics on the ground who create innovative, contextualised and relevant interdisciplinary courses, by doing interdisciplinary work or having the time and space to develop such work and partner with colleagues.

Network forms of organisation can facilitate the transfer of legitimation and status (Podolny and Page 1998). In higher education, this can be seen in the ways in which prestige and recognition in select departments and disciplines can be shared across other fields. Interdisciplinary options often provide opportunities for students to experience areas of research excellence across an institution. This exchange can also be seen when 'new' disciplines and departments partner with traditional and established fields of study, such as Media Studies working with an English department.

Such aspects seem to resonate with traditional views of how universities operate, and particularly how academics work (Becher and Trowler 2001). They offer an alternative to strong top-down management, which may not always be effective in producing curriculum change. Therefore we believe that recognising the value of networks and working through them has a great deal to offer those involved in curriculum change. We discuss networking throughout the book in relation to the curriculum, the student experience and the management of curriculum change. The methodology of the book is described below, followed by an overview of the chapters and case studies, all drawing on aspects of network forms of organisation and change.

Methodology for the book

Rather than focusing solely on theoretical aspects of the curriculum, such as what it could or should look like or do, we explore the messy side of the curriculum by examining curriculum and curriculum change in practice. This builds on a rich tradition of social practice research. Although not developed as a formal theoretical framework, social practice has emerged from ideas and theories in philosophy, social theory, cultural theory and theory of science and technology (Postill 2010). Early theorists in the field, including Bourdieu (1977), Giddens (1979, 1984) and Foucault (1979) explored relations between structure and agency and issues of power and control. This work has been furthered by the exploration of notions of practice in specific disciplines, such as Anthropology (see Ortner 1984) and areas such as strategy research (see Jarzabkowski 2005) and in the relations of practice to broader cultural and social issues (Reckwitz 2002). Social practice research includes studies in localised, context-specific environments and also more general settings. Much current social practice theory focuses on a social philosophy of the connections and networks between and amongst individuals and the social world (Schatzki 1996, 2001). Throughout the book we take a social practices approach, analysing the curriculum and curriculum change through lived experiences.

We contextualise practice by critically reviewing the curriculum literature, concentrating on the 'how' of the curriculum: how curriculum changes are conceived, organised, implemented and how they are assessed and evaluated. We analyse how the curriculum functions at the university level, including the organisational structures of universities and consider how both structures and curricula can be made more flexible, adaptable and effective. We argue for a curriculum framework as a means of organising content and of enacting processes for sharing it as a vehicle for empowering students (Fraser and Bosanquet 2006).

Studying the curriculum requires engagement with immense amounts of 'gray literature', materials that are produced by and for university committees and working parties, which are often quite local in their concerns and are rarely formally published. These sources of information about curriculum change are varied, usually works-in-progress, often restricted-access, and may be politically sensitive. Therefore, to discover the heart of curriculum change – the intersection of the purposes of change, the forces affecting it, the intended goals and the actual outcomes – a number of universities were studied that had conducted or were currently undertaking curriculum change initiatives (King's Learning Institute [KLI] 2010). As a result of this work, we discovered a group of institutions that were leading international trends in undergraduate curriculum change. We selected a subset of these institutions for comprehensive site visits, which allowed us to have in-depth conversations about four key areas: the policies, purposes, processes and outcomes of curriculum change. We met with senior administrators, discipline-based academics, administrative staff and students involved in curriculum change. All of the institutions grappled with change issues in different ways.

Throughout the book, we often speak about examples of change generally rather than directly citing institutions. Curriculum change can be a contentious and political endeavour, and we were fortunate to have very candid conversations about change processes and have respected their sensitive nature. Our book draws on data from institutions on four continents, in six countries, and from over twenty site visits. This data was presented in a project report from the two institutions involved, King's College London and the University of Warwick (KLI 2010), referred to throughout the book as 'the report'. We have since followed up on site visits, continued research and followed developing trends in curriculum change. The book is supported by chapters from two area specialists who contributed to the report and is further enhanced by contributions from leaders of four major curriculum change initiatives around the world.

Structure of the book

The book is divided into four parts. This chapter, along with the next two, provide an introduction and the context for studying the curriculum. In Chapter 2, Saranne Weller explores curriculum notions and relationships, taking a critical view and describes ways in which the impact of commodification upon the curriculum can be resisted (Parker 2003). Chapter 3 showcases these ideas in practice, with a case study by Katherine Bergeron of curriculum review at Brown University.

After laying the foundations of how we conceptualise the curriculum, the next four chapters set out the context and consider the delivery of the curriculum in practice, drawing largely from discussions with discipline-based academics on their experiences of curriculum change. Chapter 4 covers strategic approaches to curriculum structures, features and outcomes. How this functions in practice is shown through a case study in Chapter 5 by Amy Tsui about curriculum transformation at the University of Hong Kong. Chapter 6 describes the curriculum characteristics in detail, and how these can function in network-like ways throughout an institution, connecting disciplines and departments. In Chapter 7, Emma Medland draws these notions together and focuses attention on assessment and feedback, aspects of the curriculum that most closely connect curriculum content and process with students and outcomes.

The next three chapters focus on making change happen. Chapter 8 examines how change is enabled through management and resourcing. There is often a mandate for major institutional change, which usually requires structural changes that have complex political, symbolic and financial ramifications. Developing network forms of organisation can create new opportunities and go beyond traditional institutionalised patterns and archetypes that often emerge (Vaira 2004). Chapter 9, dealing with people and change, builds on arguments for the curriculum to be central to change initiatives, while also considering a more traditional focus on leadership, management and governance procedures as levers for change (Sporn 1999). Universities are slow to change, and tend to absorb new functions into existing structures; facilitating change and creating new networks requires relationship building and trust amongst those involved (Krücken 2003). Developing trust amongst actors through networks can promote strategic partnerships across institutions and higher education sectors (Cooke and Lang 2009). Chapter 10 describes the lived experience of change in an institution, through a case study of major institutional change at the University of Melbourne by Richard James and Peter McPhee.

The final part explores how change is supported in an institution and how it is through working with individuals that institutional and wider societal goals can be achieved. Chapter 11 considers evaluation and development. Institutions do not always evaluate whether the curriculum goals of a strategic change has been achieved. Often the desired outcomes are not reflected in student assessment throughout their programme of study, despite rhetoric about the importance of assessment and evaluation for curriculum enhancement

(Johnson *et al.* 2004). Networks can support building flexible and sustainable processes for evaluation and development. Chapter 12 explores how learning is supported throughout universities. This includes examining how spaces, both physical and virtual, are used, as well as how student services support is structured. Chapter 13 broadens the discussion, drawing attention to ways in which the curriculum can have a significant impact on society. Ian Scott provides a case study from South Africa on how the curriculum can be part of institutionalised inequality, but can also be used strategically to overcome this and provide opportunities for a new generation to lead a developing nation. The final chapter draws the preceding chapters together and looks forward, discussing the possibilities for strategic curriculum change in dynamic environments, and the opportunities that viewing universities as networks could offer, allowing them to be more responsive to students, academics, external stakeholders and society.

References

Andersen, M. L. (1987) Changing the curriculum in higher education. *Signs, 12*(2): 222–254.

Barnett, R. and Coate, K. (2005). *Engaging the curriculum in higher education.* Maidenhead, England: Society for Research into Higher Education and the Open University Press.

Becher, T. and Trowler, P. R. (2001) *Academic tribes and territories: Intellectual enquiry and the culture of disciplines* (2nd ed.). Buckingham: The Society into Higher Education and the Open University Press.

Bernstein, B. (1975) *Class, codes and control (Vol. 3): Towards a theory of educational transmission.* London: Routledge and Kegan Paul.

Bernstein, B. (2000) *Pedagogy, symbolic control and identity: Theory, research and critique.* New York: Rowman and Littlefield.

Borgatti, S. P. and Foster, P. C. (2003) The network paradigm in organizational research: A review and typology. *Journal of Management, 29*: 991–1013.

Bourdieu, P. (1977) *Outline of a theory of practice.* Cambridge: Cambridge University Press.

Carley, K. M. (2003) Dynamic network analysis, in Breiger, R., Carley, K. and Pattison, P. (eds). *Dynamic social network modeling and analysis: Workshop summary and papers* (pp. 133–145). Washington, DC: Committee on Human Factors, National Research Council.

Clark, B. R. (1998) *Creating entrepreneurial universities: Organisational pathways of transformation.* Oxford: International Association of Universities and Elsevier Science.

Cohen, M. D. and March, J. G. (1986) *Leadership and ambiguity: The American college president* (2nd ed.). Boston: Harvard Business School Press.

Cooke, M. and Lang, D. (2009) The effects of monopsony in higher education. *Higher Education, 57*: 623–639.

Evans, G. R. (2010a) *The University of Cambridge: A new history.* London: I. B. Tauris.

Evans, G. R. (2010b) *The University of Oxford: A new history.* London: I. B. Tauris.

Foucault, M. (1979) *Discipline and punish: The birth of the prison*. New York: Vintage.

Fraser, S. P. and Bosanquet, A. M. (2006) The curriculum? That's just a unit outline, isn't it? *Studies in Higher Education, 31*(3): 269–284.

Giddens, A. (1979) *Central problems in social theory: Action, structure and contradiction in social analysis*. Berkeley: University of California Press.

Giddens, A. (1984) *The constitution of society*. Cambridge: Polity.

Granovetter, M. S. (1995) Coase revisited: Business groups in the modern economy. *Industrial and Corporate Change, 4*(1): 93–130.

Gumport, P. J. (2000) Academic restructuring: Organizational change and institutional imperatives. *Higher Education, 30*: 67–91.

Hansson, B. (1999) Interdisciplinarity: For what purpose? *Policy Sciences, 32*: 339–343.

Howe, F. (1984) *Myths of coeducation*. Bloomington, IN: Indiana University Press.

Jarzabkowski, P. (2005) *Strategy as practice: An activity-based approach*. London: Sage.

Johnson, D. K., Ratcliff, J. L. and Gaff, J. G. (2004) A decade of change in general education. *Changing General Education Curriculum: New Directions for Higher Education*, 125: 9–28.

Karseth, B. (2006) Curriculum restructuring in higher education after the Bologna Process: A new pedagogic regime? *Revista Española de Educación Comparada, 12*: 255–284.

Keller, G. (1983). *Academic strategy: The management revolution in American higher education*. Baltimore: Johns Hopkins University Press.

Kerr, C. (2001) [Orig. 1963]. *The uses of the university* (5th ed). Cambridge, MA: Harvard University Press.

King's Learning Institute [KLI] (2010) *The King's-Warwick Project: Creating a 21st century curriculum*. London: KLI.

Knight, P. T. (2001) Complexity and curriculum: A process approach to curriculum-making. *Teaching in Higher Education, 6*(3): 369–381.

Krücken, G. (2003) Learning the 'New, New Thing': On the role of path dependency in university structures. *Higher Education, 46*(3): 315–339.

Lattuca, L. R. and Stark, J. S. (2009) *Shaping the college curriculum: Academic plans in context* (2nd ed.). San Francisco: Jossey-Bass.

Lave, J. and Wenger, E. (1991) *Situated learning: Legitimate peripheral participation*. Cambridge, UK: Cambridge University Press.

Lyall, K. (2011) Seeking sustainable public universities: The legacy of the Great Recession. *Research and Occasional Paper Series: CSHE 10.11*. Berkeley, CA: The University of California Berkeley.

Mason, T., Arnove, R. F. and Sutton, M. (2001) Credits, curriculum and control in higher education: Cross-national perspectives. *Higher Education, 42*(1): 107–137.

Maton, K. (2009) Cumulative and segmented learning: Exploring the role of curriculum structures in knowledge-building. *British Journal of Sociology of Education, 30*(1): 43–57.

Meyer, J., Ramirez, F., Frank, D. and Schofer, E. (2007) Higher Education as an Institution, in P. Gumport (ed.). *Sociology of higher education: Contributions and their contexts* (pp. 187–221). Baltimore: Johns Hopkins University Press.

Ortner, S. B. (1984) Theory in anthropology since the sixties. *Comparative Studies in Society and History, 26*(1), 126–166.

Parker, J. (2003) Reconceptualising the curriculum: From commodification to transformation. *Teaching in Higher Education, 8*(4): 529–543.

Pastor, J. C., Meindl, J. R. and Mayo, M. C. (2002) A network effects model of charisma attributions. *Academy of Management Journal, 45*(2): 410–420.

Podolny, J. M. and Page, K. L. (1998) Network forms of organization. *Annual Review of Sociology, 24*: 57–76.

Postill, J. (2010) Introduction: Theorising media and practice, in Bräuchler, B. and Postill, J. (eds). *Theorising Media and Practice*. Oxford and New York: Berghahn.

Powell, W. W. (1990) Neither market for hierarchy: Network forms of organization. *Research in Organizational Behavior, 12*: 295–336.

Powell, W. W., Koput, K. W. and Smith-Doerr, L. (1996) Interorganizational collaboration and the locus of innovation: Networks of learning in biotechnology. *Administrative Science Quarterly, 41*(1): 116–145.

Reckwitz, A. (2002) Toward a theory of social practices. A development in culturalist theorizing. *European Journal of Social Theory, 5*: 243–263.

Rudolph, F. (1977) *Curriculum: A history of the American undergraduate course of study since 1636*. San Francisco: Jossey-Bass.

Schatzki, T. (1996) *Social practices. A Wittgensteinian approach to human activity and the social*. Cambridge: Cambridge University Press.

Schatzki, T. (2001) Introduction: Practice theory, in Schatzki, T., Knorr Cetina, K. and von Savigny, E. (eds). *The practice turn in contemporary theory* (pp. 1–14). London: Routledge.

Scott, W. R. (2003) *Organizations – rational, natural and open systems* (5th ed.). Englewood Cliffs, NJ: Prentice Hall.

Shay, S. (2011) Curriculum formation: A case study from history. *Studies in Higher Education, 36*(3): 315–329.

Short, E. C. (2002) Knowledge and the educative functions of a university: Designing the curriculum of higher education. *Journal of Curriculum Studies, 34*(2): 139–148.

Sporn, B. (1999) *Adaptive university structures: An analysis of adaptation to socio-economic environments of US and European universities*. London: Jessica Kingsley.

Squires, G. (1987) The curriculum, in T. Becher (ed.). *British Higher Education* (pp. 155–177). London: Allen and Unwin.

Tang, F., Xi, Y. and Ma, J. (2006) Estimating the effect of organizational structure on knowledge transfer: A neural network approach. *Expert Systems with Applications, 30*(4): 796–800.

Trow, M. (1974) Problems in the transition from elite to mass higher education, in Organisation for Economic Co-ordination and Development [OECD] (ed.). *Policies for higher education*. Paris, OECD (pp. 51–101).

Trow, M. (2000) *From mass higher education to universal access: The American advantage*. Research and Occasional Paper Series. Berkeley, CA: Center for Studies in Higher Education.

Uzzi, B. and Gillespie, J. J. (2002) Knowledge spillover in corporate financing networks: Embeddedness and the firms debt performance. *Strategic Management Journal, 23*: 595–618.

Vaira, M. (2004) Globalization and higher education organizational change: A framework for analysis. *Higher Education, 48*: 483–510.

van Alstyne, M. (1998) Higher education's information challenge, in J. Meyerson (ed.). *New thinking on higher education* (pp. 120–147). Bolton, MA: Anker Publishing.

Weick, K. E. (1976) Educational organizations as loosely coupled systems. *Administrative Science Quarterly, 21*: 1018.

Wenger, E. (1998) *Communities of practice: Learning, meaning and identity.* Cambridge: Cambridge University Press.

Wong, B. K., Lai, V. S. and Lam, J. (2000) A bibliography of neural network business applications research: 1994–1998. *Computers and Operations Research, 27*: 1045–1076.

Chapter 2

Achieving curriculum coherence

Curriculum design and delivery as social practice

Saranne Weller

The increasing opportunities for modularised and interdisciplinary study in contemporary university curricula have opened up to scrutiny ways of being and knowing that have been traditionally defined by progression through, and mastery of, a disciplinary programme of study. As the status of higher education institutions and lecturers as the sole constructors and curators of specialised knowledge have been challenged (Bridges 2000), the curriculum has become an important site for the reshaping of student and lecturer identities in higher education. The emergent focus on identities has the potential to be transformative and engender genuinely participative curricula. Such changes have also, however, raised concerns about intellectual, social and personal fragmentation as an outcome of individual engagement with a divergent curriculum structure, an interrupted cohort experience and the lack of intellectual continuity within a modularised curriculum (Light *et al.* 2009). The 'commodification' of the curriculum into bite-size modules with assigned fees and credit has been seen as a significant threat to disciplinary understanding (Parker 2003). Even in the US, where broader general education has a well-established history in university curricula, reforms focused on generating greater coherence and enabling students to make connections between different components of their programme remain an 'unfinished agenda' (Johnson and Ratcliff 2004:92).

The aim of this chapter is to explore this 'fragmentation' of the curriculum as it impacts on student and lecturer identities and to consider a social practice understanding of the curriculum as the basis for enabling greater academic coherence. Drawing on this approach to the design, delivery and evaluation of the curriculum, the chapter considers:

- strategies for developing student and lecturer disciplinary and collective (self) positioning in relation to the curriculum experience as an alternative to a rational curriculum planning model;
- the potentialities afforded by transformative rather than normative approaches to academic literacy practices in the curriculum that recognise the resources students bring into the academy;
- the framing of lecturers' engagement in curriculum design and delivery as an ongoing collaborative and scholarly process of inquiry.

The chapter concludes by arguing that a key requirement for sustainable curriculum reform is the exploration of the ways in which a curriculum is conceptualised and experienced by both students and lecturers. It considers how best to support this engagement with the curriculum individually and institutionally. Such an approach moves beyond standardising and instrumental responses to engender coherence. Rather, it is suggested that institutions seek to promote the virtues of a flexible curriculum as an active site for contextualised critical encounters between students, lecturers and their subject discipline(s). Such reforms demand a reconsideration of the development needs of students and academics and require further investment in student support and academic development if coherence across the curriculum is to be achieved.

Constructing the coherent curriculum to enable collective learning

Accounts of the contemporary university curriculum have acknowledged the benefits of a modularised structure that enables students to create a personalised curriculum that can provide them with the 'ontological and epistemological resources for engaging meaningfully with others in a world in which nothing is certain' (Barnett 2000: 262). In a supercomplex world, Barnett suggests that traditional, discipline-based curricula should be open to contestation and students given the flexibility to construct their own learning experiences. Such opportunities can enable students to meet the challenges of employment and real-world problems that do not straightforwardly map against traditional disciplinary knowledge. It also equips them to respond to the reconstituting of their professional and personal identities throughout their working life within a changing employment market.

Yet despite the potentialities of such flexibility in curriculum choices, there are recognised challenges in supporting students to make their individual module selections meaningful, integrative and academically coherent rather than merely superficial and accumulative. A number of mechanisms have been put in place to facilitate student choice and effect greater integration of a modular programme, principally through the pre-specification of learning outcomes within a rational curriculum model. Despite appealing to a sense of rigour and accountability, there are limitations to this model and the nature of the coherence it generates.

Core curriculum and learning outcomes approaches to achieving coherence

The simplest strategy for achieving curriculum coherence is to limit individual student choice and develop deliberate pathways through degree programmes (a core curriculum). This works alongside appropriate mentoring by personal tutors or academic advisers to help students to plan and negotiate a fundamentally unified curriculum while retaining some of the benefits of a modular structure. Alternatively, another mechanism for creating coherence within the curriculum is the purposeful development of specific interdisciplinary modules that require lecturers and students to think explicitly through the ways in which different disciplinary knowledge and methodologies overlap within and across the curriculum. Such integrated cross-disciplinary degree programmes, however, are still rare (Hennessy *et al.* 2010).

In the absence of well-planned interdisciplinary curricula, an intermediate modular curriculum in which students can select and individually connect single discipline modules, whether chosen from cognate disciplines or even more widely, requires other pedagogic and structural strategies for aiding students to synthesise divergent content. Horizontal integration within the curriculum is a possible tool for enabling coherence, for example through the development of compulsory case-based modules that require all students to apply and integrate discipline-based knowledge from their individual choice of modules. These case-based modules are designed to engage students in solving real-life problems at key and regular stages throughout the curriculum (Hubball and Burt 2004). Similarly, vertical integration using a capstone experience or senior thesis as the 'pinnacle of the curriculum' (Shapiro 2003:424) in the final year of study can provide students with the opportunity to demonstrate achievement of programme level learning outcomes and integrate a range of divergent modules. As Shapiro suggests, students can also develop projects that are relevant to their intended career paths, enabling them to bridge their formal education and future employment.

Central to facilitating such horizontal and/or vertical integration of a curriculum in practice, however, is a rational curriculum planning model based upon the statement and targeting of pre-defined common learning outcomes for all students at the programme level that are often also aligned to post-education employment. This approach has been widely adopted as a way to mitigate and potentially resolve curriculum incoherence and achieve a shared student experience despite variation in individual selection of modules (Ecclestone 1999; Knight 2001). Yet learning outcomes have come under considerable scrutiny as a product-focused and managerialist tool that is counter to the complex, transformative and divergent aims of tertiary education (Hussey and Smith 2003).

Learning outcomes might provide clear statements, or perhaps more accurately 'shibboleths' (Knight 2001:371), of what students must do and demonstrate within an holistic understanding of the curriculum. However, to be meaningful for all students, such pre-defined learning outcomes ultimately must be broad in interpretation, de-contextualised from the actual classroom experience and transferable regardless of the individual modules chosen. Key generic outcomes emphasise communication, problem solving, decision making, team-working and self-management that are considered relevant for future employment. In turn, critics of learning outcomes approaches have pointed to the disappearance of the subject content in framing generic outcomes (Parker 2003), and the apparent undermining of disciplinary specialists in determining what is and what is not valued within the curriculum.

Alternatively, instead of targeting student attainment of de-contextualised graduate competencies, it is possible to generate coherence by understanding the curriculum as a more holistic process of engagement with, rather than the acquiring of, disciplinary knowledge. This approach is mutually emancipatory for students and their lecturers because it recognises learning as a complex social practice rather than the one-way transmission of a discrete canon of knowledge (Fraser and Bosanquet 2006). Instead of focusing on the curriculum as a set of pre-defined understandings and behaviours into which students are socialised, Knight (2001) has argued that curricula should show 'a concern for coherence manifested through attention to processes, messages, and the quality of communities and environments' (378). Such 'processes', 'messages' and 'communities' cannot be dislocated from the identities of the students and their lecturers or the disciplinary and institutional context within which they are produced. It is an approach that fundamentally recognises the curriculum experience as a social process requiring active participation within living disciplinary communities of practice (Wenger 1998). Individual students then learn to do more than master disciplinary facts and concepts or likewise to demonstrate transferable critical-thinking or problem-solving skills. In collaboration with their lecturers and their peers, students learn to participate in their disciplinary communities as historians who think historically or scientists who think scientifically. This coherence can be achieved in a number of ways by understanding the curriculum as a set of social practices in which students and lecturers are equal social actors participating in the ongoing construction of ways of being, communicating and validating knowledge that is situated in the context of the academy.

Realising curriculum coherence: The curriculum as social practice

In the design, development and delivery of the curriculum, a social practice understanding of the curriculum experience can enable greater coherence of a modularised system by explicitly addressing the tensions between the traditional academic disciplines and their relevance to student lives. Rather than attempting to resolve such tensions, a social practice understanding of the curriculum fosters opportunities for students and lecturers to recognise and critically comment on their personal relationship to the curriculum, its formation in specific contexts and its tacit articulation of particular values and power relations. In particular, Reckwitz (2002) points to the ways in which practice theory 'encourages a shifted self-understanding' (259) of individuals as carriers of ways of knowing and being. Such an understanding of the curriculum experience requires institutions to embed into their curricula:

- opportunities for disciplinary self-positioning: whereby mechanisms for enhancing student self-understanding across the curriculum are used to enable them to become aware of their relationship to a field(s) of knowledge through disciplinary self-positioning;

- the contextualisation of curriculum formation: whereby lecturers explore their role in historicising and contextualising the collective field of knowledge and articulating the formation of the curriculum to students;
- participation in communities: whereby lecturers and students acknowledge their mutual participation in disciplinary communities of practice and the importance of collaborative learning within the curriculum.

A social practices understanding of the curriculum suggests that instead of seeing students simply as recipients of a defined body of disciplinary knowledge, lecturers have a role in creating within their programmes deliberate opportunities for students to connect the curriculum to their own lives. Lecturers can also devise ways to stimulate critical self-awareness of the social processes involved in the design and delivery of the curriculum to develop a deeper understanding of the subject and its pedagogy. Such experiences enable students to perceive the transition of their identities as they engage with a field of knowledge that is continually re-shaped by a community of practitioners including their peers and their lecturers. In particular, this understanding of their collective experience in the classroom opens up opportunities for students to self-consciously position themselves in relation to the formation of the disciplinary fields that they encounter in their studies. Parker (2003) has argued that rejecting objective conceptions of a canon of content knowledge in favour of more generic graduate outcomes has led to the undermining of the discipline as the locus of the curriculum. Yet she also suggests that refocusing on the relationship between students and their subject of study can yield powerful learning experiences that cohere around the individual student as learner and validate their subjective experience of the curriculum content in relation to that of others.

Two recent practice examples demonstrate how this relational understanding of the curriculum can be used to generate a more complex and holistic level of student understanding by providing opportunities for students to reflect on their engagement with the discipline knowledge as it is framed by the curriculum. Both Anderson (2010) and Kapp and Bangeni (2009) have shown how the introduction of creative and self-reflective assessment tasks into modules can be used to develop and legitimise students' intellectual, emotional and physical responses to the subject matter. Challenging an approach to learning that requires students simply to reproduce knowledge rather than demonstrate understanding, Anderson argues that, in modularised curricula, discipline knowledge is increasingly 'divorced from experience', which leads to 'disembodied intelligence and [...] alienation between learner and body of knowledge' (206). One solution to this disengagement with the subject matter is the development of written assessment tasks that encourage students to connect their personal experience to the texts they are reading 'to show how building imaginative understanding through writing helps students create a meaningful place for themselves within their discipline [...] to see themselves as contributors to a field' (210). This engagement can generate critical and transformative awareness of students' self-positioning in relation to the discipline and eschews a reproductive orientation to the content. Such awareness enables students to develop a critical understanding of the experience of the curriculum and to reflect on the university as a traditional site of authority and possible inequality in knowledge creation. This critical approach to their curriculum experience and reflection on their relationship to subject experts is ultimately empowering for students rather than disenfranchising.

In parallel with the development of learning and assessment tasks that engage students in reflecting on their relationship with the subject matter, a social practices conception of the curriculum encourages lecturers to engage in self-conscious historicising of the curricula they design and deliver. From this perspective, academic coherence emerges out of a shared awareness of the curriculum as a socially constructed experience between student, lecturer and a disciplinary tradition that reflects the values and perspectives of individuals and institutions rather than through the straightforward transmission of a body of objective knowledge. Critical reflection on the syllabus, for example, enables lecturers to understand and be able to explain why certain concepts are taught and others are not, to articulate the history of the subject as a field of knowledge and to be able to justify the chronological ordering of topics through a module of study.

For example, in a case study of the curriculum in one South African sociology department, Luckett (2009) conceptualises the curriculum as a 'subjective practice [...] informed by social interests and relations' in which lecturers operate as 'agents of recontextualisation' in the process of translating disciplinary knowledge into the curriculum (442). In her analysis she identifies the deep epistemological divides within the field reflected in disconnected specialist modules within the curriculum. She suggests that one solution is to 'forge a collective pedagogic discourse [...] based on an explicit meta-language about knowledge, that locates for students the different positions represented in the department'. In curriculum design and delivery, she argues that there is a 'need to explicate for students the contestations around knowledge' (452) while also investing time in the process of curriculum design and development. This approach provides significant opportunities for lecturers to acknowledge and share the value judgements that are often implicit as a syllabus is translated into a module and programme curriculum through selection of teaching strategies, allocation of resources and assessment decisions. The juxtaposing of disciplines within new interdisciplinary degree programmes, in particular, has already opened up disciplinary identities and practices to scrutiny in ways that reveal the 'normative' function of the 'hidden' disciplinary curriculum. This hidden curriculum represents the unwritten, unspoken 'rules of the game' that can derail students if they move outside their home discipline (Portelli 1993; Barnett and Coate 2005). These tensions drive the need for increased critical engagement with the processes of curriculum-making by both lecturers and students as the basis for creating greater curriculum coherence.

Attentiveness to the role of students and lecturers in the formation of the curriculum through the process of design and delivery serves to localise and situate knowledge creation in ways that enact a desirable 'ontological turn' in higher education (Dall'Alba and Barnacle 2007). From this perspective, the curriculum represents a series of planned critical encounters in which lecturers and students can articulate their relationship to the subject knowledge rather than engage them in an attempt, respectively, to transmit and to acquire disembodied and de-contextualised knowledge. These encounters frame knowledge as constructed and enacted. This emphasises the relational interaction between lecturer, student and subject matter in the formation and reformation of a curriculum over a period of time and in a specific context. The curriculum is localised and meaningful – in the students' and lecturers' own experience, in the classroom, in the institution, and in the cultural, social and historical context within which the experiences occur.

Drawing on the development of both the students' relational experience of the curriculum and the lecturers' commitment to historicising and contextualising the formation of that curriculum, the final crucial factor in enabling curriculum coherence from a social practices perspective is to generate a learning experience that is communal and collaborative. As Ecclestone (1999: 40) has noted, emphasis on student choice within the modularised curriculum has focused on individual achievement to the exclusion of more participative experiences central to complex learning:

> The subsequent loss of collective learning separates a person's sense of their individuality and their perception of their needs from opportunities to understand the social forces which govern their situation [. . .] individualised approaches to study and assessment obscure a sense of oneself as part of a social group of learners learning together.

This isolationist model also powerfully dislocates lecturers and students and there is ultimately little sense of lecturers and students as collaborators within a community of disciplinary practice (Parker 2003). As Ecclestone suggests, an alternative approach to the curriculum is to embed the experience of participating in a 'social group of learners' within the curriculum. This includes the initiation of students into understanding their ways of being within a disciplinary community and active student participation in the re-creation of disciplinary practices as they themselves practise that discipline. Also, importantly, this approach encourages lecturers to recognise that they share the experience of students as ongoing learners in the discipline through their roles as active researchers in their field and as inquiring scholars of their curricula.

The development of a coherent curriculum experience requires students and their lecturers to mutually question objective conceptions of subject knowledge, to participate in a dialogical relationship in and outside the classroom and, from those positions, to mutually negotiate what is included in the curriculum (Fraser and Bosanquet 2006). Central to the achievement of this shared and ongoing (self-) positioning in relation to the discipline is the development of a critical awareness of the role that communication practices play in shaping the field of knowledge. At the same time, in order to enable students and lecturers to contribute critically to curriculum formation, lecturers and their students must also be provided with opportunities to understand and engage with curricula in scholarly ways that connect the discipline and its pedagogy. The following sections will elaborate how an academic literacies approach to student writing and the engagement in a scholarship of curriculum practice can be utilised not only to enhance student writing and curriculum design, but also to promote greater curriculum coherence.

Facilitating curriculum coherence through academic literacies

In higher education, communication practices are complex activities that are increasingly identified as fundamental to the development of students' disciplinary understanding rather than simply as a neutral means for the transmission of subject knowledge. As such, the literacy practices they adopt will determine how students participate in, and across, disciplinary communities in the university. Traditionally, universities have approached developing student writing either as a generic study skill or as the management of the process of acculturation of students into the discursive conventions of a specific discipline (Lea and Street 1998). The study skills and the socialisation models of student writing have inevitably been dominant at the level of curriculum design (Lea and Street 2006).

An 'academic literacies' approach, however, provides an alternative theoretical framework for understanding literacy practices within the curriculum. From this perspective, student and lecturer communication strategies are recognised as social practices through which subject knowledge and identities are constructed, shared and understood within the social context of the discipline, the classroom and the institution. In a modularised curriculum with the possibility of students selecting modules from a range of different disciplines, the divergent conventions of different subjects, therefore, can be a significant fault line for subsequent lack of curriculum coherence. As Lea and Street (2000: 35) have argued:

> a dominant feature of academic literacy practices is the requirement to switch practices between one setting and another, to deploy a repertoire of linguistic practices appropriately to each setting, and to handle the social meanings and identities that each evokes.

Students can face difficulties in synthesising their learning from across a range of modules into a more holistic understanding of their curriculum. This may arise not only from undertaking a number of discrete and unrelated units of study but also from their encounter with the range of different literacy requirements and unfamiliar genres across a modularised programme of study. These difficulties can also be extended to their understanding of the ways in which the curriculum of different disciplines is conceptualised and articulated. Despite attempts to standardise the format across subject areas, even the curriculum documentation, such as student handbooks, assessment rubrics and reading lists, can become a complex and unmanageable text. Consequently, students, and indeed other lecturers and professional staff from across an institution, may find it difficult to decode or successfully negotiate the curriculum.

As discussed above, an emancipatory understanding of the curriculum draws on the importance of ongoing dialogue between students and lecturers to shift the agenda from a normative perspective (based on beliefs about the objective reality of disciplinary methodologies and practices) to one that is transformative. This perspective allows such conventions to be contested as well as for the exploration of the ways in which those 'outside' the academy can contribute to legitimate meaning-making. Discussing the ways in which language is used can provide a focal point for enabling students to create coherence within a multi-disciplinary modularised curriculum. The implication of bringing an academic literacies perspective to the curriculum, therefore, is that programmes will need to consider the provision of 'pedagogic spaces for exploration of all the different and contrasting textual practices' that students encounter in their studies (Lea 2004: 745).

The iterative process of understanding different disciplines and their literacy practices provides a powerful unifying thread through a student's programme of study. At the same time, engaging students and their lecturers in dialogue around the literacies of a field of study emphasises the interrelationship, rather than differences, between their individual writing practices and writing objectives. The introduction of critical and reflexive writing activities throughout a curriculum, across multiple modules, provides an opportunity to develop student authorial identities and writing practices as creative rather than simply for the purposes of reproducing in assessments the knowledge that has been delivered in lectures. This approach brings to the fore the shared literacy experiences of students and their lecturers as academic writers working within, and contributing to, a field of study (Pittam *et al.* 2009) and encourages the possibility of further reflection on the relationship between writing and knowledge creation in the discipline.

An academic literacies approach to the curriculum can help students reposition themselves as scholars in a (multi-) disciplinary field. Correspondingly, engaging faculty in a scholarly approach to curriculum design, delivery and evaluation can also serve to engage lecturers as participative learners within the curriculum experience rather than simply the deliverers of pre-defined content. Curriculum scholarship can generate greater curriculum coherence in practical terms, for example, by gathering data to track and evaluate the student experience through a curriculum that can then be acted upon. Engaging lecturers in researching their practice can also resolve the increasing disconnect between lecturers' identities as disciplinary experts (teacher) and continuous learners within their field (researcher) as these impact on their approach to curriculum design and delivery.

Promoting curriculum coherence through the scholarship of curriculum practice

Many recent commentators have deplored the devaluing of academic disciplinary expertise in the face of increased requirements for lecturers to demonstrate pedagogical knowledge of theories of learning, curriculum design, assessment and evaluation of practice. Framing such knowledge within 'generic' postgraduate qualifications in learning and teaching in higher education has accentuated the apparent separation between disciplinary knowledge, academic research and teaching practice. A scholarly approach to the curriculum, however, can provide a method for developing a critical understanding of teaching, learning and assessment that is also grounded in the disciplinary context and promotes the development of a community of learners, both students and lecturers, within the curriculum experience.

The scholarship of curriculum practice is an approach to curriculum design, delivery and evaluation that parallels the familiar practices of disciplinary research – for example, conducting a literature review, choosing a theoretical framework, carrying out data collection and disseminating outcomes for peer review (Hubball and Pearson 2011). It enables lecturers to understand the student learning experience in the curriculum from the student perspective and align that with data drawn from their own contribution to the curriculum. As such it can have a meaningful and practical impact on student learning, and if focused on creating improved coherence across a curriculum, can identify and mitigate the impact of *ad hoc* revisions of individual modules over the lifetime of a curriculum. It can also facilitate the development of appropriate opportunities for students to integrate learning from different modules.

A scholarly approach to curriculum practice, therefore, affords a means to produce and monitor mechanisms for improving coherence across a curriculum at a number of levels. With an understanding of the curriculum from a social practices perspective, however, engaging lecturers routinely in researching their curriculum also reasserts the role of lecturers as scholars both in and of a field of study and challenges the now common disassociation between the teaching and research role. Christensen Hughes (2007: 109) has suggested that:

> we in the professoriate may have lost sight of what it means to be a scholar. Perhaps as a result of the dichotomy between research and teaching, heavy workloads, or simply lack of critical awareness, many faculty appear to routinely make decisions in their teaching and service activities that are not evidence based (a standard they would not accept in their research activity).

By re-engaging lecturers in the curriculum not only as teachers but also as researchers of both their discipline and their pedagogy, an individual and institutional commitment to the scholarship of curriculum practice works towards integrating a lecturer's teacher and researcher identities. At the same time, by requiring wider dissemination of the outcomes of curriculum inquiry, the scholarship of curriculum practice also brings disciplinary academics into new groupings of scholars and requires them to engage with new academic literacies as they share practice within and across disciplines. These encounters with new communities and new discourses are powerful reminders to lecturers of the experiences of their own students as they engage as learners. Researching the curriculum provides an activity around which lecturers' multiple identities – as teacher, as researcher, as learner – can cohere within a disciplinary context while also enabling them to explore their own conceptions of the curriculum and their critical awareness of the process of its formation and delivery.

From the perspective of the enhancement of teaching, learning and assessment practice, the curriculum and the module or programme team have also been identified as a focus for situated and long-term development of practice. Working with the programme team on curriculum design and development rather than the more individual-focused orientation of traditional academic or educational development interventions has been found to lead to meaningful, contextualised collaboration across a programme team (Harp Zeigenfuss and Lawler 2008). Involving students in that process may also engender the participative engagement with the curriculum that is central to improved coherence in the experience of the curriculum.

Conclusion

This chapter has proposed that understanding the curriculum from a social practices perspective can provide a framework for responding to the perceived fragmentation of the learning experience within contemporary modularised curricula. This perspective challenges a learning outcomes approach as unlikely to achieve coherence across a programme of study or realise the complex and creative learning that higher education needs to facilitate in order to equip graduates for future employment. The alternative conception of the curriculum as a social practice in which the disciplinary curriculum is co-constructed and contextualised by students and lecturers, however, can provide the basis for greater coherence by enabling lecturers and their students to critically reflect on their identities as mutual contributors to a knowledge field and its articulation through the curriculum.

This approach to the curriculum requires investment of time and resources for the purposes of locating literacy practices as central to (multi-) disciplinary learning. The development of student and lecturer academic literacies should be within and across the disciplines and surface the shared experience of writing in a community of disciplinary practice. Equally, the historicising and contextualising of the curriculum can connect pedagogy to disciplinary content knowledge through the design and delivery of modules and programmes of study. Finally, the locating of curriculum research and development as the unit of activity for educational enhancement can engender greater coherence between teaching and research identities and focus academic or educational development at the group rather than the individual level.

Creating coherence across the modularised curriculum requires a re-envisioning of current student support and academic development to give greater attention to student and lecturer academic identity formation and transition. This also embeds enhancement initiatives more directly within the disciplines rather than as an adjunct to them. As such, academic support for students and lecturers is not based on a deficit model but integral to what it is to know and be within a discipline or disciplines. Similarly, there is also a need to shift the focus of support from the individual to the group level as the basis for sustainable and collaborative development of curricula that is situated, participatory and critically accountable.

References

Anderson, K. (2010) The whole learner. The role of imagination in developing disciplinary understanding. *Arts and Humanities in Higher Education*, 9(2): 205–221.

Barnett, R. (2000) Supercomplexity and the curriculum. *Studies in Higher Education*, 25(3): 255–265.

Barnett, R. and Coate, K. (2005) *Engaging the curriculum in higher education*. Maidenhead: Society for Research into Higher Education/Open University Press.

Bridges, D. (2000) Back to the future: The higher education curriculum in the 21st century. *Cambridge Journal of Education*, 30(1): 37–55.

Christensen Hughes, J. (2007) Supporting curriculum assessment and development: Implications for the faculty role and institutional support. *New Directions for Teaching and Learning*, 112: 107–110.

Dall'Alba, G. and Barnacle, R. (2007) An ontological turn for higher education. *Studies in Higher Education*, 32(6): 679–691.

Ecclestone, K. (1999) Empowering or ensnaring? The implications of outcome-based assessment in higher education. *Higher Education Quarterly*, 53(1): 29–48.

Fraser, S. P. and Bosanquet, A. M. (2006) The curriculum? That's just a unit outline, isn't it? *Studies in Higher Education*, 31(3): 269–284.

Harp Zeigenfuss, D. and Lawler, P. (2008) Collaborative course design: Changing the process, acknowledging the context, and implications for academic development. *International Journal for Academic Development*, 13(3): 151–160.

Hennessy, E., Hernandez, R., Kieran, P. and MacLoughlin, H. (2010) Teaching and learning across disciplines: Student and staff experiences in a newly modularised system. *Teaching in Higher Education*, 15(6): 675–689.

Hubball, H. and Burt, H. (2004) An integrated approach to developing and implementing learning-centred curricula. *International Journal for Academic Development*, 9(1): 51–65.

Hubball, H. and Pearson, M. (2011) Scholarly approaches to curriculum evaluation: Critical contributions for undergraduate degree programme reform in a Canadian context, in M. Saunders, P. Trowler and V. Bamber (eds). *Reconceptualising evaluation in higher education: The practice turn* (pp. 186–192). Maidenhead: Society for Research into Higher Education/Open University Press.

Hussey, T. and Smith, P. (2003) The uses of learning outcomes. *Teaching in Higher Education*, 8(3): 357–368.

Johnson, D. K. and Ratcliff, J. (2004) Creating coherence: The unfinished agenda. *New Directions for Higher Education*, *125*: 85–95.

Kapp, R. and Bangeni, B. (2009) Positioning (in) the discipline: undergraduate students' negotiations of disciplinary discourses. *Teaching in Higher Education*, *14*(6): 587–596.

Knight, P. (2001) Complexity and curriculum: a process approach to curriculum-making. *Teaching in Higher Education*, *6*(3): 369–381.

Lea, M. (2004) Academic literacies: A pedagogy for course design. *Studies in Higher Education*, *29*(6): 739–756.

Lea, M. and Street, B. (1998) Student writing in higher education: an academic literacies approach. *Studies in Higher Education*, *23*(2): 157–172.

Lea, M. and Street, B. (2000) Student writing and staff feedback in higher education: An academic literacies approach, in M.Lea and B.Steirer (eds). *Student writing in higher education: New contexts* (pp. 32–46). Buckinghamshire: Society for Research into Higher Education/Open University Press.

Lea, M. and Street, B. (2006) The 'academic literacies' model: Theory and applications. *Theory into Practice*, *45*(4): 368–377.

Light, G., Cox, R. and Calkins, S. (2009) *Learning and teaching in higher education: The reflective practitioner*. (2nd ed.). London: Sage.

Luckett, K. (2009) The relationship between knowledge structure and curriculum: A case study in sociology. *Studies in Higher Education*, *34*(4): 441–453.

Parker, J. (2003) Reconceptualising the curriculum: From commodification to transformation. *Teaching in Higher Education*, *8*(4): 529–543.

Pittam, G., Elander, J., Lusher, J., Fox, P. and Payne, N. (2009) Student's beliefs and attitudes about authorial identity in academic writing. *Studies in Higher Education*, *34*(2): 153–170.

Portelli, J. (1993) Exposing the hidden curriculum. *Journal of Curriculum Studies*, *25*(4): 343–358.

Reckwitz, A. (2002) Toward a theory of social practices: A development in culturalist theorizing. *European Journal of Social Theory*, *5*(2): 243–263.

Shapiro, D. (2003) Facilitating holistic curriculum development. *Assessment and Evaluation in Higher Education*, *28*(4): 423–434.

Wenger, E. (1998) *Communities of practice: Learning, meaning, and identity*. Cambridge: Cambridge University Press.

Chapter 3

Case study: A tradition of reform

The curriculum at Brown University

Katherine Bergeron

At Brown University in Providence, Rhode Island, the undergraduate College and its curriculum have symbolic weight. Established in 1764 as the third institution of higher learning in New England, Brown (then the College of Rhode Island) was an open place from the start: it was the first school in America to accept students regardless of their religious affiliation. Brown today includes a graduate school, a medical school and a school of engineering, but it continues to be known for its College and for the cohorts of creative, independent and entrepreneurial students who are drawn to its unique philosophy of undergraduate education. Some people call that philosophy the open curriculum. Others may refer to it as the new curriculum, recalling the moment in 1969 when the faculty and students joined together to rewrite their educational contract and create a new, more open climate of engaged and activist learning. Most people today, though, know it as the Brown curriculum, and for good reason. The spirit of reform written into its principles is now a tradition that defines the ethos of Brown as an institution.

This chapter is about the Brown curriculum and the steps the University took starting in 2007 to review and evaluate its significance for the twenty-first century. No curricular reform can happen without a sense of urgency, and in this case the pressure came through an ambitious plan for academic enrichment at Brown. The plan, launched in 2002 by Brown's eighteenth president, Ruth Simmons, was designed to improve every aspect of the educational enterprise, from faculty to research programs, facilities and students.[1] The goals for the College included enhancing the quality of what was already perceived to be an excellent undergraduate experience, and this, of course, included the almost forty-year tradition of the open curriculum. As Brown's new Dean of the College, I was asked to lead a task force in 2007 to evaluate this icon of the Brown undergraduate experience. It would be the first comprehensive review of the curriculum in nearly twenty years.

Embarking on this task, however, raised a somewhat awkward question: How does one review an icon? The Brown curriculum is not, after all, a set of core requirements but a directive for students to create their own core programs. Brown expects its students, like undergraduates at other American universities, to gain a perspective on a range of disciplines, develop their critical abilities and hone their judgment. The difference lies in the degree of freedom Brown students have. Rather than selecting from a menu of general education requirements prescribed by the institution, undergraduates at Brown shape this education for themselves, guided by a set of principles, or ideals, about liberal education. In practical terms, students must earn a minimum of thirty units, successfully complete a concentration and demonstrate competence in writing. The spirit of Brown's curriculum, however, challenges them to do more: not merely to sample a range of classes but to make connections between them, to use perspective gained from one discipline as a window onto the next. Brown asks its students, in other words, to make intentional educational choices. This has important effects, both for the student and for the curriculum. Students are empowered to understand the scope and purpose of their education by taking an active role in its creation; and the curriculum itself is refreshed, subjected to a kind of continuous "re-opening" by the work of each subsequent generation.

In a way, this powerful educational philosophy only made the job of reviewing the curriculum more complex. When the task force was announced in 2007, students and faculty wondered why further review was necessary given the built-in attention the open curriculum already received. They also worried that any tampering with its openness might harm the special character of Brown as an institution. For the task force to succeed, it was important to make its purposes as clear as possible and to conduct an open and inclusive process. This meant ensuring transparency in the group's dealings with existing campus committees, as well as with the faculty, students and alumni who had a stake in the curriculum. To encourage the broadest participation, the task force published its meeting materials on an open website, held focus groups and forums, and invited various cohorts to respond to questionnaires. In all, the group held over thirty meetings on campus and received feedback from thousands of alumni.

The review was guided by a set of questions focused on liberal education, advising, teaching and assessment. The simplest question was in many ways the most difficult to answer: did the open curriculum still make sense for Brown today? The task force gathered data about student success and sought out stories from alumni. It examined transcripts of recent graduates to look for patterns in disciplinary distribution. It also debated the kind of academic advising that different groups of students needed to succeed at Brown, as well as the evidence that departments needed to show that success. The final report, released in September 2008, offered summaries of these debates along with fifteen recommendations aimed at enhancing the educational experience for all undergraduates.[2] Because some time has passed since the release of the report, the remainder of this chapter will focus not so much on the recommendations themselves (which by now have been implemented) as on four areas of reform that have emerged from them. These include a new approach to liberal learning in general and to Brown's writing requirement in particular, as well as new perspectives on advising and on the academic concentrations.

Liberal Learning at Brown

The report's most important – and, for many, most welcome – conclusion reaffirmed the value of Brown's open learning environment for the twenty-first century. And yet conversations with faculty and students also made it clear that the deeper aims of the Brown curriculum were no longer widely understood. The first recommendation in the report thus focused on communication, urging the College to produce a new statement on liberal learning for the benefit of a new generation. The last such document had been produced in 1989 as part of a twenty-year review of the open curriculum.[3] By 2008, it needed significant revision both to speak to students and to bring out new areas of emphasis. Brown's existing curriculum committee for the College took on the job and set to work even before the task force had finished its own process. The document that came to light –"Liberal Learning at Brown" – was finished early enough to be published as an appendix within the task force's final report.[4]

The new statement is notable for both its tone and its content. It begins by establishing the history and purposes of liberal education, then goes on to outline a set of capacities that all Brown students are expected to develop. These include not just intellectual capacities but broader aspects such as the ability to collaborate with others, and the cultivation of learning experiences beyond the classroom. Importantly, the statement is written in the second person and in the imperative mood, to show that these are not lofty or unattainable ideals, but concrete goals that each student will embrace. The organization of the statement is interesting as well. To demonstrate a key assumption of the curriculum – that a student will "make connections between courses" – the form mimics the content: the capacities self-consciously cut across disciplinary divisions. Comments about the nature of evidence, for example, appear in paragraphs that discuss both historical and scientific inquiry. This is as important for students as it is for departments. The interconnected exposition makes clear that academic departments have a stake not just in the disciplinary education of their concentrators but also in the liberal learning of all students. I will return to this point at the end of the chapter.

The writing requirement

One of the values most commonly shared across the disciplines is effective communication, and the first imperative of "Liberal Learning at Brown" directs students to "work on [their] speaking and writing." But the task force was even more emphatic in demanding accountability in this area. Brown has always expected its students to demonstrate competence in writing: this is, in effect, the University's only general education requirement. But the environment of the open curriculum made the expectation difficult to enforce, and students were often confused about how to fulfill their obligation. Following the report, then, one of the first tasks the College undertook was to clarify the writing requirement. Working collaboratively with faculty and students, the College's curriculum council produced in 2009 a new statement on the value that writing has for a Brown education. It begins:

> To earn the baccalaureate degree, all Brown students must demonstrate an ability to write well. Why? Good writing is essential to learning. Across the disciplines, scholars, teachers, and students write to explore ideas, uncover nuances of thought, and advance knowledge. Writing is not only a medium through which we communicate and persuade; it is also a means for expanding our capacities to think clearly.[5]

The statement goes on to explain how students will demonstrate proficiency. Notably, they must work on their writing not just once but throughout their Brown careers. This may occur through appropriate courses, and the College now has a rubric (WRIT) to identify more than three hundred courses in the curriculum, at all levels and across departments, that emphasize the writing process. But the spirit of the requirement extends beyond coursework to include writing completed in other contexts as well. All students are encouraged to save examples of their best work so that they can monitor their own development. The question of how Brown might save and assess student writing ultimately led the College toward its next important curricular innovation: an online tool to enhance advising.

Advising and assessment

Brown's new statements on liberal learning and writing were created to clarify the ideals of the open curriculum and to help students embrace their responsibilities within it. But an official statement – however inspiring – can only go so far. Students need not just a set of directions, but also meaningful occasions to set goals, assess progress and plan for the future. Academic advisors provide one kind of outlet; required self-assessments can offer another. In order to realize the promise of the Brown curriculum, students in fact need both. Following the task force report, considerable time was spent imagining not only how to improve advising, but also how to encourage students to reflect more deeply on their education. In 2009, Brown introduced something to help with that goal: a custom electronic advising tool that we call ASK (Advising SideKick).

We purposely did not call this tool an "electronic portfolio," although we could have. We focused on advising because Brown's open curriculum requires an even more robust advising system to make it work, and students and faculty acknowledged the need for more support. ASK was first introduced to aid faculty advisors in their work, bringing all student information, handbooks and other resources onto a single site. (The student version, also introduced in 2009, offers essentially the same features in reverse.) From the home page, advisors and advisees can find to-do lists and notices of deadlines and events, as well as information about each other. Brown's liberal learning goals are also prominently featured.

Each time a student or advisor logs in to ASK, a different goal appears at the top of the page. The repetition helps to convey the importance of liberal learning at Brown, while making the goals accessible to the thousands of students and advisors who make up Brown's advising network each year.[6]

ASK supports the continuity of advising, too, by making student information available to multiple advisors – and to students themselves – across their time at Brown. There are two important pieces of writing we collect from students in the first two years. The first is a letter. In the summer before coming to Brown, new students are asked to write to their academic advisor, discussing a summer reading project and outlining their academic goals.[7] This letter is uploaded and stored in ASK. When, at the end of the sophomore year, students choose an academic concentration, they are again asked to write. This time it is an essay defending the choice of concentration in the context of their liberal studies – an essay that also goes into ASK. Thus, by the time students declare the concentration, advisors have the beginning of a narrative about a student's educational development. More importantly, students have that narrative, too. Sophomores can easily look back at that first letter to see how their goals have changed – and the concentration essay makes them do exactly that. For seniors, seeing the arc of a whole education, the revelations can be even more profound. This kind of reflective practice is essential for students to understand their development in the open curriculum.

The portfolio function of ASK – and especially the required writing – can help with University-wide assessment as well, by offering direct evidence of student growth from matriculation to graduation. While the College does not require all seniors to upload a thesis or a senior project, individual concentrations do have exit requirements. A number of programs are beginning to use ASK to enhance this summative function: allowing seniors to put together a portfolio of work that reflects on their concentration and, in turn, on their entire Brown education. The critical role played by the concentration in defining a student's liberal education was, in fact, a key concern of the task force discussions, one which led to the report's most ambitious recommendation and to what is now an ongoing project of curricular reform.

The concentrations in review

All Brown students are required to complete an academic concentration as a final step toward the baccalaureate degree. There are about eighty programs to choose from, 40 per cent of which fall between or beyond traditional department structures. This level of flexibility and choice is another manifestation of the "openness" of Brown's curriculum. But it also raises a question: are students are equally well served by all programs? The College's curriculum council was tasked with finding an answer – indeed, with initiating another curricular review – and in 2009 it began the process of evaluating every one of the concentrations. In the spirit of reform that has characterized the Brown curriculum from its inception, this project will be continuing for quite some time.

The reviews are essentially looking for three things: coherence, culmination and connection. Does the concentration converge on a set of clearly stated goals? Does it offer a proper culmination to the Brown degree? We like to say at Brown that the academic concentration is the "focal point" for a student's education – a place where parallel strands of activity converge – and this review process offers an opportunity to make that image true. One of the more interesting byproducts of this review, in fact, is a new web tool we have created for exploring the concentrations, which is called, appropriately, Focal Point. It draws together information about all of Brown's programs onto a single site, bringing order to the student's extensive array of options so that they might be encouraged to make more intentional educational choices.[8] From the home page students can search the concentrations according to academic interests and potential career pathways. They can also drill deeper to learn more about individual programs. Clicking on a concentration link, for example, brings the viewer to a new page that offers a short description of the program and its requirements, information about capstone and honors opportunities, and, importantly, an account of its learning goals for students.

But there is another, crucial piece of information that Focal Point provides, one that helps bind the concentration more closely into the student's overall experience. It is a reminder of Brown's broader educational mission. On each of the concentration pages, in addition to the description of capstone and honors opportunities, viewers can find a few words about liberal learning. This feature responds to an emphatic appeal within the original report of the task force, an appeal that, by way of conclusion, is worth quoting in full:

> The conventional view of a divided curriculum – with the concentration on one side and "everything else" on the other – is, we think, profoundly misleading. Not only is the undergraduate expectation of four years and at least thirty courses larger than any concentration requirement, but the commitment to diverse areas of inquiry and knowledge must also be seen as the main event, not the leftovers, of the college experience. If, as one student eloquently argued, the real "core" of the Brown curriculum lay in the connections students make between their courses and their activities, then we should see the concentration as part of that network rather than separate from it. We must insist, in other words, on a fully integral view of the concentration.[9]

This view of the concentration offers, in the end, the most important effect of the open curriculum: the opening of disciplines to the broader aims of a liberal education. Such an aspiration for integration and engagement lies at the heart of the great reformist tradition that defines Brown as an institution, a tradition in which the curriculum will always be, in the most profound sense, a work in progress.

Notes

1   For a more detailed account of President Simmons' Plan for Academic Enrichment, see http://brown.edu/web/pae. The Boldly Brown campaign, which accompanied the plan, was completed in 2011 and ultimately raised $1.6 billion in new resources to support Brown's objectives.

2   See "The Curriculum at Forty: A Plan for Strengthening the College Experience at Brown" (Brown University: Office of the Dean of the College, 2008) http://brown.edu/College/tue/downloads/Task_Force_Final_Report.pdf

3   That review was undertaken by an earlier Dean of the College. See Sheila E. Blumstein, "The Brown Curriculum Twenty Years After: A Review of the Past and an Agenda for the Future" (Brown University: Office of the Dean of the College, 1990).

4   The statement can be found on pages 39–41 of the task force report (see http://brown.edu/College/tue/downloads/Task_Force_Final_Report.pdf). "Liberal Learning at Brown" can also be found elsewhere on the web and in several new guides created for students and faculty advisors since 2008.

5   The full statement on writing is reprinted in all the relevant advising handbooks for both faculty and students, and is available on the Dean of the College website.

6   Brown has about 450 faculty and staff members (and about 350 student peer advisors) engaged in the general academic advising of the first-year and sophomore classes. Another 125–150 faculty members serve as advisors to the concentrations. Brown's student body includes some 6,000 undergraduates.

7   All entering students participate in the First Readings program, in which they read a nominated book during the summer and then discuss it with faculty and staff members in small seminars during their orientation to Brown.

8   The tool is available at: http://www.brown.edu/Administration/focal-point/

9   *The Curriculum at Forty: A Plan for Strengthening the College Experience at Brown* (Brown University: Office of the Dean of the College, 2008, page 14).

Part 2

Strategic curriculum structures and processes

Chapter 4

Curriculum organisation and outcomes

Camille B. Kandiko and Paul Blackmore

In the context of the conceptual arguments made in Chapters 1 and 2, and application in Chapter 3, we now explore curriculum structures and features theoretically and in practice in universities. We draw the connections between providing coherence in an environment of increased breadth and choice in curriculum design with associated goals and outcomes, and consider how more flexibility in structures can enhance student choice. Taking a social practice approach, we analyse curriculum structures, features, goals and outcomes in institutional settings. This is in contrast to much curriculum research that speaks of an idealised curriculum, which may not ever function in actual institutions. Curriculum change processes face similar tensions. Although rational curriculum planning (RCP) has been regularly critiqued (Stenhouse 1975; Eisner 1985; Knight 2001) for not offering the flexibility needed in complex learning environments that stimulate critical thinking, a desire to achieve prescribed learning outcomes continues to drive much curriculum change. RCP works through a linear process from goals to planning objectives to curriculum design, including teaching and assessment, with evaluation to promote future improvement. However appealing from a management perspective, an efficient linear cycle for curriculum design and delivery rarely captures the lived reality of the university environment. Therefore, this chapter analyses the curriculum and curriculum change in practice rather than analysing theoretical curriculum models and frameworks.

The first section provides an overview of approaches across a number of institutions and some of the key tensions in implementing a change. We look at the scope of the formal curriculum and efforts to implement change, including approaches on school and faculty level, as well as cross-faculty initiatives. This draws on research on curriculum change in different institutions, from which Johnson *et al.* (2004: 27) note the complex nature of the change process:

> each curriculum differs in educational philosophy or philosophies, students served, programmes offered, constituencies served, institutional mission, and other factors. The value of learning from others' experiences in general education reform then, is one of analogy, allegory, and adaptation rather than adoption of approach and practice.

Building on these ideas, and drawing on Chapter 2, the next section analyses the tension between structure and choice. We do this in the context of general education, exploring the role of a core curriculum, generic versus specific provision, and broad offerings and niche programmes. Following from this, we discuss how coherence is addressed as a means of offering students a holistic learning experience. The third section focuses on goals and outcomes, and how notions of graduate attributes can provide coherence for curriculum change.

Many features of a curriculum can develop new connections within institutions, highlighting key factors from network organisational theory. These include developing know-how, being quicker and more responsive, and creating environments of trust. Such network forms can enhance creativity and interdisciplinary ways of working, as can be seen in curriculum structures which foster cross-departmental collaborations. Networked curriculum structures can encourage sharing of information, and the flexible structure can enhance innovation and better adaptation to changing environments. This allows new connections and linkages to be made, creating a context for continual organisational learning. The examples on pages 47, 51 and 57 highlight how such structures can support the goals and outcomes of the curriculum, even when these are loosely defined.

Curriculum structures and organisation

Universities are large organisations that do certain tasks well, repeatedly. As this replication occurs, processes become formalised. Examples include university timetabling, course and module descriptions, marking deadlines and set exam periods. There are further norms of behaviour at various levels within institutions, at college, school and department levels. Each level has boundaries and embedded rules and practices, particularly in relation to programme and course design. While much of this infrastructure has organisational benefits, it can impede change and innovation. In our review of institutions, we found a number which used changes in the curriculum to strategically realign, connect and create flexible pathways across institutional boundaries.

Institutions made major changes in how the content and processes of the formal curriculum are structured. Some institutions also paid attention to the co-curriculum, the learning opportunities that take place alongside the formal curriculum. This raises questions about coherence, particularly where a traditional emphasis on the learning of a discipline as the principal purpose of a higher education has been challenged. There is a need for curriculum models that are 'multi-faceted, comprehensive and intellectually cogent' (Parker 2003: 539), but that can also function in university settings. There have been arguments for universities to go beyond making small changes to general education, academic disciplines and professional education and to think about 'a new way to conceive, rationalize, and legitimize the organization of the curriculum' (Short 2002: 140). At an organisational level, this raises questions about how broadly or narrowly the curriculum and curriculum change initiatives are conceived.

Organisation of the formal curriculum

As most students do not become discipline-based academics or go on to do post-graduate research, it can be argued that they need a more general education that prepares them for a work environment in which they are likely to change jobs and careers. Thus students need to develop a broad range of abilities and the capacity to make connections across a range of knowledge and experience. A common approach to curriculum change is through the specification of general education requirements, introduced in a way that allows an institution to retain traditional disciplinary degree structures while offering exposure to multiple ways of thinking. A broad intellectual base rather than a narrow disciplinary one is the foundation of most general education requirements. Additionally, many universities that conducted a university-wide curriculum change spoke of wanting common learning experiences for all students, including features such as experiential learning, common core courses, interdisciplinary exposure and research opportunities. All of these require a place in the curriculum.

There are four primary ways of making space for general education in the curriculum, the most common being to condense disciplinary knowledge, in terms of either time or content. A more radical approach is lengthening a degree, often from three to four years. Owing to the wide implications of such an endeavour, this is usually only done at a national or supra-national (e.g. European Union) level. A related action is to move some disciplinary knowledge, particularly professional and vocational aspects, to Master's level. The fourth approach is to extend the curriculum beyond traditional formal boundaries. Extra-curricular and co-curricular activities vary across countries and university sectors, although there is a shared challenge in integrating and recognising such activity within the formal curriculum (Clegg *et al.* 2010). These changes can be mostly structural, or be used to make broader changes within the content and processes of the curriculum.

Process-focused change, such as adopting a critical stance or more interdisciplinary approaches, tends to take place through a series of phases. The first phase includes recognition of the subject to be changed, then conceptualisation of what the change could be and the development of an understanding of the context of change. Later phases include challenging the traditional methods and processes and finally redefining the subject and its place in history. This was seen in developments in Women's Studies and Area/Cultural Studies over the last forty years. As seen in pioneering efforts in field-specific studies, 'the final phase of curriculum transformation ... would be one based on the differences and diversity of experience, not sameness and generalization' (Andersen 1987:236). This conceptualisation challenges notions of authority and power in the curriculum, and instead places learners and their experiences at the centre. Many recent change initiatives work to manage tension between being an educational project that is structurally or organisationally based, or a project that is going further and pushing for societal, emancipatory change, such as with climate change and sustainability.

Another option is to offer an alternative or separate Honours curriculum, which a number of institutions have combined with broader curriculum changes. For example, the University of Western Australia plans to offer a high-profile, research-oriented Bachelor of Philosophy degree. It will be a four-year Honours degree taken in any discipline. Small cohorts will work in groups to conduct a joint research project, intended to be multidisciplinary in nature. The degree includes major and broadening units and residential and study abroad options. In the Netherlands, Utrecht University (UU) offers an alternative curriculum through its University College Utrecht (UCU). It is designed for elite students and is small and selective, offering a broader liberal-arts-style education and a residential-based programme. Students choose a major and a minor field of study, which can be in different faculties.

Some universities offer curriculum enhancement for selected students. These include advanced research opportunities that are often pathways for those intending postgraduate academic study or an academic career. The University of Warwick's Undergraduate Research Scholarship Scheme (URSS) offers students the opportunity of undertaking 'real' research with academic staff. Through the well-regarded Undergraduate Research Opportunities Programme (UROP), Imperial College is currently seeking to create opportunities for students to link in with research centres and to make the programme more institutionally embedded.

Over the last forty years, curriculum changes have sought to address consistent challenges of integration and balance across types of enquiry, fields of study and outcomes. As argued in the development of Women's Studies, it may be impossible to seek a balanced curriculum in an unbalanced world (Bowles and Duelli-Klein 1983). However, it has been observed that traditional views of the power in universities residing in individual faculty members and their departments has shifted, with strength emanating from the connections faculty members have with one another and with other professionals around the world (van Alstyne 1998). This highlights the networking function of universities, and the role that the curriculum can have in facilitating connections across and beyond an institution. However, particularly at the undergraduate level, attention needs to be paid to how complex changes are organised and structured, issues that are discussed in the next section.

School-level and faculty-level approaches

It was striking that in all the institutions that we surveyed, interviewees at school level and faculty level rarely mentioned their institution's priorities or initiatives in describing their own thinking and activities. Instead they referred to their own discipline and students. This suggests that centrally mandated change may remain little more than institutional rhetoric if it does not connect with faculties and schools. Any attempt to define broad curricular goals at the institutional level has to accommodate ideas about the curriculum at a local level.

In some institutions, following an initial institutional steer, the change process was devolved to a school or faculty level. At the University of Aberdeen, for example, the overall change initiative was run centrally, but the implementation phase has been led through each of the institution's Colleges. The central offices oversee the initiative, but the specifics of how the changes function in the curriculum have been devolved and can be tailored by the Colleges. At another university, the curriculum change was led from the departments and professions with a focus on 'graduateness' so change was managed at the departmental level, but done within the university framework. At Utrecht University a broad framework was interpreted at local level, with a master plan for the change customised in each faculty. Features of the Utrecht Model (UM) reflect this local preference, with the intention of developing a stronger bond between students and education. This is done in part through smaller-scale education, with more freedom of choice for students through the major/minor field of study; more active engagement of students in their learning; more student–faculty interaction; a redesign of assessment; and a mentoring system. The Model offers choice in implementation and is interpreted differently across the faculties.

Case study: Medicine at Utrecht University

Until 2006, there was one 6-year programme for Medicine at Utrecht University. When the Bachelor/Master's initiative through the Bologna Process was adopted by the University, Medicine was the last programme to change over. However, the changes were aligned with those adopted as part of the university-wide curriculum framework, the Utrecht Model. These overlapped with changes across Medicine in all of the Netherlands, with the development of a more practice-oriented interaction of clinical skills and basic science. As part of reforms from the adoption of the Utrecht Model, the Bachelor programme also makes room for working across faculties (previously, electives were only available within Medicine). Short courses have been introduced in Medical Humanities (e.g. Medical Ethics, Sociology of Medicine and Medical Law). These courses are mandatory for all medical students and they introduce the context of life in the medical curriculum. It is a successful and ongoing programme.

The Master's programme operates a similar programme as before the Bachelor/ Master's split, in large part because the curriculum was fully redesigned in 1999. It is theme-based, working across four to seven disciplines in each theme. There is a mix of theory and practice throughout the curriculum, which is interdisciplinary, integrated, and more student-focused and problem-based than the old curriculum. It also focuses on communication and uses small study groups. Even though there had been recent curriculum changes, the Bachelor/Master's phase was used to make some more small changes. More than 90 per cent of Bachelor's students go on to the Master's course. There were political reasons for separating the Bachelor and Master's, which led to other changes in the curriculum. About 80 per cent of the programme is the same as before the Bologna policies, which is less change than in many other programmes, as there was already a natural break between the third and fourth years.

Full modularisation has been a very difficult change across the institution. Bologna adoption was seen by many staff as political and structural, rather than educationally oriented. It raised questions about pedagogy and whether mobility is a valid academic goal or offers a better education. Bologna was a good motivation for changes in some programmes, like Biomedical Science, because it allows students to combine programmes across different faculties. The educational philosophy of teaching within the Utrecht Model is coherent in terms of assessment, quality assurance and the use of small study groups.

The University of Cape Town offers a further example. Devolved strategic planning supported change happening across the institution in response to institutional strategic goals. Faculties drew up their own strategic plans and each school, such as Engineering, then asked its departments to say how they would implement the plan. Funding was awarded on the understanding that new activity would be absorbed by the faculty in due course. Many institutions wanted such innovative initiatives to have impact beyond a single faculty. Major change efforts often involved attempts to build bridges and make connections across disciplines and fields of study, as discussed on page 76.

Cross-faculty approaches

Disciplinary allegiances are strong in research-intensive institutions. This presents significant challenges for cross-institutional provision, especially at an undergraduate level. A cross-institutional, interdisciplinary based restructuring, such as detailed in Chapter 9, is extremely difficult to complete successfully. A centrally driven initiative is likely to be resisted for that reason, no matter how well intentioned. Furthermore, epistemological issues and practical needs mean that neat, consistent patterns of interdisciplinary networks across an institution are not common. Devolution to the school level, as discussed above, is possible, but developing networks may also be more difficult because of the boundaries between schools. Many institutions found it more efficient and effective to encourage local initiatives where there are natural connections, such as a university-wide network for Biomedical Health Sciences. Other examples are specialist degrees in Global Business at the Hong Kong University of Science and Technology, and Conservation Ecology and Entomology at Stellenbosch University. Given the reservations that some faculty have about interdisciplinarity at undergraduate level, it may be easier to justify these if they are highly selective courses with demanding entry requirements, such as some at the University of Western Australia.

Less demanding to instigate and more common at the undergraduate level are interdisciplinary courses as part of a core curriculum or general education requirements. Examples of these are detailed in the Chapter 5 case study from the University of Hong Kong as part of their shift from three-year to four-year undergraduate degrees, and as part of the restructuring described in the University of Melbourne case study in Chapter 10. Another cross-faculty initiative at the University of Aberdeen offered 'Sixth Century' courses, drawing on faculty from at least two of the three Colleges. This has led to multi-faculty networks of academics forming, based on designing a course but often shifting into research efforts as well. Other examples include using postgraduate students to teach small-scale 'boutique' courses, which can often relate to the postgraduate's area of expertise, therefore offering students insights into advanced academic work and the research process.

Curriculum initiatives that reach beyond disciplinary material and integrate academic learning with personal reflection, such as Women's Studies, Area Studies and Environmental Studies, can be met with resistance and lead to conflict. However, such experiences, when properly supported and developed through the entire curriculum, can lead to emancipatory-style change, as discussed in Chapter 2. Such broadening efforts can have benefits for faculty as well, in terms of enhancing current teaching and research, as well as bringing in new students and enabling networking with a wider group of colleagues. These initiatives raise questions about mandating structural change for all students or offering options only for interested students, bringing to light tensions between structure and choice.

Structure versus choice

This section draws on the discussion about curriculum organisation to explore aspects of structure and choice in the curriculum. This expands on the possible consequences of a structure that emphasises general education and associated broadening units, exploring the challenges and opportunities of offering courses in discrete units of study and the proportion of the curriculum left for discipline-based study. Tensions between breadth and depth surface in discussions on the respective merits of generic versus specific provision, or whether institutions should offer fewer, broader offerings or more specific, niche programmes. There are also distinctive features that some institutions have adopted for all students. Curriculum breadth highlights the challenges of developing and sustaining networks to promote collaboration, and how structural changes need to address wider issues of student choice, fairness and cost-effectiveness.

Broadening units

General education requirements have been implemented in many recent curriculum change initiatives, as seen in the Hong Kong University of Science and Technology and the Chinese University of Hong Kong. However, in the US, where they have been a common feature as detailed in the Brown University case study in Chapter 3, many institutions have decreased the amount of student choice in their coursework (Johnson *et al.* 2004). This is often in response to faculty demand, administrative burden and a concern for lack of coherence amongst subjects for students, as discussed in this chapter. There has also been a shift from open distribution models to courses grouped in themes and clusters, often taking an interdisciplinary approach to integrate theories, methods and the study of phenomena across disciplines (Szostak 2003).

All curriculum initiatives we studied retained the 'major' or area specialisation structure and an articulation of what a major means. Some adopted interdisciplinary degree options or, more commonly, joint degree options. Most new curriculum initiatives developed broadening and elective units, including the following range:

- concentration on literature through revisiting canon texts and 'Great Books';
- broad distribution model of selecting courses from a number of different areas;
- focus on understanding disciplines in greater depth;
- courses to put disciplines in a wider context;
- interdisciplinary modules, often based on current world problems;
- structured major questions and ways of thinking in the world; and
- complete student choice across a broad range of electives.

The University of Hong Kong case study in Chapter 5 details an institution's decision-making process when adopting a structure for general education requirements. The tensions between administrative and pedagogical influences on change are brought to the fore. The Melbourne case study in Chapter 10 provides another example of the change process surrounding the creation of interdisciplinary broadening units. The latter case highlights how difficult it can be to create new structures and networks across academic disciplines. There are pedagogical challenges for some approaches, particularly interdisciplinary courses, but also for experiential learning, integrating inclusive perspectives, and adopting distance and blended learning.

Course teams in Medicine often have to choose whether to teach in disciplinary units, such as Chemistry, or in a more integrated process-oriented fashion. In developing a new Medical curriculum, the Centre for Health Science Education (CHSE) at the University of the Witwatersrand in Johannesburg faced tensions between broadening learning through theme units or through the core curriculum. This also raised the question of whether responsibility for determining the core curriculum should rest with the disciplinary specialists, such as the physicists or chemists, or with staff from Medicine. 'Roadshows' held in each department to discuss the options met with variable engagement from the different units, but overall such an approach helped to support the change effort. In the end, the 'core' was reviewed by the non-core departments to see if there was agreement that the right information was in the curriculum. To retain coherence in the courses, the curriculum was reviewed by the leaders of the courses preceding and following each one. Overall they found the keys to successful change were the roadshows and a public record of the change process.

In one Humanities school, two core courses were developed, one on texts and contexts and another organised as an introduction to thinking in the Social Sciences. However, in contrast to the disciplinary courses that students were required to take, the core courses were felt by students to be impositions. If core courses are not integrated into the disciplinary curriculum, and coordinated by discipline-based academics, not only will there be structural challenges but students may find it difficult to achieve a sense of coherence.

Many 'turf wars' in curriculum change occur over the home of certain required courses; an example is Statistics, which can be taught generically or in a specific disciplinary context, such as Biostatistics or Educational Statistics. Another university faced tensions within Chemical Engineering over provision for Maths and Physics. The chemical engineers had felt that they needed to take control of Maths and Physics, which had been taught separately in ways that were not adapted for the context of Chemical Engineering. Ideally, the chemical engineers would prefer their own mathematicians in their department. It was difficult to make this change because the Science faculty depended on the income from large introductory courses and, therefore, did not want to lose students or

Case study: Broad offerings versus niche programmes

A tension in curriculum design and programme development is whether to offer broad subjects and let students specialise within them, or to organise niche programmes, often with a more direct link to employment. One example of the latter is the Applied Computing Programme at the University of the Witwatersrand in Johannesburg. This degree is founded on modules and ideas from Software Engineering, Electrical and Engineering Science and the School of Economic and Business Studies. Applied Commuting was developed as a unique degree, geared for 'high-flyers' and offered as a separate option to the three continuing undergraduate programmes. A research centre was created, which had a more direct link with the community and industry than the individual departments.

There has been a lot of 'top-down' support for the programme. However, this has generated tensions with the three base programmes, which still each offer their own degrees. Marketing the different programmes to students has been challenging. The decision to create the course was led in part by strong academic principles and concepts, and in part by the changing nature of disciplines and socio-political conditions in the country. However, the University wished to reduce the number of schools by two thirds as part of a university restructuring. The change process required academics to make 'intellectual' sense of programmes after the structural change. In trying to shift the focus from gaining a degree to preparing for a career, course developers have found tensions between whether to provide broad offerings or specialised niche programmes.

differentiate their provision. However, Chemical Engineering students had had a problem of transfer, in that they could not use their basic science in practice in their discipline. The department's response had been to organise 'just-in-time' Maths and Physics, providing students with the content needed to advance in their studies. There have also been problems with sequencing – for example physicists using calculus when it has only started being taught elsewhere in the curriculum. Final year projects were developed to increase coherence. This sort of intervention helps, but the structure of the curriculum, which offers large, generic introductory courses rather than discipline-specific ones, is the real issue. Some institutions noticed the benefits of curriculum features such as final year projects and adopted them on a broader institution-wide scale. However, there is a danger that such efforts act as a cover for dysfunction within the curriculum.

Common features of curriculum change

Universities have adopted a number of distinctive curriculum features for a range of reasons. For example, first-year initiatives aim to help with student retention efforts and final-year projects aim to link to postgraduate opportunities. Many of the structural changes we studied were designed to promote rapid transfer of knowledge, often as a way to get advances in cutting edge research into under-graduate classroom settings. Some features were added to the formal curriculum while others were offered as optional elements or through the co-curriculum.

First-year seminars might last for a semester or a full year. One institution runs a 'virtual' first-year experience programme with an institutional focus. Another offers a spring capstone seminar experience that challenges first years to expand on the knowledge and skills acquired during the first half of the academic year and to complete a substantive project of their own. Other institutions adopted final-year capstone courses, often centred on a research project or incorporating a research project into a taught course. To help engage first-year students, UCLA runs First-Year Interest Groups (FIG). Students enrol in a cluster of three classes organised around a central theme such as Literary Imagination. This aims to help students make the transition to an intense learning environment at the university.

Adopting problem-based learning (PBL) has been a structuring device for several institutions' curriculum change. PBL is a pedagogical method used to engage students and provide a broad range of practical skills. Maastricht University introduced PBL fifteen years ago when the university was founded. The curriculum is dynamic: the institutional framework is interpreted and put into practice by the disciplines. A matrix structure of themes is offered throughout the semester and disciplinary study fits in at certain points. However, students from a rote learning background may find the student-centred team approach challenging. PBL also makes demands on staff; one academic noted that an institution had gone 'too far' with PBL and lost the support of its teachers. An academic at another institution argued that PBL is only one of many ways to encourage students to participate in and conduct research.

Several institutions included work experience, internships, placements and community volunteering experience in the curriculum. To link with the academic curriculum, these have to be organised at the local level, and therefore are very difficult to implement universally across the university. Such activities are commonplace in some fields and disciplines, but do not align easily with other areas of study. In part this relates to the purpose of a degree. For example, some curricula include a significant level of vocational and professional training while others lend themselves more to a liberal arts 'learning how to learn and think' approach. It is very challenging to engage all students, and several institutions found it better to create opportunities for interested students rather than to make it a standard requirement.

Distinctive curriculum features and pedagogies are useful organising elements for curriculum changes for both the institution and students. However, they can also be very costly in terms of resources, time and administration. Several institutions warned that new features should not be implemented without guaranteed funding, or major initiatives could disappear in a year or two. New curriculum features can also be challenging for students, who often need guidance and support in understanding requirements, choices and new learning styles.

Coherence

As discussed in Chapter 2, coherence is a major issue in curriculum design, referring to the way in which the component parts of the curriculum fit together into a cohesive whole. This includes consistency through the five aspects of the curriculum: content, process, pedagogy, assessment and learning outcomes. However, this also includes paying attention to tensions in the various ways that a curriculum can be viewed – as a planned, created or understood curriculum – and a curriculum's hidden aspects. Coherence is not achieved by simply aligning curriculum plans. Attention needs to be paid to how such plans are put into action and how they are delivered and received by students. Furthermore, coherence accounts for hidden aspects of the curriculum, such as whether critical thinking is actually encouraged or to what degree diversity is valued. Most institutions attempt to ensure coherence within disciplines through sequencing of knowledge and skill development. The availability of unstructured elective options raises questions not just about the relationship between electives and majors, but about degree programmes themselves. What, for example, is expected that all Bachelor of Arts students will have acquired? There is a tension between student choice on the one hand and disciplinary coherence on the other. An entirely open choice model may make it hard to connect the curriculum as a whole. In addition to the difficulty of achieving coherence, it is also hard to account for, to measure and evaluate open choice curricula in any systematic way.

There are also challenges for coherence when options are permitted for joint degrees, whether in structured programmes, such as Economic History, or in unstructured options that students might individually develop by working in minor areas of study, such as Education with a focus on Sociology. Some universities permit more student choice by allowing double degrees both within schools and across disciplines. Students may make broad choices (as in a liberal arts degree) or discipline-specific choices. For other universities, joint degree options are built into the curriculum and only one or two more courses are needed for a qualification in another field.

In many programmes, coherence requires the balancing of academic and disciplinary knowledge with vocational and professional competence. As one institution noted, there is a need to develop graduates with an education that is fit for purpose. Harvard University has addressed this through its General Education curriculum, which aims to navigate the tension between general education and vocational education, recognising the need to provide connections between educational experience in the university and the demands of life outside Harvard.

For some institutions, curriculum coherence was not simply a university issue, but involved the relationship with a changing school system as well. Some countries have overhauled their school curriculum, resulting in a change in what incoming cohorts of students learn and how they are taught. In South Africa, the first students to pass through the post-apartheid school curriculum are now enrolling in universities. As noted in the case study in Hong Kong in Chapter 5, the governmental Education Commission has restructured the entire education system, including primary, secondary and tertiary levels. Faculty, particularly in Medicine and Sciences, report that they do not yet know what the incoming students will know and what skills they will have.

Goals and outcomes

Universities have to be increasingly clear about what they are attempting to achieve, and to be able to communicate this widely to a variety of audiences. A survey of US institutional leaders showed that they perceived there to be external pressure for increasing emphasis on learning outcomes and competencies (Johnson *et al.* 2004) and reports in the UK (CBI 2009; Harvey *et al.* 2002) have pressed for employability to be a main outcome. Some universities have focused on the broad purposes of a degree, often expressed through particular learning outcomes.

Outcomes and goals are often the most publicised elements of a contemporary curriculum. Generally universities expressed a wish to focus on student learning and improving the student experience. The experience tends to be framed in a range of ways, using concepts such as educational aims and principles, student learning outcomes, curriculum goals, graduate attributes and skills. Some universities use them as guides and signposts while others view them as strict requirements and assess them for all students. In the latter case, they are often structured into the formal curriculum. In the former, they are often met in both the formal and co-curriculum. This section discusses outcomes and goals. Graduate attributes are covered in more detail on page 58.

Institutions took a range of approaches to implementing a focus on goals and outcomes. One institution noted that externally there is a desire for broader, less specialised skills and for more widely trained graduates. Another university began the change process with a set of educational principles and spent some months discussing the nature and purpose of the curriculum. The principles agreed upon included a focus on understanding disciplines in a wider context and the need to free space in the curriculum for new courses, so that the desired learning outcomes might be achieved. Interdisciplinarity can be seen as a way to provide students with greater skill acquisition than disciplinary study alone, as seen in the case studies from The University of Hong Kong and Melbourne. In many institutions, learning outcomes were not the initial driver for curriculum change, but became rallying points during the change process, an example of the strategic use of positive drivers for change.

Institutions that found outcomes useful appeared to have guiding principles, pathways for students and achievable outcomes for students in the curriculum. Only with faculty support would they become embedded in the formal curriculum. Outcomes and goals have the advantage of appearing to be relatively neutral terms. However, the idea that the outcomes of learning either can or should be expressed in advance is contestable, and some terms acquire particular connotations. As discussed further on page 58, graduate attributes are often linked negatively with employability and skills agendas. The issue of language about outcomes arose in discussions with several institutions. For example, one academic suggested that although learning was clearly central to a higher curriculum, the term 'learning to learn' might be interpreted as a competence approach to learning, and might therefore be resisted by academics.

Drawing on three external forces, a new university in England embedded employability skills into the curriculum. The drivers identified included recognition that the pathway from higher education to employment is not straightforward; that the curriculum is a vehicle for delivering attributes, constant across subjects; and that the world of employment is rapidly changing (Fallows and Steven 2000). They found that universal templates for application could be made flexible enough that they could be tailored to the local setting. However, there were unintended consequences, including faculty rethinking their approach to the curriculum and students 'becoming more aware of their personal responsibilities as learners' (81). However, as many universities found, this skills initiative had more success in vocational fields.

Goals

A number of universities set specific curriculum goals. At the University of Aberdeen, the fundamental goal of the curriculum change was to set disciplines in a wider context. The University of Western Australia developed discipline-based curriculum goals so that on exit from the first degree, all graduates would 'think like (Major X)' in terms of methodologies, applications of methodologies and skill sets, and should be able to communicate like 'an X' within the discourse of the discipline. Students are intended to acquire the skills to solve interdisciplinary real-world problems from a disciplinary perspective. In contrast, Temple University is strongly committed to meeting employability goals such as analysis and critical thinking through a broad general education curriculum that is not constricted or prescriptive.

The new Harvard General Education curriculum has four overarching goals for a general education, which:

- prepares students for civic engagement;
- teaches students to understand themselves as products of – and participants in – traditions of art, ideas and values;
- prepares students to respond critically and constructively to change;
- develops students' understanding of the ethical dimension of what they say and do.

Outcomes

Hong Kong offers an interesting example at a national level of an outcomes-led approach. The Hong Kong government has required all higher education institutions to articulate learning outcomes. One institution developed specific learning outcomes in their new curriculum, at the course, programme and degree level. Outcomes have become a key element in the institution's Teaching and Learning Strategy and the outcomes are integrated in a process of programme design, reflection and development. Assessment within the university is geared for outcomes, which are built in at the course and programme level. Another Hong Kong institution took an outcomes-based approach throughout the curriculum. The learning outcomes stem from the educational aims, reflected in faculty-based learning outcomes and then course-based outcomes. These are also linked with assessment modes and types of learning as well as particular pedagogies. In tune with the changes, auditing is moving away from a focus on standards and toward a 'fitness for purpose' model. Another institution in Hong Kong developed educational aims, which were meant to move beyond generic skills. The institution intends to infuse these within the curriculum rather than require them in a structured way. To provide coherence there is a progression in the curriculum from developing knowledge to acquiring skills to gaining experience in the real world.

Outcomes devised by universities tend to be culturally bound, both at a national and local level. For example, at institutions visited in the US, there was less emphasis on employability and more on the role of universities in educating graduates who were equipped for social responsibility and citizenship. One institution linked its graduate attributes with developing lifelong learning. At all institutions there was felt to be a tension when outcomes-based approaches were linked explicitly with what was seen to be an instrumental employability agenda.

Case study: External networks and outcomes

The University of Wisconsin-Madison partnered with external agencies to develop its curriculum aims. The Wisconsin Experience (WE) comprises:

- substantial research experiences that generate knowledge and analytical skills;
- global and cultural competencies and engagement;
- leadership and activism opportunities;
- application of knowledge in the 'real world' Wisconsin.

These broad themes are supported in the curriculum by a series of Essential Learning Outcomes that were developed by the Association of American Colleges and Universities (AAC&U) in consultation with employers, faculty, staff and alumni. These were based around the simple question, 'What qualities and skills do you want in college graduates?'. Wisconsin was designated as the first partner state in the Liberal Education and America's Promise (LEAP) campaign fifteen years ago. Wisconsin has subsequently piloted a series of efforts through the curriculum to support liberal education. The LEAP campaign at the University works to support the WE and increase 'understanding of the value and purpose of liberal education for the University of Wisconsin system students and Wisconsin citizens'. Four core areas have been identified under which the Essential Learning Outcomes fall for students at the university:

- *Knowledge of Human Cultures and the Physical and Natural World.* This outcome is achieved through an engagement with major questions that are both contemporary and enduring.
- *Intellectual and Practical Skills.* This outcome is achieved across the curriculum by providing increasingly more challenging problems, projects and standards of performance.
- *Personal and Social Responsibility.* This outcome is achieved through active student involvement with diverse communities based around real-world challenges.
- *Integrative Learning.* This outcome is demonstrated through the application of the knowledge, skills and responsibilities developed elsewhere within new settings to meet complex problems.

Outcomes were often aligned with specific graduate attributes, which will be discussed in the next section. Several institutions structured their curriculum around aims, both for the institution and for the curriculum. These often became banner headlines for curriculum changes, used internally and externally to promote the institution.

Graduate attributes

Graduate attributes was the most discussed student outcome of curriculum change initiatives. There were many different approaches to articulating, defining, requiring and assessing graduate attributes. It is also a very contentious subject, particularly for many discipline-based academics. One institution felt that graduate attributes could be one driver for curriculum change, of many possible drivers. At the University of Stellenbosch, the Centre for Teaching and Learning offers seminars on the scholarship of teaching and learning, as well as functional workshops. There are also generic skills modules, for example study skills and thinking skills. This is part of an effort to infuse writing and other attributes into the curriculum. An academic there proposed that the curriculum could be conceptualised as a brick wall, where the bricks are the disciplines, with generic skills providing the mortar to keep it all together. Sometimes, when things work really well, the mortar could be found in the bricks as well.

At several US Ivy League institutions, where the concept of a broad liberal education is valued and well accepted, the idea of aiming for a very instrumentalist notion of employability is rejected in favour of a belief in the value of learning and the ability to apply this to a range of settings. At Harvard, Brown and the University of Pennsylvania for example, the emphasis is on a breadth of intellectual, global and community experience and on pedagogies that enhance the learning of students. The express aim of these institutions is to educate graduates who can function at the highest levels of society as leaders in employment and the community. Such institutions often reject specific graduate attributes because they are seen to limit the purpose of an education. Ideally, what is learned during university can have multiple uses throughout a student's life. Furthermore, the meaning of attributes and outcomes varies across disciplines. A university that embedded an institution-wide employability skills initiative found that:

> An interesting disciplinary paradox is becoming ever more apparent: It has to be recognised that the demand for, say, history graduates to utilise, in subsequent employment, their subject knowledge (regardless of era) is minimal but the opportunity to utilise their employability skills is tremendous. History graduates are rarely employed as historians and this is not a general expectation; rather they recognise the need to utilise the more general skills gained during their university education. By contrast, graduates whose degree is vocationally focused (including the acquisition of very job-related skills) leave the institution with an initial expectation of employment within their chosen vocation and such persons are often slowest to recognise the generic (skills) attributes that have been developed during their time with the University.
>
> (Fallows and Steven 2000:82)

Elsewhere in the global survey a range of ways of understanding and implementing graduate attributes was found. One institution in Australia felt that the adoption of graduate attributes had been a success and had achieved influence within the university. It was noted that the weakness had been the relationship of graduate attributes and degree programmes and assessment, but the adoption of graduate attributes offered a point to focus on outside of individual faculty specialty and could be helpful in thinking about the larger curriculum picture. The institution is trying to embed attributes in the curriculum and is introducing e-portfolios, where students can self-report their attributes. At this institution an important new initiative is a Vice-Chancellor's award for teaching at the system-level and they may do something similar for graduate attributes. However, across the university there is variability in how graduate attributes are implemented. Although students know the vocabulary of graduate attributes, there is often a surface engagement, which is influenced by the staff interpretation. Some students do not feel that the graduate attributes capture what they are intended to mean. Faculty suggested that although students could speak superficially about attributes, they could not articulate what graduate attributes really mean; students need to be more than just informed about graduate attributes. Furthermore, student activities offices and support services need to be made aware of how graduate attributes link with educational experiences. Overall, the concern was for meaningful engagement rather than only adoption of the terminology.

In contrast, graduate attributes were a very contentious issue at another university in South Africa. Graduate attributes approaches were seen by many in the humanities as 'ridiculous and irrelevant'. Some faculty felt that attributes had been imposed in a heavily 'top-down' approach that had since softened, but overall attributes were felt not to be the answer to concerns about the curriculum because they had not been developed appropriately. It was felt that attributes needed to come from departments and to be put into the curriculum through disciplines, rather than imposed from outside. As one disciplinary academic put it, graduate attributes are 'fine' but she wants a Chemistry graduate to be able to do Chemistry. In another department, students gained graduate attributes in a way that fitted the national context. It was claimed that through 'learning to do a lot with little' in South Africa, they would learn to be creative and innovative and would be very skilled in international settings. Staff felt that the challenge for students was a large one. Tasks needed to be contained and put in perspective for students so they did not become overwhelmed and disillusioned.

As an academic at another institution put it, there are some graduate attributes that can be taught but most are absorbed, so the learning environment is important. Highlighting the network nature of attributes, the question becomes how to measure the 'embeddedness' of attributes across a variety of settings and contexts. Graduate attributes were also conceptualised as links not just between the curriculum and students but also with the co-curriculum and between staff and students. For example at the University of Aberdeen, postgraduate students were trained to teach the various graduate attributes to undergraduate students. At the University of Sydney, the big challenge was to think of graduate attributes in the big picture of the curriculum, rather than only in units of study. The institution developed

Sydney Talent, which concentrates on behavioural attributes and focuses on immediate entry into the workforce. Interestingly, this initiative is actually leading to more student interest in graduate attributes.

At one institution, the development of graduate attributes was seen by many academic staff to be done at the expense of disciplinary content. A centrally driven and approved strategic plan aimed to enhance the quality and profile of graduates. However, although graduate attributes were a focus in some of the professional faculties, several other faculties were resisting 'central planning'. A new approach from the central units had been to invite faculties to identify members to produce 'think pieces' about attributes within faculties and disciplines, in relation to the strategic plan. This engagement with academics about how attributes could be conceived was gaining more support. From a disciplinary perspective, one academic noted that employers are looking for evidence of broad critical thinkers, people who can 'think outside the box' and also for 'team workers' in the business world. The department's goal was to develop independent critical thinkers and learners within a discipline, offering a firm basis for individual thinking and learning and developing the idea of how to 'learn how to learn'.

Another institution detailed graduate attributes in a number of areas such as research, communication and diversity, creating matrices for each module, year and programme. These were implemented across departments through showing examples and allowing disciplinary experts to define it in their own terms. This was seen as 'over-matrixing' by some, but leaders of the initiative saw it as presenting tools to show academics how it could be done. They felt it was better to 'give tools to people to implement themselves rather than give the tools to assessors to use them in the disciplines'. This provided the academics with more control over how their programmes were reviewed, rather than having evaluation driven externally.

At one institution, it was sometimes assumed in departments that that the adoption of graduate attributes in degrees would be restrained by professional accreditation requirements of the programmes. However, some of the professional bodies were very supportive when approached. Changes were made to disciplinary options, which mapped onto changes the professional body wanted to explore. Academic staff appeared to be more concerned than the accrediting body about maintaining the disciplinary content. Space could be found in the early years of the curriculum, since the accrediting process is more focused at the examination and Honours level in the final year.

Conclusions

Many broad influences shape a curriculum, setting its scope and framing how coherence is achieved. Although there are similarities across the globe, the curriculum is always shaped by the local context. Drivers may be international, national and institutional. We recognised the important role that professional and accrediting bodies play in influencing and supporting curriculum change. All of the institutions that were visited grappled with these issues in different ways. We have looked at the curriculum as a set of policies, or requirements, and also as a process that students move through. In analysing innovative practice elsewhere, we looked at the structure and content of curriculum change, as well as various curriculum characteristics. We saw that these could be formally structured in the curriculum, set as requirements students needed to meet, or more generally infused throughout the curriculum. We also saw that responsibility to meet requirements was often placed on students, although some institutions provided more support from staff and others to embed these in the curriculum and assist students in meeting them.

References

Andersen, M. L. (1987) Changing the curriculum in higher education. *Signs, 12*(2): 222–254.

Bowles, G. and Duelli-Klein, R. (eds). (1983) *Theories of Women's Studies.* Boston: Routledge.

CBI (2009) *Future fit: Preparing graduates for the world of work.* London: CBI.

Clegg, S., Stevenson, J. and Willott, J. (2010) Staff conceptions of curricular and extracurricular activities in higher education. *Higher Education, 59*: 615–626.

Eisner, E. (1985). *The educational imagination* (2nd ed.). New York: Macmillan.

Fallows, S. and Steven, S. (2000) Building employability skills into the higher education curriculum: A university-wide initiative. *Education + Training, 42*(2): 75–83.

Harvey, L., Locke, W. and Morey, A. (2002) *Enhancing employability, recognising diversity: Making links between higher education and the world of work.* London: Universities UK.

Johnson, D. K., Ratcliff, J. L. and Gaff, J. G. (2004) A decade of change in general education. *Changing General Education Curriculum: New Directions for Higher Education, 125*: 9–28.

Knight, P. T. (2001) Complexity and curriculum: A process approach to curriculum-making. *Teaching in Higher Education, 6*(3): 369–381.

Parker, J. (2003) Reconceptualising the curriculum: From commodification to transformation. *Teaching in Higher Education, 8*(4): 529–543.

Short, E. C. (2002) Knowledge and the educative functions of a university: Designing the curriculum of higher education. *Journal of Curriculum Studies, 34*(2): 139–148.

Stenhouse, L. (1975) *An introduction to curriculum research and development.* London: Heinemann.

Szostak, R. (2003) 'Comprehensive' curricular reform: Providing students with a map of the scholarly enterprise. *Journal of General Education, 52*(1): 27–49.

van Alstyne, M. (1998) Higher education's information challenge, in J. Meyerson (ed.). *New thinking on higher education* (pp. 120–147). Bolton, MA: Anker Publishing.

Chapter 5

Transforming student learning

Undergraduate curriculum reform at the University of Hong Kong[1]

Amy B. M. Tsui

From September 2012 onwards, undergraduate education in Hong Kong will be extended by one year. In response to this government policy change, higher education institutions in Hong Kong have been redesigning their undergraduate curricula in different ways. This chapter provides a brief outline of some of the challenges currently faced by universities worldwide and the ways in which the University of Hong Kong (HKU) has tried to meet these challenges in its undergraduate curriculum reform. Because of the space limitations, this chapter focuses on only a few of the major, and perhaps more contentious, changes in the curriculum. These include the review of the aims of undergraduate education, the reconceptualization of the curriculum, the adoption of a flexible curriculum structure, the introduction of a common curriculum component as a university requirement for all students and the promotion of experiential learning as an integral part of the curriculum.

The context of undergraduate curriculum reform in Hong Kong

The Hong Kong education system has been, and still is, highly selective and academically focused. Until 2011, only 40 per cent of Secondary 5 graduates were able to continue to Secondary 6 and 7 after selection by public examination. At the end of the two senior secondary years, which were entirely focused on preparing students for university study, a second public examination selected 18 per cent of these students to enter university. This system no longer meets the needs of a knowledge society. The social and economic developments in Hong Kong require the school system to produce graduates with a broader knowledge base and more diverse skills to enable them to move easily into other fields besides academic studies. To address this situation, the Hong Kong government introduced a new educational structure in 2009. The secondary education structure now consists of three years of junior secondary schooling and three years of senior secondary schooling (3+3), with a public examination at the end of the six years. In September 2012, undergraduate education will change from three years to four years (i.e. 3+3+4). The new senior secondary structure allows all students to enjoy three years of senior secondary education. The secondary curriculum has become broader and more diversified, providing a wider range of academic and practically oriented subjects to suit the aptitudes and interests of the students. In addition, under the new system, students sit one public examination at the end of secondary schooling instead of two. This alleviates examination pressure on students and will hopefully also result in less examination-driven teaching and learning.

University education in Hong Kong has until now largely been modelled on the British higher education system, with students specializing in specific disciplines or professional training from their first year of study. In recent decades, however, it has become increasingly clear that this model of early specialization and narrow disciplinary focus does not enable students to develop the generic skills, capabilities and attitudes required for coping with the rapidly changing demands made on university graduates. The Hong Kong government therefore proposed that undergraduate education be extended by one year to allow time for a strong foundation of subjects to support specialization. This structure also articulates with the education systems in the US and in Mainland China (Education and Manpower Bureau 2004). This new undergraduate structure will be introduced in 2012. Since the announcement of the reform schedule, universities in Hong Kong have been redesigning their undergraduate curricula accordingly.

One major concern shared by academics across institutions is whether, with one year less of secondary education and a broad-based curriculum that is no longer focused on preparation for university study, students will have enough basic knowledge in the disciplines for them to pursue specialization at tertiary level. This concern is particularly strong amongst academics in science-based and technology-based disciplines, as well as those in professional schools. To make up for any perceived knowledge gap between the new secondary curriculum and university specialization, some institutions have planned to introduce 'remedial' or 'foundational' courses in these disciplines.

Transforming student learning: Undergraduate curriculum reform at HKU

At the University of Hong Kong, there was a similar concern amongst some quarters of the academic community regarding university entrants' potential lack of a solid grounding in disciplinary knowledge. However, others felt that what students needed rather than disciplinary knowledge was the ability to think critically, to learn independently and to uphold the core values of a humane and democratic society. When members of the academic staff were asked what they wanted the new curriculum to achieve, an Architecture professor said, 'I want our students to be thinking Architects!'; a Medical professor said, 'I want my students to treat patients like human beings!'; and an Arts professor said, 'I want my students not to expect me to tell them what the right answer is!'

After much discussion at university retreats and seminars, it was agreed that the design of the new curriculum at HKU would be better guided by consideration of how student learning might be transformed in the four years of undergraduate education, rather than by consideration of what should be added to the extra year. This decision was inspired by Stephanie P. Marshall's insightful comments on public education reform. Marshall pointed out that the reinvention of public education is 'not about changing what is, but about creating what is not' (1996). She further commented, 'Adding wings to caterpillars does not create butterflies – it creates awkward and dysfunctional caterpillars. Butterflies are created through transformation.'[2] Hence, the overall framework for the undergraduate curriculum reform at HKU was entitled 'Transforming Student Learning' (hereafter TSL).

To facilitate university-wide discussion, the reform framework document proposed a conceptual framework for curriculum design. According to this framework, a curriculum is guided by the educational aims that it sets out to achieve. The aims, in turn, are shaped by the environment they are designed to shape. Based on our analysis of the external environment, that is, the demands made on higher education as a result of globalization, and the impending changes brought about by the new educational structure, the following questions were posed collectively to the university community: What are the aims of our undergraduate education? What attributes do we wish to nurture in our students? What kind of learning experience should be afforded to students in order to help them to develop the knowledge, skills and values required to meet the challenges of globalization? What kind of learning environment should be created to facilitate these developments?

After consultation with all Faculties and heated debate at the University Senate, the following six educational aims for undergraduate education were agreed upon.

To enable our students to develop the capabilities in:

- the pursuit of academic excellence, critical intellectual inquiry and lifelong learning;
- enacting personal and profession ethics, critical self-reflection and greater understanding of others;
- tackling novel situations and ill-defined problems;
- intercultural communication and multicultural understanding;
- communication and collaboration;
- leadership and advocacy for the improvement of the human condition.

All programmes are required to state their learning outcomes in relation to these educational aims, the learning activities that will help students to achieve these outcomes, how these outcomes will be assessed and/or the evidence that will serve to indicate whether these outcomes have been achieved or not.

Responding to change and a flexible curriculum structure

In the past two decades, the rapid changes brought about by globalization have led to reviews of higher education and undergraduate curriculum by governments and universities worldwide.[3] The traditional curriculum structure that confines student choice largely to disciplines offered by the student's home Faculty is no longer fit for purpose. A university should be a place that opens up students' minds, encourages students to explore untrodden territories and provides abundant possibilities for personal and intellectual development. In order for the University to serve these functions, we need a curriculum structure that allows students to explore their own interests and to maximize their potential capabilities. We also need a flexible curriculum that can respond quickly to advances in knowledge and societal needs by setting up new interdisciplinary and multidisciplinary programmes and offering cross-disciplinary collaborations in programmes and courses. A rigid curriculum structure, where teaching and the corresponding funding allocations are compartmentalized, works against a responsive curriculum. A flexible curriculum structure has increasingly become a standard feature of undergraduate education worldwide.

At the University of Hong Kong, a credit–unit system and a more flexible structure that allows students to take minors and electives outside their home Faculties was introduced more than ten years ago. The new undergraduate curriculum structure is more flexible, allowing students to choose different combinations of majors, minors and electives within and outside their home Faculties to fulfil their credit–unit requirements. In the old curriculum structure, most students selected their majors on entry to the university, with the exception of Arts students, who could declare their majors any time after the first year of study. The new structure requires that students enrolled in all programmes, bar professional programmes, declare their major(s) after the first year. While a flexible curriculum structure that caters for student choice is commonplace in many North American universities, its implementation nevertheless poses some challenges. Successful transition requires Faculties to give top priority to students' intellectual and personal development rather than their own interests. It also requires a resource allocation mechanism that does not hinder student movement across Faculties and Departments. A university-wide academic advising system that is truly student-centred and has multiple channels for students to obtain advice on their academic studies is also crucial.

The curriculum as the totality of learning experiences

In the new curriculum framework at HKU, we adopted a view of learning as not only cognitive but also experiential. We believe that it is in the course of participation in social practice that students develop the knowledge, skills, attitudes and values that enable them to contribute to society as responsible citizens. Thus, learning permeates all activities in which students are engaged, irrespective of setting, context and modes. Based on this view, we have defined the curriculum 'as the totality of experiences that are afforded to students to achieve educational aims' (TSL: 9). All learning, whether it takes place inside or outside the classroom, should contribute to the achievement of educational aims. For example, to enhance intercultural understanding, opportunities are afforded for students

from different disciplines and ethnic and cultural backgrounds to engage in intellectual inquiry and collaboration through participation in common courses, tutorials and projects; the admission policy adopted by the student residences ensures
a balanced mix of local, international and mainland Chinese students; and activities are organized by students that raise their awareness of and respect for cultural
differences.

We also believe that not all experiences are educative. As John Dewey pointed
out, 'The belief that all genuine education comes about through experience does
not mean all experiences are genuinely or equally educative … for some experiences are mis-educative. Any experience is mis-educative that has the effect of
arresting or distorting the growth of further experience' (1938:25). Therefore,
it is our responsibility as curriculum designers to organize the experience so that
it is conducive to students' continued growth. Accordingly, we proposed the
following overarching statement to guide our design and planning: 'To make
available multifarious educational experiences and to structure them in a way that
enables students to engage with these experiences in meaningful and coherent
ways throughout their undergraduate education and beyond' (TSL: 10).

To facilitate the achievement of this curriculum goal, the Dean of Student
Affairs, who oversees student activities, student organizations and student accommodation, has become a member of all university-level committees relating to
teaching and learning.

Breadth requirement and the common core curriculum

In most North American universities, 'General Education' is a standard component of undergraduate education. In universities that used to adopt early
specialization, however, the allocation of a substantial portion of the curriculum to studies outside the major disciplines inevitably generates debate on
the balance between 'depth' and 'breadth'. A similar situation occurred at
HKU, where members of the academic staff held different conceptions of what
constitutes knowledge and how knowledge is acquired. After heated debate
across the university, it was agreed that, given the rapid generation of new
knowledge and the increasingly short half-life of new knowledge, students
needed to be equipped with the intellectual skills to engage in critical enquiry
and independent thinking, to ask questions from different perspectives, and to
formulate their own answers to these questions. Inspired by the words of Mark
van Doren, the American Pulitzer Prize-winning poet and critic, who said,
'The student who can begin early in life to think of things as connected … has
begun the life of learning' (1943: 115), we realized that it was crucial to help
students to see the interconnections between concepts or things that appear to
be discrete and unrelated, and to see the commonalities underlying concepts
or things that appear to be different. After reviewing the various ways in which
educators had tried to help students develop these intellectual skills[4] in the past
few decades, it was decided that students would benefit most from exploring

human experiences that are common to all societies. These common experiences include the following:

- the aesthetic (or symbolic) expression of ideas and emotions;
- the relationship between individuals and communities and the role of the former in the latter;
- the interaction amongst communities of different scales;
- the relationships and interdependencies between human beings, science, technology and nature;
- the beliefs and values that are essential to human bonding and to mediating tensions within and between groups;
- the relationship between our past, present and future.

This component of the new curriculum has been given the nomenclature 'Common Core Curriculum'[5]. The word 'common' delimits the scope of the curriculum, that is, it focuses on the commonality of human experiences. The word 'core' defines its essence, that is, the curriculum focuses on issues that have been, and continue to be, of deeply profound significance to humankind and on core values that students should uphold. It also denotes the learning experiences that are common to all HKU undergraduates and the common attributes that they are expected to acquire.

To determine the organization of this component, we reviewed models of organization of general education in US universities. The most commonly adopted model is the distribution requirements model, in which students are required to take a number of introductory courses in various disciplines. This popular model is easy to administer, requires no extra resources and no redesign of courses by teaching staff. However, it has been heavily criticized by a number of scholars, including former university presidents in the US, for not being able to achieve the goals of general education. Those who are critical of this model argue that, as students intend to major in the respective disciplines, taking a smorgasbord of introductory courses spanning a number of disciplines simply leads to fragmentation of knowledge. As Derek Bok, former President of Harvard University remarked, 'For most colleges with simple distribution requirements, the price does seem too high. Administrative advantages have been purchased at the cost of diluting the legitimate aims of general education' (2006:262). Despite the fact that there was support for the distribution requirement model to be implemented at HKU, a decision was made that student learning should not be compromised by administrative convenience, and that a coherent curriculum consisting of specially designed courses should be offered to all students to enable them to achieve the following goals:

- to develop a broader perspective and a critical understanding of the complexities and the interconnectedness of the issues that they are confronted with in their everyday lives;

- to cultivate an appreciation of their own culture and other cultures, and the interrelatedness amongst cultures;
- to see themselves as members of global and local communities and to play an active role as responsible individuals and citizens in these communities;
- to develop the key intellectual skills that will be further enhanced in their disciplinary studies.

To organize the curriculum, four Areas of Inquiry (AoI) were defined: Humanities; Science and Technology; Global Issues; and China: State, Culture and Society. These AoIs are interrelated rather than mutually exclusive, and courses often straddle two or more AoIs. The coherence of the curriculum is achieved by outlining a conceptual framework for each AoI and using these frameworks to address the goals of the Common Core. While the four AoIs seem to be commonplace, what is perhaps more exciting is the fact that each AoI specifies its aim and the key issues that will be addressed. For example, the China AoI aims to enable students to gain an understanding of China from past to present, as well as from different disciplinary perspectives. It engages students in critical inquiries of the issues and problems faced by China through five outlined themes: Chinese Culture: Thoughts, Values and Ways of Life; Chinese Civilization: State, Society and Economy; China's Changing Environment; China's Quest for Modernization; and The Rise of China in the twenty-first century: Challenges and Prospects. Within each theme, key issues are listed.[6] Each course proposal must indicate the related AoI, as well as the key themes and issues the course aims to address, and how. Each course proposal goes through a rigorous vetting process by a university-level committee to ensure that it has intellectual depth, but is also accessible for non-major students. The rigour of the vetting process is evidenced by the fact that in the first round of applications, only 72 of the 225 proposals submitted by all ten Faculties were accepted. The Common Core Curriculum was introduced in 2010 for the current three-year curriculum as a pilot to allow sufficient time for fine-tuning for full implementation in 2012. The new courses were rated highly by the students, with the most common comments being 'intellectually challenging', 'exciting', and 'exhausting' (a reference to the heavy workload).

Experiential learning: An integral part of the curriculum

One long-standing criticism that employers of university graduates have voiced is their inability to solve problems independently. For this reason, HKU has always placed a strong emphasis on helping students to develop problem-solving skills. In recent years, however, an additional criticism has been voiced, namely that university graduates are unable to function fully outside their comfort zone: that when they are put in unfamiliar situations or presented with problems that are not clearly defined, they become lost. This criticism is not difficult to understand if we reflect on the kinds of problems that students are typically presented with in educational contexts. These problems are often set within familiar contexts and defined by the teacher. The assumption is that someone (often the teacher) knows what the problem is and what the 'right' solution(s) should be. However, in real life, we often find ourselves in situations where we do not even know what the problem is. As the anthropologist Jean Lave pointed out, problems often do not present themselves as such. A classic example relevant to Hong Kong is the outbreak of SARS. When the epidemic hit the territory, there was a shared assumption in the community that somebody should know what the problem was and should have a ready solution to it. Blame was put on the government, the Hospital Authority and hospital management for not being able to contain the epidemic, when, in fact, the epidemic was not fully understood and the problem had not even been identified. Again, as Lave noted, the relationship between the problem and the answer is dialectical: the problem is defined at the same time as an answer to the problem is developed (1988). We therefore need to enable students to develop the capability to identify problems. While it is important to develop skills in problem solving, it is equally important, if not more so, to help students to understand that there are problems that have no perfect solutions and that often a proposed solution generates a new set of its own inherent problems (Engström 2001). It is important for us to be fully aware of the likely consequences of the solutions proposed and to accept that we may have to live with less than perfect solutions.

In planning the new curriculum, we are concerned not only about what our students know and the skills they have acquired, but also, and more importantly, about whether they have developed the capability to deal with novel situations (i.e. situations that they have not come across before) and whether they are able to identify problems and come up with solutions. One powerful way to ensure this is to provide opportunities for students to engage in real-life projects or solve real-life problems (rather than projects or problems designed by the teacher). In real-life situations, problems are typically not easily identifiable or well defined. Identifying and tackling these problems requires a broad interdisciplinary knowledge base. It requires us to take into account not only the technical factors, but also the social, political and economical factors in a specific context. Therefore, providing opportunities for students to work in unfamiliar real-life contexts and to tackle real-life problems is a powerful way of helping them to develop these skills. We refer to this kind of learning as 'experiential learning', and define it as the development of situated knowledge and skills through direct experience rather than through reading about them in books or listening to lectures.

Experiential learning is supported by a theory of learning that sees participation in practice as central to knowledge development, and the context of participation as part of the knowledge developed. Hence knowledge is not something that is passed on second-hand from the teacher to the student but something that is constructed first-hand by students themselves. It is in practice that students make sense of theoretical knowledge, put it under scrutiny in various contexts, and consequently construct their own theories. In the new curriculum, Faculties are encouraged to incorporate experiential learning into their curricula so that it complements theoretical learning. Experiential learning goes beyond internship (or practicum), which has a long tradition in professional programmes. In internships, students are often assigned specific roles and carry out well defined tasks. They are then assessed on how well they have acquired the necessary practical skills to carry out these tasks.

Experiential learning, however, aims to put students in contexts in which they are engaged in a broader scope of work and forced to solve real-life problems. For example, the traditional internship for civil engineering students at HKU takes the form of summer jobs in construction firms, where the students often contribute to a very small part of the construction process and interact mainly with their supervisor(s) or a few co-workers. Experiential learning in civil engineering involves students participating in construction projects in underdeveloped regions, for example by building schools and student hostels for village children, reconstructing roads and bridges, and so on. These projects require students to engage with local residents to find out their needs and negotiate building designs, to cope with adverse working and living conditions and to maximize the limited resources available. They give students a more thorough understanding of the complexities of the process of construction and open their eyes to the fact that technical considerations are only one part of a construction project. More importantly, the students' engagement with the community during these projects helps them to better understand their civic role as engineers within society. While a number of Faculties have made experiential learning credit-bearing, three Faculties – Social Sciences, Science, and Engineering – have made it a graduation requirement. The ultimate goal is for experiential learning to become a graduation requirement for all undergraduate students.[7]

Concluding remarks

In this chapter, I have barely skimmed the surface of the enormous challenges faced by higher education institutions, and the ways in which the University of Hong Kong has tried to leverage the opportunity of a structural change in the education system to address some of these challenges. I have highlighted only a few of the major changes that generated heated debate amongst staff, and the more distinctive aspects of the new curriculum. Other changes in the curriculum that I have not touched on here are also significant, and equally important and contentious. Examples include the introduction of outcome-based learning, standards-referenced assessment, the review of the honours classification system, the use of English (not only as a medium of instruction but also as a lingua franca on campus to enhance cultural inclusiveness and to resolve cultural tensions), and so on. I have also not been able to touch on the synergy between the physical learning space and the intellectual learning space, which is an integral part of the curriculum reform. At the University of Hong Kong, a new campus and new student accommodation are currently being built and the old campus is being retrofitted to cater for the double cohort in 2012. The design and modification of the physical spaces has been guided by student-centred learning and the aim of fostering collaborative learning, flexible learning and the creation of learning communities. This chapter is also brief on the immensely complex processes of culture change that are involved in a curriculum reform of such scale. The journey on which the University has embarked to transform student learning has only just begun. In 2016, after the first cohort of students enrolled in the new four-year curriculum has completed their study, a review of the reform will be conducted. This review will yield important findings and evidence for the University to fine-tune its implementation plan and strategies.

Notes

1   The author wishes to thank Mr. Gwyn Edwards for his comments on the first draft of this manuscript. She also wishes to thank members of the Steering Committee of the 4-Year Undergraduate Curriculum Reform for their input into the conceptualization and the planning of the entire reform.
2   Stephanie Pace Marshall was the Founding President and currently President Emerita of the Illinois Mathematics and Science Academy in Aurora, Illinois.
3   See for example, in the UK, *The Dearing Report* in 1997 and *The Future of Higher Education* in 2003; in Australia, *The West Review* in 1998, *Our Universities: Backing Australia's Future* in 2003, and *The Bradley Review of Higher Education in Australia* in 2008, and the policy paper *Transforming Australia's Higher Education System* in 2009; in the US, the Boyer Commission Report, *Re-inventing Undergraduate Education* in 1998 and the review of this report in 2002; and in Europe, the Bologna Process, which started in 1998 with four or five states and grew to forty-five in 2005, resulting in the establishment of the European Higher Education Area in 2010.
4   The curriculum frameworks reviewed include those suggested in the highly influential curriculum framework proposed by Jerome Bruner in the 1960s, *Man: A Course of Study*, known by its acronym as MACOS, to address Bruner's famous question 'What makes humans human?'; the work of Ernest Boyer and Arthur Levine (1981) on General Education; Dennis Lawton, one of the founding scholars of curriculum studies in the 1980s and 1990s; Donald Levine (2006), emeritus professor of Sociology at University of Chicago; and Derek Bok (2006), former President of Harvard University.
5   The HKU Common Core is different from the Common Core used in some US universities (such as Columbia), which refers to the study of core classical texts.
6   For example, under the theme 'China's quest for modernization', some of the issues listed are:
    - What are the competing visions of modernization put forward by contending Chinese political forces and movements?
    - What are the similarities and differences between the responses from China and other late developers such as Germany and Japan to the challenge of Western powers since the mid-nineteenth century?
    - How was the Chinese polity shaped and transformed by the successive attempts to modernize the country by the different political forces in the last century?
    - What are the roles played by intellectuals, capitalists, workers, peasants and other important social forces in China's modernization?

- How have the different Chinese societies, namely Hong Kong, Macau, Taiwan and overseas Chinese communities, contributed to China's modernization in the different historical eras?
- What are the characteristics of the different paths of modernization in Greater China? What are the similarities and differences between these development models?
- What are the social, economic, cultural and political roles played by Hong Kong in bridging China and the West during China's quest for modernization?

7   For examples of experiential learning at HKU, see http://tl.hku/reform/experiential-learning/

References

Bok, D. (2006) *Our underachieving college.* Princeton: Princeton University Press.

Boyer, E. L. and Levine, A. (1981) *A quest for common learning: The aims of general education. A Carnegie Foundation essay.* Washington, D. C.: The Carnegie Foundation for the Advancement of Teaching.

Dewey, J. (1938) *Experience and education.* New York: Simon and Schuster.

Education and Manpower Bureau, Hong Kong Special Administrative Region Government. (2004). *The new academic structure for senior secondary education and higher education: First stage consultation document.* Retrieved from http://334.edb.hkedcity.net/doc/eng/main.pdf

Engeström, Y. (2001) Expansive learning at work. *Journal of Education and Work,* *14*(1): 133–156.

Lave, J. (1988) *Cognition in Practice.* Cambridge: Cambridge University Press.

Levine, Donald (2006) *Powers of the mind: The reinvention of liberal learning in America.* Chicago: University of Chicago Press.

Marshall, S. P. (1996) Chaos, complexity, and flocking behavior: Metaphors for learning. *Wingspread Journal,* *18*(3). Retrieved from http://www.learningtolearn.sa.edu.au/core_learning/files/links/ChaosComplexity.pdf

Steering Committee on 4-year Undergraduate Curriculum, The University of Hong Kong. (2006) *Transforming student learning: 4-year undergraduate curriculum reform.* Retrieved from http://www.hku.hk/reserved_2/tlearn/reform/doc/discussiondocs/Transforming%20Student%20Learning_first%20draft_May%202006.pdf

Van Doren, M. (1943) *Liberal education.* New York: Henry Holt and Company.

Chapter 6

Shaping the curriculum

A characteristics approach

Camille B. Kandiko and Paul Blackmore

Introduction

Curricula are often reviewed and revised in order to ensure that they have particular characteristics, as institutions seek to show that they are distinctively different from their peers. Paradoxically, remarkably similar issues were discussed at the institutions we visited. Research-intensive institutions are always concerned that students should benefit from the presence of research. Curriculum broadening often means that an interdisciplinary approach is encouraged. Universities increasingly seek to ensure that students' experience includes engagement with the world beyond the university, whether in the local community or globally. Another group of concerns centres on students' capacity to learn.

We consider these issues here, using the following terms:

- research intensiveness
- interdisciplinarity
- community engagement
- global connectedness
- academic literacy

Each of these concerns is known by a range of different terms. Each points to a desirable aspect of a well-rounded curriculum and may be woven into the rhetoric of an institution. However, whether these characteristics are actually reflected in the curriculum is largely an act of faith. Most institutions appear to do relatively little to define in detail what they mean by such terms, which is understandable, because it is extremely hard to arrive at a settled and universally agreed definition of any of them, given their nature and also the diversity of disciplines and professional groups. There was little serious attempt to define or to assess the outcomes of exposure to such characteristics, in terms of students' cognitive gains or other metrics. Not only is it extremely difficult to specify them, as discussed in Chapter 4, it is equally challenging to assess them, an issue which is taken up in Chapter 7. However, since many of the outcomes of higher-level learning are inherently unpredictable, we argue that it is appropriate to pay attention to creating the conditions under which desired learning is likely to occur. This is, perhaps, to return to a more traditional conception of a university as an environment that facilitates inherently unpredictable learning, rather than to train its students towards sets of known outcomes.

Implementing characteristics within existing provision, by current staff and within disciplinary settings, can be challenging. We were fortunate to have discussions with many discipline-based academics about their experiences in planning for, implementing, teaching, and assessing new curriculum characteristics. Many of the tensions within curriculum change noted throughout the book were raised, including: challenges between breadth versus depth; structure versus choice; provision in the formal versus the co-curriculum; disciplinary versus professional education; and theory versus practice. These issues arose across the five curriculum characteristics. However, how these characteristics were interpreted varied immensely across disciplinary, institutional and national settings, highlighting some of the key challenges of curriculum change initiatives.

Following on from the structures discussed earlier, we explore the various ways the curriculum characteristics were implemented. These approaches indicate different patterns of theme-based networks operating across institutional boundaries. First, they could be integrated or infused in the existing curriculum or embedded in new modules, such as communication skills. In this case, the focus is on the outcome. Second, they could become required elements, such as foreign language requirements, made available through existing courses or through new provision. This is a more content-centred approach. Lastly, they could be structured, such as in core modules for all students or through distributed elective elements (e.g. 'Solving World Problems' courses). Such a process-based approach often requires extensive networks throughout an institution to provide universal provision, especially if it is interdisciplinary in nature. We saw that institutions often placed the responsibility to meet such requirements on students, although some provided more support to embed these in the curriculum and assist students in meeting them, such as with the advising system developed at Brown University.

Research-intensiveness

All research-intensive institutions seem concerned to show that their research benefits their teaching. In part this reflects a deeply held view that it does benefit their teaching; for many staff this seems axiomatic. There is also recognition that the strength of research in a research-intensive institution offers a market advantage over other institutions. Research-intensive institutions are also aware that an assertion that research benefits their teaching can be a means of arguing for the continuing availability of research funding.

Driven in part by the political aspect, there has been an immense amount of research and discussion on the link between research and teaching in recent years. Jenkins and Healy in particular have focused on institutional strategy in this field (Jenkins and Healy 2005; Jenkins *et al.* 2002; Gibbs 2002). While there is a widespread belief in universities that the presence of research and the quality of teaching are linked, many studies have shown little or no close association between high-quality research and teaching outcomes, as demonstrated by Hattie and Marsh's (1996) widely cited meta-analysis, although a weak link has been demonstrated in liberal arts institutions. The presence of excellent research in an institution does not guarantee excellent teaching. However, even though a link is not inevitable, it is reasonable to suppose that a research-rich environment can benefit students' learning.

Although the link is often emphasised, policies and practice are not always aligned in ways that support a teaching–research nexus. There are several broad approaches that work to build such networks. The first emphasises students encountering the products of research. This is often termed 'research-led' teaching. Students frequently say that they find exposure to academics' own research to be inspirational. It is not always possible to base an entire curriculum on current research by an institution's academic staff, particularly at an undergraduate level. However, there are many other ways that research can be brought into the curriculum. Some institutions emphasise the importance of students doing research and, in the process, having research tools available to them (Blackmore and Fraser 2003). Others emphasise the less tangible aspects of a research culture, through immersion in a place where research is visible, spoken about and valued. If all these possible ways of making connections are to be exploited, a university will build a concern for both process and product into the curriculum in a developmental manner through the course of a student's career, within a strong research culture. The view currently reflected in the higher education literature is that this can be facilitated when teaching activity more closely resembles research activity. This may require a significant change in approaches to teaching. To achieve this change, the curriculum needs appropriate support and resourcing, and student and staff roles need to be clear.

Terminology is not easy in this field; there are a number of terms with meanings that vary in use. 'Research-led' focuses on the products of research and is therefore rather narrow. 'Research-informed' is an unambitious term that all universities might aspire to offer. An alternative is to use a term that has not been colonised. 'Research-rich' was chosen for this reason during the King's-Warwick Project [KWP]. One institution has also used the term 'research-intensive' to describe curricula. This has the advantage that it is a high-status term that has no fixed meaning in relation to curricula and can thus be defined in desired ways.

Any definition of a 'research-rich' or 'research-intensive' environment must be flexible enough to allow for local interpretation across a range of academic disciplines, since the nature of the link varies considerably according to context. Models of such networks vary from no linkage, to total integration. As noted in the KWP report, a 'research-engaged' model offers a balance, involving a conceptual shift from seeing students as consumers of knowledge to an acknowledgement of students as producers of knowledge. However, the terms 'consumer' and 'producer' may both suggest a one-way flow that is not adequate when teaching and research are closely integrated. Teachers and students may be better viewed as co-constructors of knowledge. Activities that support a research and teaching nexus may be of many kinds. A number of them are categorised in the following sections:

Learning about research in the discipline

At a basic level this may mean including academics' own publications on reading lists. It also incorporates: embedding an introduction to the purpose and processes of research in the curriculum (University of Western Australia); introducing students to research communities and research centres (University of Pennsylvania); introducing students to peer-reviewed journals and the publication process; opening the doors of research centres to undergraduate students; and teaching students how knowledge was researched, rather than simply delivering it as subject content.

Engaging in research discussions

Approaches to encouraging student engagement in discussion about research include: presenting multiple perspectives and techniques to approach research questions (Brown University); using evidence-based research and evidence-based practice (University of Sydney); linking knowledge and the wider society (Harvard University); providing interdisciplinary perspectives (University of Melbourne); supporting student-led research journals (University of Warwick); inviting students to attend academic seminars and conferences; and including Master's and PhD students and post-docs in teaching activities.

Developing research and inquiry skills and techniques

These are approached by: probing students to frame their questions in terms of researchable hypotheses (University of Cape Town); presenting material to students in the forms in which it is researched, such as using first-hand source materials in History and using lab techniques and findings in the Sciences; setting up mock grant application workshops and journal review clubs (Imperial College); student participation in virtual research communities (Utrecht University); applying research in the community (Temple University); and including optional additional lab modules with appropriate courses (Cornell University).

Interdisciplinarity

The trend towards encouraging breadth in curricula has led to arguments for interdisciplinarity to be a feature at the undergraduate level. Interdisciplinarity has been an issue in higher education for more than forty years. A key Organisation for Economic Co-operation and Development (OECD 1972) report listed five areas that led to demand for interdisciplinarity: developments in science; student demand; problems of university operation and administration; vocational and professional training requirements; and social demand.

Interdisciplinarity is an often contested term. It has been described as: 'a means of solving problems and answering questions that cannot be satisfactorily addressed using single methods or approaches' (Klein 1990: 196), thus neatly expressing one of the main reasons given for its encouragement. Petrie comments that: 'The key feature of a truly interdisciplinary general education program is, ultimately, the extent to which the program itself attempts to synthesize the elements of the curriculum instead of simply leaving it to the students' (1992: 316).

It can thus be distinguished from multidisciplinarity, an approach in which differing disciplinary perspectives may be brought to bear, but without an aspiration to meld them together to create an 'integrative synthesis' (Klein 1990: 188) through an approach that is distinctly different from its component parts. In practical terms, the distinction might be that a topic can be approached from a multidisciplinary perspective if a series of lectures is given by staff from a range of disciplinary backgrounds. Interdisciplinarity comes about when a body of knowledge is produced that transcends the components and offers a distinctive view.

This is one of the more contentious curriculum issues. Staff attitudes to interdisciplinarity vary widely, from enthusiastic support, often by those whose research is itself interdisciplinary, to outright hostility, on the grounds that it is a kind of 'dumbing down' of the curriculum. At the most negative was a view that students should not be exposed to other disciplines until they had mastered one, although opinions differed on what level constituted mastery. This range of views is reflected in the literature. It is suggested that such courses: develop critical abilities and increase empathy for ethical and social issues; enable students to tolerate ambiguity and to accommodate, synthesise or integrate diverse perspectives; offer broader perspectives and encourage creative thinking; and increase the ability to listen and sensitivity to bias (Newell 1990). However, Heckhausen (in Klein 1990) wrote of 'indiscriminate interdisciplinarity' coming about in courses that did not contain a genuine synthesis of ideas. There was much wider acceptance at an undergraduate level that the lesser aim of multidisciplinarity was desirable and achievable.

Nevertheless, around the world can be seen a general trend towards the introduction of more interdisciplinary elements in degree programmes, sometimes signalled through the institution of common first-year courses or other core and synthesising elements, including general education requirements. Examples are described in the Melbourne and Hong Kong case studies in this book. Interestingly, although the academic discipline continues to be the main way in which universities are organised, research itself is becoming increasingly interdisciplinary in many fields – Biomedicine being an example. As universities respond to demands that their research have more immediate practical applications, there is inevitably a trend towards more problem-focused research that draws in all the disciplines that are needed in order to make a difference in the real world.

Approaches to interdisciplinarity

Interdisciplinarity has become embedded most widely in US curricula, both through a strong liberal arts degree tradition and, more recently, through general education requirements becoming commonplace in degree programmes. Notable examples of interdisciplinary curricula from the 1920s through to the 1970s have included: Antioch College, Bard College, Sarah Lawrence College, Goddard College, Pitzer College, Hampshire College, University of California at Santa Cruz and Evergreen College (Smith and McCann 2001). Although there have been notable experiments, such as at some of the 'new' universities of the 1960s, like the University of Sussex and the University of East Anglia (Klein 1990), the UK has been relatively more cautious and has tended, particularly in research-intensive institutions, to favour mono-disciplinary undergraduate degrees. As detailed in the case study in Chapter 10, Melbourne has been a leader in its development of the 'Melbourne Model', introducing modules that are specifically topic-based and interdisciplinary.

Interdisciplinarity looks rather different across a university. In the Humanities and some of the Social Sciences, a 'self-contained' form of it is most common, in which perspectives and approaches from elsewhere are incorporated into a single honours degree. In the Sciences and some of the Social Sciences, it may be 'externalised', consisting either of synthetic interdisciplinarity or transdisciplinarity, in which disciplines are broken down and knowledge takes an entirely new form. These approaches are also common in professional areas. It is also noteworthy that interprofessionalism is a major concern in many professional fields in health sciences. Some of the issues are similar, but the rationale for it springs from the need to provide a rounded and integrated professional service rather than the more epistemologically-based roots of interdisciplinarity.

In undergraduate education, interdisciplinarity is often introduced through themes or clusters of courses. These aim to 'increase coherence and provide greater meaning across the curriculum ... [and] leaders saw curricular themes connecting study across disciplines and permitting the inclusion of innovation such as learning communities, service-learning, reflective essays, and capstones' (Johnson *et al.* 2004: 22). The major challenge with enhancing interdisciplinary provision is that of breadth versus depth in the curriculum. Many academics feel that undergraduate students do not have the disciplinary knowledge and understanding of subject methodology of one area to tackle interdisciplinary learning. However, most practical societal concerns and methodological approaches do not fit within disciplinary boxes. This includes many problems, such as studying the acidification of lakes, and also major academic breakthroughs, following in the historic interdisciplinary traditions of Newton and Kepler (Hansson 1999). Most joint and combined degrees and cross-subject concentrations are smaller scale multidisciplinary or interdisciplinary initiatives, generally available to all students but not often taken up by a significant number of them.

Academics around the world felt it was natural to cross into other disciplinary areas when their subject took them there, although on the surface this was often not initially identified as interdisciplinarity. This presents challenges when 'interdisciplinarity from above' is mandated into curricula that may already have a significant amount of interdisciplinary provision in practice. Interdisciplinarity also occurs within individual courses, as will be discussed, where its presence is more difficult to gauge. Each of the examples we offer presents different challenges, often based on disciplinary settings, institutional structures and national contexts.

Overall, the most common approach to enhancing interdisciplinarity has been to 'condense' the traditional disciplinary component of a degree and make room for interdisciplinary electives and breadth courses. Broader curricular approaches are seen in courses such as 'World Problems' courses or foundational 'Ways of Knowing' modules. Interdisciplinary courses, whether infused into traditional structures or added through core modules, are often seen as taking away from traditional disciplinary learning and rigour in the curriculum. However some institutions were able to implement university-wide interdisciplinary modules, courses and programmes with great success. Others had to scale back grand plans, and some initiatives never made it into the classroom. As mentioned, there are key disciplinary, institutional and national differences, discussed further below.

Further examples of unique approaches to interdisciplinarity provision are seen in the case studies in this book from Brown, Melbourne and the University of Hong Kong. One finding from KWP research was that interdisciplinarity is not attractive to staff for itself, but rather because a field of interest is inherently interdisciplinary. This may apply to students too, who may be less moved by the idea and more moved by the kinds of problem that can be worked on and the learning that will emerge from the experience.

Examples of structuring interdisciplinary curricula

The most radical approaches to interdisciplinarity can be found in a small number of US institutions, where a degree programme is often built around an agreed theme, drawing in disciplines as necessary. Interdisciplinarity is often approached by condensing the disciplinary aspects of a degree and adding interdisciplinary electives for up to a third of the curriculum. This typically US pattern is increasingly being adopted in Hong Kong, Holland, Australia, Scotland and England. There are many joint and combined degrees and cross-subject major and minors operating at a local level in the institution.

Chinese University of Hong Kong. Interdisciplinarity often occurs at the programme level for undergraduate students. At the Chinese University of Hong Kong, the main driver is from market demand for such programmes, as well as from the research interests of faculty. For example, the School of Public Health and Primary Care is now offering a Bachelor of Science and there are new degrees in fields such as Risk Management, Food and Nutrition, Biomedical Engineering, and Cell and Molecular Biology.

The University of Aberdeen. The University of Aberdeen decided to offer inter-disciplinary modules. As part of a major curriculum restructuring, the university has also created space for Enhanced Study, with options for students to choose Sustained Study modules outside their disciplinary home, such as intensive language study. Students can also choose to study new interdisciplinary flagship courses termed 'Sixth Century' courses. The courses are broad, multidisciplinary and topic-based in areas such as 'Sustainability', 'Science and the Media' and 'Risk in Society'. The Sixth Century courses stemmed from logical links with other disciplines, but the courses were developed with a 'blue skies' approach of coming up with new disciplinary links. The desire is that these networks may extend beyond teaching.

There are many drivers for such courses. These include faculty research inter-ests, staff enthusiasm, and interesting connections for students. Of course there is always a combination of factors. The Aberdeen development process involved consultation with students about the courses, and there has been student repre-sentation in the course development process. To design courses for students with very different academic backgrounds is challenging. This approach of offering broad interdisciplinary courses to students from a range of disciplines resulted in a need to balance providing enough breadth to sufficiently cover the material while at the same time providing depth appropriate for the university level. The programme was rolled out after extensive consultation with employers, students and academics. The modules slot into the existing, flexible curricular structure.

Harvard University. The Harvard General Education Curriculum offers interdisciplinary courses in a distributed form. The curriculum has attempted to emphasise the problem-oriented nature of scientific knowledge and to create interdisciplinary (rather than foundational) courses in the Sciences, combining Biology, Chemistry and Physics to assert the integration of science knowledge in the curriculum. An example is a programme that attempts to enable students (including those whose concentration is not in the Sciences) to 'do' science rather than simply understand science within the traditional science curriculum.

Team teaching by experts in the different fields is seen as central to the success of this curriculum, but it requires extensive commitment from research-active staff and raises questions about sustainability. There is an associated development of pedagogic and research spaces that enable an interdisciplinary and research-rich teaching and learning environment. For example, the new laboratory spaces recently developed for the sciences have facilitated the integration of research and teaching practices. The new lab spaces are flexible research spaces that facilitate simultaneous faculty and student research. Academic enrichment is provided by teaching and research centres that foster the initiatives, particularly with a focus on the necessary academic support and infrastructure to serve the needs of such programmes. These centres function as hubs for the networks that evolve from large-scale interdisciplinary provision.

The London School of Economics and Political Science. Recently the London School of Economics and Political Science (LSE) introduced 'LSE100', a foundation course taking a thematised, problem-based approach to key social, economic and political questions. The course was created, with strong support from the Director, to address the perceived fragmentation of knowledge within the Social Sciences as well as to meet employer concern about writing and presentation skills. The LSE100 course takes place in the first two years of a degree for all undergraduate students. Participants attend weekly lectures delivered by established academics and have classes in mixed subject groups taught by contracted teaching fellows. Additional teaching support includes teaching staff training to enable staff to teach outside their discipline, office hours, formative assessment and in-class exercises, and writing surgeries at the Writing Lab. This is an intellectually adventurous and exciting venture which has so far commanded considerable staff and Student Union support. It does not necessitate any reformulation of curricula or classification but brings both interdisciplinarity and skills support to them. However, with its dedicated office and contract teaching team, it has high cost implications.

The University of California, Los Angeles. At the University of California, Los Angeles (UCLA) a programme was launched in the late 1990s as a five-year initiative; today it is an established and highly successful example of embedded interdisciplinarity in an undergraduate curriculum. UCLA developed interdisciplinary teaching and learning clusters with the goal of offering year-long courses that challenge first-year students to understand complex and controversial issues from selected disciplinary perspectives. Orientation and training for graduate teaching instructors is extensive and exemplary, a recognition that teaching on an interdisciplinary module requires different preparation. The student experience of interdisciplinarity is, in this case, that it carries with it a greater workload. Anecdotal evidence suggests that graduate teachers, too, find cluster teaching more demanding than teaching purely in their own discipline. While many students experience the increased workload as a positively distinctive feature of the clusters, others feel that the modules should carry greater accreditation; some eventually opt out of the programme owing to the workload challenges.

Temple University. Temple University offers place-based learning, using the city of Philadelphia as a focus for learning, particularly through community involvement as a means of 'giving back' to the city. Temple University has courses that are thematically organised, for example around the interdisciplinary idea of 'journey' and draw together a range of key texts. These courses are usually based on faculty interest and at their core is the notion of intellectual exploration. Interdisciplinarity is key and the focus of the course is not a disciplinary one, although it is content based. Place-based learning uses the idea of the city of Philadelphia as a focus for learning – learning about the city, learning in the city, contribution to the life of the city and involvement with community projects in the city.

Community engagement

Ernest Boyer, reflecting a perennial concern about the relationship between the academy and society argued: 'the academy must become a more vigorous partner in the search for answers to our most pressing social, civic, economic and moral problems' (1996:11). Boyer coined the term 'the scholarship of engagement', alongside other scholarships of teaching, application and integration. The term gathers together a wide range of activities that strengthen and make use of the relationships between universities and their surroundings. Engagement refers to 'a reciprocal, collaborative relationship with a public entity' (Barker 2004); stressing its inclusiveness, Barker contends community engagement may 'describe a host of practices cutting across disciplinary boundaries and teaching, research, and outreach functions in which scholars communicate to and work both for and with communities' (124). In the US, universities working in this field have commonly used the terms 'service learning' and 'civic engagement'. A further helpful definition was offered by the Committee on Institutional Cooperation:

> The partnership of university knowledge and resources connects with those of the public and private sectors to: enrich scholarship, research and creative activity; enhance curriculum, teaching, and learning; prepare educated, engaged citizens; strengthen democratic values and civic responsibility; address critical societal issues; and contribute to the public good.
>
> (Civic Engagement Benchmarking Task Force 2005)

Approaches to community engagement

Community engagement can be approached in many ways. How it develops in an institution varies considerably, owing to a number of factors, including the institution's disciplinary and professional mix, its location, its student population and the beliefs and values that are most influential in the institution. Engagement may have student, faculty and institutional dimensions.

Students commonly 'combine academic study with some sort of direct, practical involvement, usually with a community close to the university' (Bednarz *et al.* 2008:87), often as a result of connections that have been made by members of faculty, for that purpose. This may form part of the formal curriculum or else be dealt with through the co-curriculum.

Faculty may engage in projects that aim to support development in the community, whether in teaching or in research. In the latter case, conventional boundaries between the academy and the community may be eroded. Deciding what is researched and how it is researched may become a more collaborative activity, shaped in part by the community that the research is intended to benefit. It involves generating, transmitting, applying and preserving knowledge for the direct benefit of the community (Muirhead and Woolcock 2008).

At an institutional level, community engagement may refer to university collaboration with local, regional/state, national and global communities. It has been described as a reciprocal, mutually beneficial, knowledge-driven relationship that increases both partners' capacity to address issues (Garlick and Langworthy 2004). This definition usefully brings together a number of aspects. First is the idea of partnership to achieve benefits for all. Secondly, although curriculum may be an important aspect, engagement has benefits for other areas of university activity.

Examples of community engagement activity

The University of Pennsylvania. The Netter Center for Community Partnerships was set up in 1992 with the aim of connecting the academic mission of the University with the aspirations of its local community to effect positive change in its West Philadelphia neighbourhood. The resulting partnerships are seen as a means to improve the lives of local residents and enhance the intellectual development of academic staff and students. Academically-Based Community Service (ABCS) courses are a cornerstone of this mission, integrating academic work with the needs of the community by linking teaching and research to hands-on, real-world problem solving.

The starting point for each course is a problem identified with a community partner. An undergraduate course is then collaboratively developed, a course that includes work and research in the relevant community. Students are enabled to analyse the problem and recommend a solution to be jointly implemented. Finally the effects are evaluated and efforts are made to broaden the scope of the implementation and to attract funding if necessary for sustainability. Students enjoy the experience and this unique approach to education is a major attraction. The ABCS courses are extremely varied, covering most disciplines. They range from health and the environment (e.g. Sustainability in Action; DNA, Diet and Disease; Clear Water – Green Cities; Prevention of Childhood Lead Poisoning) through education (e.g. Physics and Maths initiatives in local schools; Socio-linguistics of reading; tutoring in urban schools; Healthy Schools initiatives) to courses on the Art of Persuasion; Mural Art in Philadelphia; the Social Life of Urban Spaces; and Research as Public Work.

Maastricht University. University College Maastricht (UCM) has developed the Think Tank project which aims at establishing and utilising several levels of collaboration and reciprocity in learning: among students, among students and staff, and between university and the local and regional community. Each semester UCM students are offered the opportunity to join the project. During Think Tank, students work together, putting their knowledge into practice by analysing, researching and writing a policy recommendation for external clients, ranging from small private businesses to the city government of Maastricht. Students have their own office and set up their own schedule, meeting with the external client and experts in the field. As a result, part of the university learning experience and the assessment takes place in a new and real-life setting.

The University of Cape Town. The central administration has led an initiative to link social responsiveness and the curriculum through 'portraits of practice'. Social responsiveness has involved academics' identities, especially the 'boundary challengers'. There is also reflection about the degree to which social responsiveness has been institutionalised, becoming part of the ethos and mission of the University. Social responsiveness has been a contested terrain. It also involves student groups that focus on voluntary student activities; each has over 300 volunteers and there are other societies as well. An annual symposium on social responsiveness is held, and large reports are put together and distributed widely. The implications for teaching in general are also considered. The issue is taken seriously in the professional faculties, where such issues align directly with the curriculum.

Temple University. Community involvement is a very important aspect of Temple and the idea of 'giving back' to the community was stressed as much as using it as a resource. As one academic commented, they aimed for the city to 'take central stage'. The idea of place-based learning is interdisciplinary or cross-disciplinary and can involve all disciplines. For example there were projects involving the Arts, Architecture, Sustainability, Engineering and Science that all focused on what the city could offer students and what in turn the college could offer to the community.

Most students at Temple were involved in some form of community-related activity and staff stressed the importance of central co-ordination. At Temple much of the community engagement is associated with the formal curriculum. Considerable effort is expended in developing ongoing partnerships with various community organisations. The Teaching and Learning Center works with faculty to design courses that contain an element of community involvement and are also pedagogically relevant and explore how community involvement meets learning objectives. Community involvement is also considered at a global level. Not only do students have the opportunity for year-long or semester-long placements, but increasingly there are short international placements over the summer break and placements of a week or two weeks. This is less financially draining for students, does not disrupt their study as much and is therefore a more flexible way of providing an international experience for students.

Institutions structured community engagement activities in a variety of ways within the curriculum. The University of Aberdeen saw community engagement as a major activity delivered through the co-curriculum in association with the Students' Association, and included work-based research, work placements, community projects, volunteering and overseas study. All students have such opportunities available to them and all degree programmes were required to state how the programme would support such work. The University of South Florida's Office of Community Engaged Scholarship and Research offers a 'one-stop-shop' for community engagement, aiming to encourage community partnerships involving members of faculty and working to enable students to achieve success through such links.

Community engagement is a major theme at the University of Chicago, where it is the responsibility of a senior member of faculty. Over 330 groups that offer community engagement opportunities are supported by the Students' Union. For example, the City Justice Institute enables Law students to gain direct experience through provision that is managed by students. Members of the community visit the university to offer their expertise in areas such as entrepreneurship. Community engagement is also a concern at Michigan State University, through a scholarly approach led from a senior level. Community-based research is undertaken, and a number of modules are offered on community engagement and the skills that it requires.

Global connectedness

There is an obvious trend towards recruitment of both staff and students internationally, particularly in research-intensive institutions. Any university that seriously wants to be global in its scope has to address issues of internationalisation, but it is a challenging area to tackle. A useful starting point may be to view the multicultural nature of both student and staff groups as an advantage and a potential resource rather than as a problem. Responding to internationalisation must also be a shared responsibility. While institutions can offer positive signals through mission statements, if they are to move beyond espoused beliefs and into actual practice, such rhetoric has to be willingly taken up across the institution.

Universities now often have policies for internationalisation. For some, this has been largely driven by the financial advantages in attracting overseas students. In systems such as the UK and Australia, home student fees have been set by government while overseas fees have been allowed to respond to the market, so this is not surprising. However, contemporary curriculum discussions tend to be broader. They are concerned with preparing students to be able to work internationally, but are often also attempts to prepare students for an interconnected world, where national boundaries have much less significance, and where it is vital to be able to live and work with people from across the world.

A range of terms tends to be employed, reflecting in part differing ideological stances and concerns. Internationalisation can be defined broadly as the process of integrating an international, intercultural or global dimension into the purpose, functions and delivery of higher education. Universities address a range of differing concerns that sit within this area. First, they may be concerned about the experience of students who study abroad, whether they are home students studying overseas, or foreign students coming to a host country. Second, they may focus on the extent to which home students engage with other cultures as part of their university experience. There is of course a key distinction between these two positions. In the second case, internationalisation becomes a concern for all students. This may also be a more realistic ambition to achieve in that it is logistically challenging to ensure that all students study abroad at some point. Inevitably, some students gain their exposure to international issues through a curriculum based in their home institution.

Additionally, there may be concern for the international dimension of curricula. Clearly some areas are by their nature focused on international concerns – language departments would be one obvious example. In other areas it is possible to choose to include an international component. Law, for example, may be taught entirely within a home context or it may include elements of other legal systems and possibly also include a comparative element. Disciplines such as Engineering can emphasise their international dimension if student projects deal with issues that are of concern outside their home country, such as a number of the issues raised in the South Africa case study in Chapter 13. Finally, some universities would claim that developing students' awareness of their own culture and how it relates to other cultures represents a high level of understanding of international issues.

Approaches to global connectedness

Aspects of global connectedness can be approached at a range of levels. It may be particularly difficult to achieve desired change because of the tradition of autonomy in research-intensive institutions, and the often-noted resistance to institutional policy in areas that have a significant values component. Van der Wende (1999) suggests four such levels. At a paradigmatic level, values and beliefs have to be articulated and shared. At a macro level, definitions have to be established. At a medio level, attention is paid to structures and processes that enable and support internationalisation. Finally, at a micro level, there are concerns about individual capabilities (Gacel-Avila 2005).

One of the difficulties in encouraging global connectedness is that some of the benefits most often cited are the development of 'soft' skills that are difficult to identify and assess. At the University of Warwick, a cultural competencies framework has been devised, focusing on the behaviours of those in the role studied. The framework forms the basis of a Global Advantage Award, which enables students to develop and demonstrate their achievement. There are obvious limitations in a competence approach, but having a framework and a set of terms may be helpful in focusing attention on the key issues and desired outcomes of learning.

The cultural component of teaching approaches and methods is often invisible, yet is extremely important. The Western academic tradition of critique is not universal and students from a culture where ideas from some sources are held to be self-evidently true, may experience difficulty in engaging with the Western tradition. It has also been claimed that those from a strongly collectivist culture may not feel comfortable with a more individualistic culture focused on individual achievement and including its overt celebration. Unless a forum is found for exploring these issues, they are likely not to be addressed. They are highly suitable issues for inclusion in programmes of initial university teacher development, an issue addressed in Chapter 11.

Almost all research-intensive universities have international offices, and the remit and effectiveness of these can be expected to make a considerable impact on overseas students' experience. Other administrative functions, such as internships and study abroad offices may assist the outward flow of students. Students also need to know that taking part of their programme at an overseas institution will not disadvantage them in terms of their final degree outcome. Most institutions also have schemes to encourage staff exchanges, often with partner peer institutions internationally. Some institutions offer events that provide a focus for international issues. Warwick offers One World Week, a nine-day festival of arts, sports and entertainment that has the intention of bringing all nationalities together for greater integration and internationalisation of the student body.

Examples of global connections

A key feature of universities that have addressed internationalisation is the existence of a clear mission statement. The University of Wisconsin for example identifies 'global and cultural competencies engagement' as one of its key statements.
Similarly, the University of Chicago's key mission is 'to promote cross-cultural
understanding, mutual respect and friendship among students and scholars,'
while Jacob University has a distinctive international mission which states that
'our goal is to prepare the leaders of tomorrow to responsibly meet global challenges'. These universities also have key statements which reflect international
perspectives on ethnic, socio-economic and gender diversity; intercultural respect
and global citizenship; environmental responsibility and sustainable campus practices; and creating a worldwide community of lifelong learning.

Another important theme is the importance of strong alignment between
philosophy, mission, curricular and co-curricular activity. For example, Univer-
sitas 21's multidisciplinary Global Issues Programme is offered by the network
to students studying at the Universities of British Columbia, Hong Kong, Not-
tingham, Melbourne and Queensland, Lund and Tecnológico de Monterrey.
The programme offers an integrative progressive curriculum which puts great
value on global issues. Seventy subjects are available, fifteen of which are also
offered online and are open to students in other countries. The University of
Pennsylvania provides another example of internationalisation in which students' international trips are based around business and cultural themes and are
carried out over four years. Many of these universities have a strong focus on
student exchanges, either as part of the curriculum or extra-curriculum. Hong
Kong University of Science and Technology is a key example of this approach
as the University aims to increase the percentage of students studying abroad to
over 40 per cent.

Another pertinent aspect of alignment is the recognition that focusing only
on international students will not support effective internationalisation. Attention has to be paid to staff and home students. The European Association for
International Education (EAIE) in The Netherlands, for instance, is concerned
with internationalisation at home. Their goal is to help advance the development
of internationalisation to the 90 per cent of students who do not go abroad, and
thus intercultural training is offered to all students. Their training and professional development modules are also aimed at their educators, even those at
senior management level, in the form of an executive forum.

Academic literacy

Themes from this broad field regularly gain attention in universities, as noted in
Chapter 2. Concerns over the quality of students' writing are perennial. The growth
in the number of overseas students adds a further complexity. Plagiarism, whether
intentional or otherwise, is a concern that can be approached either punitively or

as a practice that can be reduced through an induction into appropriate writing practices. Academic literacy, therefore, is being given greater attention in universities. It should be noted that other literacies may be equally important, or more so, in some disciplines, particularly numerical and graphical literacy. Professional and vocational practice also may include aspects of literacy, through an understanding of physical acts. In addition, the growth of technology-based communication has resulted in the development and growth of a range of textual practices, and digital literacy is now an established area of thinking and practice.

Technology has been presented as one key pedagogic solution to embedding literacies support within the curriculum. There are examples of excellence in the use of e-learning to support the development and embedding of literacies within the disciplines through collaboration between subject specialists and experts in writing pedagogy that draw on disciplinary practice. It is important, however, that the use of e-learning as a locus for the development of writing does not implicitly reaffirm an unhelpful distinction between discipline content that is prioritised through classroom face-to-face interaction, set against writing practices that are seen as extra-curricular and optional activities carried out online.

There is a common skills agenda for literacies. One institution has developed core writing skills in Arts and Social Sciences. A driver was the difference between the institutional and student perspectives on literacy practices. There were differing views on the balance of skills, social knowledge development, and the critical agenda in a core programme. Existing writing development often varies across faculties, and Humanities and the Sciences use very different methodologies. The key issue is how to enable staff to teach writing in disciplinary settings, rather than as an 'outsourced' activity.

To address these issues, a number of universities have invested in academic writing centres, often focused on the development of students' writing skills at a technical level. However, the field of academic writing has broadened considerably in recent years, and a number of different conceptions have been identified that do not always support such a practice. Wingate (2006) has critiqued academic writing provision that locates it outside the curriculum, claiming that such a writing support approach 'has severe limitations because it separates study skills from the process and content of learning' (457). Wingate argues that high-level literacy in a higher education setting can only be developed 'through engagement with a full range of literacy practices achieved within the subject and through explanations, modelling and feedback by the subject tutor' (463).

Taking a broader view of approaches, Lea and Street suggest the following taxonomy for student writing, within which universities' approaches can be located:

- as technical and instrumental (study skills);
- as acculturation into the discourses of the discipline (academic socialisation);
- as a social practice (academic literacies).

Where literacy is seen as a social practice, it is understood in its context, which requires that attention be paid to the academic discipline and also to the broader institution. Issues of identity – of both students and staff – are significant, together with the nature of the knowledge domain and its relationship to those involved in teaching and learning. Some of the most successful initiatives have taken this approach, engaging closely with staff and students in particular disciplines and seeking to understand literacy in its specific context, rather than to remain with generalised ideas about literacy as a set of transferable study skills. The study of composition has, of course, been well established in US universities for many decades, but is less developed in other national systems. One successful example in the UK has been the Thinking Writing initiative at Queen Mary, University of London, which has taken a collaborative approach to working with staff across a range of disciplines.

The question of academic literacy is often centred on how to bridge the gap with secondary schools. In many institutions there are intervention programmes for academic literacy (mainly because of deficiencies in the schooling system). In one institution this is a very important part of the curriculum after the first semester, where students can take a one year loop off, and then get back on the traditional track. In the UK, the prominence of the National Student Survey (NSS), which regularly awards relatively poor scores to many universities in relation to assessment and feedback, has also brought into question how to develop shared understandings of the nature and purposes of assessment and feedback in literacy practices.

Conclusions

All of these curriculum characteristics are central to contemporary conceptions of curricula in research-intensive institutions, reaching to the heart of what a higher education is considered to be. Current concerns to be more definitive about the meanings of the terms and more active in ensuring that they are developed and assessed produces a range of challenges. There are practical concerns, including whether academic and support staff are always appropriately skilled to undertake the required work. The variety in disciplinary perspectives and practices also present a challenge for universal provision. However, and perhaps more fundamentally, to assess some of the outcomes of learning in these areas is extremely challenging, since the kinds of changes in knowing, being and doing are not easy to capture through assessment. It is therefore very tempting for institutions to operate at a rhetorical level, assuming – especially in relation to the teaching and research relationship – that practice is as the institution would want it to be. A challenge for institutions is to find a way of ensuring the adoption of such characteristics in a meaningful and achievable way. A further assessment challenge is to do so without adding to the overall burden of marking, which means working with existing assessment practices, discussed in the next chapter.

References

Barker, D. (2004) The scholarship of engagement: A taxonomy of five emerging practices. *Journal of Higher Education Outreach and Engagement*, 9(2): 123–137.

Bednarz, S. W., Chalkley, B., Fletcher, S., Hay, I., Le Heron, E., Mohan, A. and Trafford, J. (2008) Community engagement for student learning in Geography. *Journal of Geography in Higher Education*, 32(1): 87–100.

Blackmore, P. and Fraser, M. (2003) Research and teaching: Making the link in R. Blackwell and P.Blackmore (eds), *Towards strategic staff development* (pp. 132–141). Buckingham: Open University Press.

Boyer, E. (1996) The scholarship of engagement. *Journal of Public Service and Outreach* 1(1): 11–20.

Civic Engagement Benchmarking Task Force (2005) Resource guide and recommendations for defining and benchmarking engagement. *CIC Committee on Engagement in collaboration with National Association of State Universities and Land Grant Colleges: Council on Extension, Continuing Education, and Public Service Benchmarking Task Force*. http://www.cic.uiuc.edu/groups/CommitteeOnEngagement/index.shtml

Gacel-Avila, J. (2005) The internationalisation of higher education: A paradigm for global citizenry. *Journal of Studies in International Education*, 9(2): 121–136.

Garlick, S. and Langsworthy, A. (2004). *Building a culture of improvement through evaluation in university/regional community engagement*. Melbourne, Victoria: Centre for Regional Development, Swinburne University of Technology.

Gibbs, G. (2002) Institutional strategies for linking research and teaching. *Exchange* 3: 8–11. www.exchange.ac.uk

Hansson, B. (1999) Interdisciplinarity: For what purpose? *Policy Sciences*, 32: 339–343.

Hattie, J. and Marsh, H. W. (1996) The relationship between research and teaching: A meta-analysis. *Review of Educational Research*, 66(4): 507–542.

Jenkins, A. and Healey, M. (2005) *Institutional strategies to link teaching and research*. York: Higher Education Academy.

Jenkins, A., Breen, R., Lindsay, R., and Brew, A. (2002) *Linking teaching and research: A guide for academics and policy makers*. London: Kogan Page and the Staff and Educational Development Association.

Johnson, D. K., Ratcliff, J. L. and Gaff, J. G. (2004) A decade of change in general education. *Changing General Education Curriculum: New Directions for Higher Education*, 125: 9–28.

Klein, J. T. (1990). *Interdisciplinarity: History, theory, and practice*. Detroit: Wayne State University Press.

Muirhead, B. and Woolcock, G. (2008) Doing what we know we should: Engaged scholarship and community development. *Gateways: International Journal of Community Research and Engagement*, 1: 8–30.

Newell, W. H. (1990) Interdisciplinary curriculum development. *Issues in Integrative Studies*, 8: 69–86.

Organization for Economic Cooperation and Development [OECD]. (1972). *Interdisciplinarity: Problems of teaching and research in universities*. Paris: Author.

Petrie, H. G. (1992) Interdisciplinary education: Are we faced with insurmountable opportunities? *Review of Research in Education*, 18: 299–333.

Smith, B. L. and McCann, J. (eds) (2001) *Reinventing ourselves: Interdisciplinary education, collaborative learning, and experimentation in higher education.* Bolton, MA: Anker Publishing.

Van Der Wende, M. (1999). An innovation perspective on internationalisation of higher education institutionalisation: The critical phase. *Journal of Studies in International Education, 3*(1), 3–14.

Wingate, U. (2006). Doing away with 'study skills'. *Teaching in Higher Education, 11*(4): 457–469.

Chapter 7

Assessment in curriculum change

Emma Medland

Strategic curriculum change requires that all aspects of teaching and learning should be reviewed to make sure that each is playing its full part in contributing positively to students' experiences. Assessment is a vitally important aspect because of its influence on the ways in which students approach learning. The following chapter highlights how assessment and feedback are integral to the support of learning and the development of the learner and, therefore, require greater prioritisation than is often afforded. In order to move away from the dominant testing culture and towards an assessment for learning culture, the intertwined nature of assessment, teaching and learning must be acknowledged, which highlights the fundamental role that assessment plays in curriculum design and development.

Writers influential in this field of research have described assessment as 'the most powerful lever teachers have to influence the way students respond to a course and behave as learners' (Gibbs 1999:41), arguing that it 'shapes the experience of students and influences their behaviour more than the teaching they receive' (Bloxham 2007:3). Indeed, for more than three decades, it has been claimed that the most efficient means of changing student learning is through making changes to the assessment system (Elton and Laurillard 1979). As a result, assessment and feedback are amongst the most hotly debated issues within the educational literature, highlighted by the regularity with which they are raised as problematic both nationally and internationally (Nicol 2010).

Knight (2002) has described assessment as 'the Achilles' Heel of quality', requiring greater prioritisation in higher education than is currently afforded. Indeed, there is a growing consensus that the current higher education assessment system is no longer fit for purpose. In the UK, the Burgess Group[1] (Universities UK 2007), the Quality Assurance Agency[2] (2003), and the National Student Survey[3] (NUS 2010; Ramsden *et al.* 2010; Surridge 2008, 2007; Williams and Kane 2008) have called for changes in the assessment system. In addition many scholars in the assessment field (e.g. Boud *et al.* 2010; Ramsden *et al.* 2010; Price *et al.* 2008; Hounsell *et al.* 2007; Gibbs 1999; Black and Wiliam 1998) have argued for ways in which the assessment system in higher education can more effectively support the development of the twenty-first century learner. This is supported by appraisals of the current UK classification system that has long been criticised for being out of date and outliving its 'usefulness' (National Committee of Inquiry into Higher Education [The Dearing Report] 1997:139–40). Furthermore, Rust adds that many of the traditional summative marking practices in higher education are not only unfair but 'intellectually and morally indefensible, and statistically invalid' (2007:233).

While academic staff and institutions generally recognise the fundamental nature of assessment in shaping student learning, evidence typically points to a weak alignment between actual assessment practices and what the assessment literature recommends (Boud and Falchikov 2007; Black 2000). This does not mean that there is a lack of examples of developmental practices that engage in supporting the enhancement of learning. However, despite Hounsell *et al.* describing this literature as being 'large and buoyant as well as richly varied and diffuse' (2007:66), they also draw attention to the considerable difference in authors' understanding of the relevant sources of information available. This, it is concluded, 'works against a truly cumulative literature and the evolution of a widely shared understanding of what is known and understood within the field' (69). The low level of alignment between assessment theory and practice is, therefore, not solely the responsibility of individual staff members, although they are undoubtedly key agents of change in this process, but also of institutions and the higher education sector as a whole.

Numerous documents in circulation offer guidance for the development of good assessment practices and the likely impact that these might have on the quality of student learning. However, despite this, and in support of the lack of alignment between assessment theory and practice, 'there has been no paradigm shift' (Nightingale 2000:118) in assessment in higher education. Indeed, the assessment system is characterised by being frequently end-loaded (Dochy *et al.* 2007; Hounsell 2007), with feedback that is often received too late for the students to usefully act upon (NUS 2010; Gibbs and Dunbar-Goddet 2009; Sadler 1989), and where the academic rules shaping assessment regularly remain tacit (Bloxham and West 2004; O'Donovan *et al.* 2004). The result is that assessment tasks will typically encourage an attitude to learning that is rather superficial and limited in nature (Boud 1995) and which arguably reflects the dominant discourse of assessment in higher education.

A great deal of criticism aimed at current assessment practices is encapsulated by Price *et al.* (2008) who claim that the dominant discourse of assessment has a preoccupation with the measurement of learning rather than a focus on promoting learning. It is characterised by terms such as marking (Knight 2002:275), measurement, outcomes and certification (Boud 2007:17), and promotes 'students demonstrating current knowledge, generating material for grading and getting (often inadequate) feedback from teachers' (Boud and Falchikov 2007:1). The dominant discourse is, therefore, traditionally viewed as distinct from teaching. This focus on assessment as measurement has been referred to as the 'testing culture' (Gipps 1994) and has arguably undermined the potential of assessment to support the development of the learner. This is placed in contrast to the 'assessment culture' (ibid.) or 'assessment for learning culture' (Black and Wiliam 1998), which is characterised by a focus on the development of the learner as an individual rather than on the knowledge they possess, and the integration of assessment with teaching. As a result, the student is believed to engage in a variety of innovative assessment methods that go beyond the evaluation of the purely cognitive, and consider the social, affective and metacognitive learning outcomes of assessment. As such, the learner becomes an active participant in their own assessment (Dochy *et al.* 2007).

The lack of paradigm shift in assessment noted by Nightingale (2000) has resulted in learner approaches continuing to reflect a fixation with learning to pass (i.e. the testing culture) rather than learning to learn (i.e. the assessment for learning culture). Dochy *et al.* (2007) conclude that the dominant testing culture in higher education has given rise to students being inadequately prepared to learn in situations where teachers and examinations are absent. In other words, the dominant testing culture fails to tackle the 'double duty' of assessment (Boud 2000:160), requiring students to, amongst other things, 'attend to both the learning process and the substantive content domain'. In essence, the dominant discourse has produced students who are:

> concerned not with mastery, but with being certified as having mastered. The knowledge that he gains, he gains not for its own sake and not for constant use in a real life situation –but for the once-for-all purpose of reproducing it in an examination.
>
> (Dore 1997:8)

Many institutions are reviewing their curricula and assessment provisions at an institutional level, aware that they are in a competitive climate in which league tables can encourage students to see themselves as consumers and the university as a product (Haggis 2006). The rise in prominence of the student learning experience, highlighting assessment and feedback to be an aspect of higher education that students are least satisfied with, has placed it firmly on the agenda of teaching and learning committees. Indeed, in 2009, 64 per cent of student complaints made to the Office of Independent Adjudicators for Higher Education (OIA) related to academic appeals, assessment and grades (OIA 2009:55). Resultant institutional reactions have included changes to policy, such as the addition of 'assessment' to the institutional learning and teaching strategies of many universities. Several institutions have also appointed a Pro-Vice Chancellor whose responsibility it is to enhance the student experience (Ramsden 2008:18).

As discussed in the previous chapter, higher education curricula are being reviewed and revised to align with particular characteristics that are deemed appropriate for the institution. The five curriculum characteristics considered within this book are intended to foster a range of graduate attributes, thus posing a challenge for assessment practices that reinforce the testing culture. In order to consider the challenges that the implementation of these curriculum characteristics pose for assessment practices, this chapter is divided in four sections: section one conceptualises the terms assessment and feedback; section two highlights the assessment-related issues pertinent to each of the five curriculum characteristics; section three draws from practice at a national and international level; and section four provides an overall conclusion, identifying barriers and offering some recommendations for future enhancement.

What is assessment?

At its simplest, assessment is an overarching concept that touches on nearly every aspect of education (Sebatane 1998). The application of the term 'assessment' to the educational context is a relatively recent pairing, which began during the 1970s; prior to this, terms such as 'evaluation', 'testing', and 'examining' were used (Heywood 2000). While there is general acceptance of the importance of assessment in directing teaching and learning, there is a great deal of debate surrounding the associated goals and impact on learning. As Scriven (1967) once noted, the purpose or 'goal' of assessment (or evaluation as he referred to it) will serve to focus attention on different aspects of that which is being assessed. The dominant discourse and underlying culture of assessment will serve to guide the 'goal' and ultimate influence of assessment, and the key drivers can initiate this process of change.

Any conceptualisation of assessment must recognise that assessment encapsulates any activity that collects evidence or information so that a judgment can be made about a person's achievement (Nitko and Brookhart 2007; Scriven 1967). In other words, evidence is collected and compared against a set of standards or goals in order to evaluate a person's progress at different points in time. The Quality Assurance Agency (QAA) also emphasises the importance of constructive alignment (Biggs 2003), or the students' ability to demonstrate that 'they have achieved the intended learning outcomes' (QAA 2006:4). A key distinction that pervades the assessment literature, as indicated in a meta-analysis conducted by Black and Wiliam (1998), is formative assessment and summative assessment. These two forms were first defined by Bloom and his colleagues as follows:

- Formative: the use of systematic evaluation in the process of curriculum construction, teaching and learning for the purpose of improving any of these processes (Bloom 1971:155).
- Summative: the type of evaluation used at the end of a term, course or programme for purposes of grading, certification, evaluation of progress, or research on the effectiveness of a curriculum, course of study or educational plan (Bloom et al. 1981:155).

Sadler (1989) outlined one of the first theories of formative assessment, pointing out that it is a means of taking control of what would have been trial-and-error learning had a judgement regarding the quality of a student's performance, and how to improve in future, not been there. This was set in contrast to summative assessment, which he described as a passive process given at the end of a learning topic that summarises the achievements of the student during that specific episode of learning, particularly for certification purposes. A central premise of Sadler's theory of formative assessment is the fundamental nature of feedback to student learning, which Hattie and Jaeger (1998) found to be the most influential factor in the improvement of student achievement.

It is important to note that this conceptualisation of assessment involves a judgement that is made within a specific context and is based on the assessor's prior knowledge and experience, or their tacit knowledge (Medland 2010). In this respect, the production of feedback is a summary of this judgement, which must then be interpreted by the student receiving it. Assessment and feedback are therefore intertwined. For the purposes of this chapter, assessment feedback is viewed as separate and distinct from the evaluation of practice, where the former relates to academic staff (or student peer) responses to a piece of work produced by a student, and the latter to student responses to the teaching practice of a member of staff. This chapter will focus solely on assessment feedback where relevant.

Assessment-related issues posed by the curriculum characteristics

The integration of characteristics into the curriculum (including formal and co-curricula), with the aim of supporting the development of certain graduate attributes, requires university engagement at all levels. If graduate attributes are to be embedded in the curriculum, this requires involvement from academic staff, recognition in the formal curriculum and hence associated assessment practices. The graduate attributes that an institution aims to instil in its students are discipline-specific in nature and shaped by the disciplinary epistemology in which they are conceptualised and taught (Jones 2009). From this perspective, graduate attributes should be taught and assessed within the local context, and should focus on supporting the processes of learning and integration into the discipline. This is of particular importance because the meaning of assessment-related terminology, such as 'analysis' and 'critical engagement', can vary between disciplines.

Employing organisations express clear views on what they want of graduate applicants and of how a good candidate might demonstrate this. However, they are relatively unconcerned with how these capabilities have been developed, whether in an academically assessed environment, as part of a programme of study or through the broader university experience. It is, therefore, important that a framework for graduate attributes is adopted that will enable academic excellence and provide a tool for reflection upon the process of learning throughout the degree and also at teaching, administrative and policy levels. The means of enabling this framework depends on the extent to which it is embedded, and clearly articulated assessment is central to the enactment of this integration within the undergraduate curriculum.

In line with the previous chapter, which focuses on the integration of curriculum characteristics being at the heart of institutional distinctiveness, the following discussion will consider the role and issues raised concerning the assessment of the following five characteristics: 1) academic literacy; 2) community engagement; 3) global connectedness; 4) interdisciplinarity; and 5) research-rich environment.

Academic literacy

The assessment of academic literacy may be conceptualised by two approaches:

- Intrinsic: for this approach, the development of academic literacy is conceptualised as central to learning and part of the process of learning, which can only be indirectly assessed through the completion of an assessment task.
- Extrinsic: for this approach, academic literacy is conceptualised as a characteristic of 'graduateness' and part of the product of learning, which can be directly assessed using competency-based assessment tasks.

Academic literacy should not simply be viewed as the means of transmission or communication, but as firmly embedded within the discipline and student learning. From this perspective, academic literacy will inevitably be used in assessment tasks. Assessment, therefore, plays an essential role in the enhancement of literacy practices and can provide opportunities for a meaningful dialogue between students and academic staff concerning the nature of writing and other communication practices that it can encourage. Formative feedback, therefore, must become embedded within the curriculum. If this is taken as true, then formative feedback can be used to enhance academic literacy. In order to encourage an assessment for learning culture, the exploration of alternative forms of assessment beyond traditional essay assignments that provide space for ongoing formative feedback and collaborative work between students and staff (e.g. student presentations, peer mentoring) will be necessary. However, this must be supported at an institutional level by quality assurance procedures governing policy. Assessment-related policy must encourage the development of assessment practices that support the development of the learner, rather than implicitly supporting entrenched attitudes (Entwistle 1997) that serve to reinforce the dominant discourse.

In view of the embedded nature of academic literacy it cannot be extracted and assessed separately and so a clarification of marking criteria is called for in order to emphasise the importance of this curriculum characteristic. However, while institutional support is a prerequisite of such change, policy development must also be flexible enough to allow for interpretation that is appropriate to the local, disciplinary context. The embedding of academic literacy into the curriculum, therefore, requires the revision of school and institutional assessment regulations to facilitate the use of a range of innovative assessment modes beyond the written assignment, to provide opportunities for students to engage with multiple genres. Clear strategies for enabling more opportunities for formative assessment and dialogue around literacy practices through feedback, such as peer mentoring, may be one pathway for achieving this end.

Community engagement

The integration of community engagement into the undergraduate curriculum may be considered alongside both accredited and non award-bearing co-curricular initiatives. However, more often than not discussion concerning community engagement focuses on accreditation rather than assessment and is, therefore, only indirectly related to assessment and its role in this curriculum characteristic.

Community engagement is typically conceptualised via a co-curriculum approach to integration of this curriculum characteristic, specifically with regard to how this might relate to, and co-exist with, existing curricula. A key issue that needs to be addressed concerns how to assess co-curriculum community engagement without being formulaic or reducing the characteristic down to a specific set of skills/knowledge. A key difficulty in assessing community engagement then becomes how to assess the less tangible aspects that lie at the heart of this curriculum characteristic, such as empathy, service, broadening perspectives, etc. While assessing aspects of knowledge and skills is by far the easiest approach, this surely misses the point, as it serves to detract attention away from the developing learner. However, this issue is less problematic where community engagement is integrated into accredited academic programmes.

Pockets of accredited initiatives encouraging community engagement, accompanied by assessment, may be found nationally and internationally. For instance, students of medicine and pharmacy are required to work in hospitals or pharmacies as part of their degrees and are often assessed on their communication skills and ability to work as part of a team. Assessment methods used include Observed Structured Clinical Examinations (OSCEs) and log books, and are frequently based on verbal interaction. However, students are not always able to articulate their learning experiences in the community, which could hinder their development as learners. For the curriculum characteristic of community engagement, assessment is a means by which students are encouraged to consolidate and articulate their learning and consider how their understanding might transfer to different situations. The portfolio approach to assessment, for instance, is considered to encourage engagement with and reflection on learning experiences within the community and elsewhere, enabling the integration of a range of learning experiences to make learning more meaningful and coherent. The portfolio, if used effectively, could therefore align with an assessment of learning culture, in which students are actively engaging with the assessment method and reflecting upon their own development.

Of the successful examples of assessing community engagement, formative assessment plays a central role that, as discussed earlier, aims to support the development of students by providing them with feedback. However, as staff-to-student ratios continue to increase, a key question for the integration of community engagement in the undergraduate curriculum concerns how formative assessment methods can assess the less tangible aspects of learning within the community in an environment where time is an increasingly scarce resource.

Global connectedness

Global connectedness is a new concept in higher education that was first coined a decade ago and, as a result, many institutions have not yet considered the role of assessment within this curriculum characteristic. This would seem to reflect the dominance of the testing culture, in which teaching and assessment are distinct activities resulting in assessment becoming an afterthought of curriculum design. Global connectedness is a curriculum characteristic that should be considered within its local context due to its department-dependent or discipline-dependent nature.

As with academic literacy, two approaches to the assessment of global connectedness can be conceptualised:

- Quantitative: this approach is concerned with the development of a cultural profile regarding how culturally aware students are. These could be and are being assessed using a pre-test and post-test inventory that is more concerned with the products or outcomes of learning.
- Qualitative: this approach encourages students to reflect on cultural issues and outline their responses to them. This could be assessed using a reflective portfolio, case studies and problem-based learning, and is more concerned with the processes of learning.

Knowledge can be an assessable product of learning. However, there is a need for a greater focus on the processes of learning. But it is difficult to assess the less tangible aspects of learning, such as attitudes and values. As a result, to date, assessment of global connectedness has largely focused on skills and knowledge or, in other words, the products rather than the processes of learning, which would appear to reflect the dominant testing culture.

While there are a small number of examples of global connectedness being part of the curriculum, these examples also highlight how this curriculum characteristic is far from being fully integrated within the curriculum. Without curriculum integration, the success of global connectedness will only be fragmented and based on individual staff/departments' initiative. It is, therefore, recommended that the integration of this curriculum characteristic should follow a bottom-up approach, in which the successes of individual staff/department initiatives should be shared with wider audiences and inform the development of an overarching strategy for global connectedness. Assessment would then be grounded within the local context and designed to support specific populations of students who could be involved in negotiating a more balanced and diverse range of assessment methods intended to support their learning. This active engagement of students in their assessment would mark a shift of assessment culture away from a testing culture.

As with community engagement, the integration of global connectedness into the undergraduate curriculum may be envisioned via curricular and co-curricular initiatives. At present, assessment is largely indirectly considered in terms of the accredited portions of this curriculum characteristic. The competency statements developed illustrate and make more concrete potential outcomes of a globally connected experience, but their use as an assessment tool requires further exploration. From this perspective, assessment is one means whereby students can gain recognition of their global connectedness experience (abroad or at home). A barrier to the integration of global connectedness within the undergraduate curriculum is the general lack of understanding of this curriculum characteristic. In order to embed this characteristic within the curriculum, a more detailed understanding of international students' experience is required so that their achievements can be appropriately evaluated. This would require change, innovation and a conscious effort to support its integration at the institutional level.

Interdisciplinarity

Assessment plays a highly significant role in the integration of interdisciplinarity into the undergraduate curriculum, because work must be assessed for it to be valued by students and staff alike, also referred to as the 'backwash effect' of assessment (Watkins *et al.* 2005). However, differences in assessment between departments with regard to weighting of assessed elements and different assignments, for instance, can lead to difficulties and student dissatisfaction. Furthermore, differences in disciplinary paradigms can result in differing assessment strategies grounded in different disciplinary discourses, which can disadvantage students working across disciplines. A further complication is that academic staff who are less convinced of the value of such initiatives can make alignment between departments problematic, as can issues relating to differing assessment terminology, formats, credits awarded and the physical location in which assessment is undertaken (i.e. home department or interdisciplinary context), for instance.

Tensions can also arise where a school offers students interdisciplinary provision but their work is assessed within the home departments, as each department has a different format and scale for the same work that the students complete. This has led to calls for interdisciplinary students to be assessed in the same way for the same work, which gives rise to questions concerning how students can be encouraged to broaden their academic horizons without damaging their academic careers. It also highlights how assessment, while being highly significant, can act as a potential barrier to integration of a curriculum characteristic in view of the challenges that it brings to the fore.

While there is often plenty of scope for students to study for modules beyond their home departments, this opportunity is often avoided owing to the potential threat to their grades that is posed. One means of avoiding this threat might be the development of optional interdisciplinary modules that could be discounted if the student does not achieve the standard they had hoped for. There is also a need for investigation into alternative formative methods of assessment such as diaries and log books that encourage reflection, collaboration and a greater degree of flexibility with regard to the teaching methodologies employed.

In order to achieve shared learning across disciplines, there is a need for explicit assessment criteria and a nodal theme or problem approach to assessment that encourages students to draw from a variety of disciplinary perspectives. However, difficulties are associated with the development and assessment of broad institutional policies concerning the integration of interdisciplinarity within the curriculum, due to the potentially unique combination of disciplinary perspectives. It is, therefore, recommended that case-by-case policies should be developed to account for the context-dependent nature of interdisciplinary study.

Research-rich environment

Before a consideration of the role of assessment within this curriculum characteristic, the dichotomy between research and teaching requires a more nuanced focus on the processes and products of teaching and research (Kinchin and Hay 2007). This could be achieved through redefining research as learning for which knowledge could be defined as original and new to the discipline, or not new per se, but nonetheless new to the student (Bowden and Marton 2004). The appropriate qualitative description of research may vary from context to context (i.e. from one discipline to another) and through time as the undergraduate matures and the student progresses through the degree course. In view of this, a central question relates to how the processes of learning can be assessed in a manner that supports the development of the learner as a researcher. Healey and Jenkins (2009:73) recommend that this question can be addressed by:

> [building] research opportunities into the formative processes and summative-outcomes of course assessment for students. This can be done in ways that retrace how academic staff develop and disseminate their research and learning in their own discipline or professional area, for example, through undergraduate research journals and student research conferences and exhibitions.

The discipline-specific nature of developing the learner as researcher is key to its integration within the undergraduate curriculum, and assessment is an important factor in embedding a research-rich environment in a sustainable manner (Healey and Jenkins 2009). Collaborative and peer-based learning and assessment are possible alternatives to traditional assessment methods that could support the development of the learner as researcher. However, students currently undertaking their undergraduate degree in research-rich universities have few opportunities for collaborative work and, as a consequence, may lack the graduate skills and capabilities associated with shared and peer-based learning and assessment.

It would therefore appear that the development of environments that facilitate collaborative research between staff and students should be a priority for research-intensive institutions. This collaboration would view staff and students as co-contributors of knowledge, particularly with regard to the implementation of collaborative and peer research into the curriculum as a means of embedding the 'research as learning' redefinition of the research-rich university. Consideration is needed of how assessment methods might support the less tangible processes of learning, as well as the products of learning, to support the development of the learner as researcher. The following section provides an overview of assessment practices at a selection of higher education institutions.

Examples from practice elsewhere

The assessment and feedback practices of note emerging from a range of higher education institutions are summarised and indicate how different institutions have embedded developments in their assessment practices towards an assessment of learning culture:

University of Aberdeen

The University of Aberdeen is of note owing to its focus on the development of innovative assessment around both the core curriculum and the co-curriculum. A range of assessment methods have been implemented that aim at assessing a broad range of skills and go beyond traditional methods such as essays, examinations and practical reports. One set of courses in particular have removed final examinations in preference of more innovative forms of formative assessment such as online journals, portfolios and group work. This has served to draw student attention away from focusing on passing the test, which is so typical of the testing culture, and towards developing as learners, which is more typical of an assessment for learning culture.

These courses have become part of the standard university evaluation and modification regulations, which manages the development and implementation of assessment methods across the curriculum. This is reflective of the institution's overarching philosophy, which conceptualises the curriculum as a process of change that requires continual renewal and revision.

Institutional as well as discipline-specific strategies have been developed to embed co-curricular initiatives that engage with the university's graduate attributes. For instance, links between the institution and future employers are encouraged through work placements in disciplinary settings, through the careers office, and employability initiatives in the curriculum which are coordinated by the teaching and learning office. Competency-based interviews set within an interview framework have replaced portfolios as a means of assessing graduate attributes, and a record is kept in an e-portfolio as part of students' Personal Development Plan (PDP).

The University of Hong Kong

The University of Hong Kong is of note owing to its outcomes-based approach to learning for the whole curriculum, for which there are goals for the core curriculum, with learning outcomes for each course that align. The outcomes-based approach was mandated by the government and seems to reflect Biggs' (2003) notion of constructive alignment. The institution is currently in the process of specifying faculty and course-based learning outcomes that stem from the institution's overall educational aims. These aims also align with assessment modes and types of learning, and many are interdisciplinary in nature. This institutional shift therefore marks an effective strategy for embedding a shift in assessment culture that could be applied elsewhere.

The new assessment scheme has an impact on every faculty member and is central to the institution's move from a three-year degree (as is common in the UK), to a four-year degree (as is usual in the USA). In support of this process, the university is running workshops and seminars on assessment and encouraging faculty-based individuals to act as sources of expertise. The student learning experience and alumni and employer perspectives are also being used to inform learning outcomes, and a staff retreat discussed surveys concerning the above perspectives and how to engage students and instructors in the process of curriculum change. Students have seats on committees and councils, so student and staff feedback are readily available and the process of curriculum change is conceptualised as collaborative in nature. Students are, in particular, very involved in assessment issues, particularly issues around Grade Point Average (GPA) standards and also the honours system.

Utrecht University

Utrecht University is of note owing to its advocacy of continuous assessment and removal of final examinations as a means of supporting the development of the learner. There is a requirement that each course must utilise at least three different assessment methods at different times of the course, where at least one of the assessments must occur prior to the mid-term and no assessment can be worth more than 40 per cent of the total grade. This allows the institution to identify students who are struggling at an early point of their academic careers and provide additional tailored support to those students as a means of reducing their vulnerability to failure and to dropping out.

The university has recently introduced a GPA system and has engaged in discussions concerning which courses should be included in the GPA. One option considered by the university was that students could discount one course where their marks were not satisfactory, but the student council opposed this, as grades impacting on total marks is less of an issue in the Netherlands.

The introduction of smaller classes and the focus on a continuous process of assessment has been accompanied by workshops on assessment and curriculum change. This has had a positive influence on the quality of feedback produced and students have indicated a greater level of satisfaction with the feedback received.

University of Western Australia

The University of Western Australia is of note due to its matrix approach to curriculum reform. Assessment is seen as a key means of embedding research into the new curriculum, together with pedagogy and curriculum content. Assessment has been designed to align with course learning outcomes, which means that the institution can look at the range, type and quality of assessment across all programmes. This has been implemented on an institution-wide basis by providing generic assessment/feedback examples and allowing disciplinary experts to define it in their own terms. This is presented as tools to show academics how implementation of curriculum changes within the local context can be undertaken. Consultation to forge consensus was key to the implementation of the new curriculum and funding will be made available to investigate the role of assessment in the curriculum.

Conclusions: Barriers and recommendations

Despite discussion concerning assessment of each of the curriculum characteristics being limited, assessment and feedback is generally accepted as a means of enhancing learning and curriculum characteristic practices that, if designed well, could support coherence and the consolidation, articulation and transferability of learning. Formative assessment is a particularly important aspect of students' experiences of learning, and feedback (both written and verbal) is central to supporting the development of the learner. While the student perspective is gaining increasing prominence in higher education in the UK via the National Student Survey (NSS) results, its focus is often perceived to be on written feedback. As a result, it is arguable that the NSS is biased against those disciplines/professions where verbal feedback is central to the teaching–learning relationship, which has implications for the results. However, knee-jerk reactions to improving NSS scores offer short-term solutions that fail to challenge the dominant testing culture discourse. Attention must, therefore, be focused on improving the learning experience to support the development of the learner rather than a focus on the learner's skill at passing the test, which generally results in memorisation and rote learning. From this standpoint, there is a clear need for the assessment of the processes as well as the products of learning, although a greater emphasis should be placed on the processes of learning, particularly with regard to co-curricular learning.

Assessment of the processes of learning (e.g. values, attitudes) is undoubtedly more difficult to assess than the products of learning (e.g. knowledge, skills), as they are often less tangible in nature and, therefore, not reducible to a particular set of skills or knowledge. The benefits of focusing academic staff and student attention on the processes of learning must surely outweigh the short-term difficulties in developing new approaches to assessment. However, there is some debate as to whether co-curricular activities should be assessed at all and the possible impact of the inclusion of assessment on learning needs to be explored further. If co-curricular activities are assessed, how can these be undertaken in a manner that does not reduce the pedagogical benefits to a tick-box activity? The exploration of alternative, non-traditional forms of assessment has been called for as a means of promoting increasing levels of collaboration between staff and students and encouraging greater amounts of reflective, collaborative and more flexible learning. There is a general perception that quality assurance procedures governing policy are potentially restrictive regarding the use of alternative, non-traditional methods of assessment. However, policy documentation often indicates this perception to be a myth, because assessment decisions (particularly with regard to formative assessment) are largely at the discretion of the department.

With regard to embedding a shift in assessment culture, there is now a diverse, research-rich body of literature that can guide how this shift might be achieved in higher education, from the current dominant testing culture discourse, towards an assessment for learning discourse. This body of literature recommends the holistic examination and development of the assessment system in higher education that moves beyond knee-jerk reactions to student expectations and simply diversifying assessment methods. It emphasises that assessment should be a key concern of curriculum revision as a primary element of learning and teaching, rather than an appendage or afterthought. It calls for the harmonisation of assessment across programmes of study that focus on supporting students to develop as learners rather than memorisers. And it strongly advocates active engagement in assessment by students who share responsibility for guiding their own learning and who act as stakeholders in institutional enhancement.

These recommendations for change are key to developing a scholarly approach to assessment (Price *et al.* 2011), which is central to the scholarship of teaching and learning (Rust 2007). However, these recommendations are being threatened by low levels of stakeholder assessment literacy, because 'teachers and those who design assessment processes have insufficient information about the effects of their assessment practice' (Boud 2007: 19). The development of evidence-based, research-informed institutional assessment policy, supported via the professional development of stakeholders is, therefore, essential in creating greater assessment literacy towards an assessment for learning culture. If it is accepted that 'assessment affects people's lives … the future directions and careers of students depend on it' (Boud and Falchikov 2007: 1), then it is surely the higher education sector's responsibility to ensure that the assessment culture promotes the development of its students as learners, rather than as vessels of knowledge, skilled only in learning to pass the assessment task at hand.

Notes

1   The Burgess Group produced a report for Universities UK focusing on the UK higher education classification system.
2   The Quality Assurance Agency have responsibility for safeguarding standards across UK higher education.
3   The National Student Survey was introduced in 2005 as a forum for final year undergraduate students in England to provide feedback to institutions on their perceptions of the quality of their higher education experience.

References

Biggs, J. (2003) *Teaching for quality learning at university*. Maidenhead: Open University Press.

Black, P. (2000) Research and the development of educational assessment. *Oxford Review of Education, 26*(3–4): 407–419.

Black, P., and Wiliam, D. (1998) *Assessment and classroom learning. Assessment in Education, 5*(1): 7–74.

Bloom, B. S. (1971) *Handbook on the formative and summative evaluation of student learning*. New York; London: McGraw-Hill.

Bloom, B. S., Madaus, G. F. and Hastings, J. T. (1981) *Evaluation to improve learning*. New York; London: McGraw-Hill.

Bloxham, S. (2007) A system that is wide of the mark [online]. (26 October) Available: http://www.timeshighereducation.co.uk/story.asp?storycode=310924

Bloxham, S. and West, A. (2004) Understanding the rules of the game: Marking peer assessment as a medium for developing students' conceptions of assessment. *Assessment and Evaluation in Higher Education, 29*(6): 721–733.

Boud, D. (2007) Reframing assessment as if learning were important, in D. Boud and N. Falchikov (eds) *Rethinking assessment in higher education: Learning for the longer term* (pp.14–25). Oxon: Routledge.

Boud, D. (2000) Sustainable Assessment: Rethinking assessment for the learning society. *Studies in Continuing Education, 22*(2): 151–167.

Boud, D. (1995) *Enhancing learning through self-assessment*. London: Kogan Page.

Boud, D. and Associates (2010) *Assessment 2020: Seven propositions for assessment reform in higher education*. Sydney: Australian Learning and Teaching Council [online]. Available: http://www.iml.uts.edu.au/assessment-futures/Assessment-2020_propositions_final.pdf

Boud, D. and Falchikov, N. (2007) *Rethinking assessment in higher education: Learning for the longer term*. Oxon: Routledge.

Bowden, J. and Marton, F. (2004) *The university of learning: Beyond quality and competence*. Oxon: Routledge.

Dochy, F., Segers, M., Gijbels, D. and Stryven, K. (2007) Assessment engineering: Breaking down barriers between teaching and learning, and assessment, in D. Boud and N. Falchikov (eds) *Rethinking assessment in higher education: Learning for the longer term* (pp. 87–100). Oxon: Routledge.

Dore, R. (1997) *The diploma disease: Education, qualification and development*. London: Allen and Unwin.

Elton, L. R. B. and Laurillard, D. M. (1979) Trends in research on student learning. *Studies in Higher Education, 4*: 87–102.

Entwistle, N. (1997) Contrasting perspectives on learning, in F. Marton, D. Hounsell and N. Entwistle (eds) *The experience of learning: Implications for teaching and studying in higher education* (pp. 3–22). Edinburgh: Scottish Academic Press.

Gibbs, G. (1999) Using assessment strategically to change the way students learn, in S. Brown and A. Glasner (eds) *Assessment matters in higher education* (pp. 41–54). Buckingham: Society for Research into Higher Education/Open University Press.

Gibbs, G. and Dunbar-Goddet, H. (2009) Characterising programme-level assessment environments that support learning. *Assessment and Evaluation in Higher Education, 34*(4): 481–489.

Gipps, C. (1994) *Beyond testing: Towards a theory of educational assessment.* London: Falmer Press.

Haggis, T. (2006) Pedagogies for diversity: retaining critical challenge amidst fears of 'dumbing down'. *Studies in Higher Education, 31*(5): 521–535.

Hattie, J. and Jaeger, R. (1998) Assessment and classroom learning: A deductive approach. *Assessment in Education: Principles, Policy and Practice, 5*(1): 111–122.

Healey, M. and Jenkins, A. (2009) *Developing undergraduate research and inquiry.* York: Higher Education Academy. [online]. Available: http://www.heacademy. ac.uk/assets/documents/resources/publications/DevelopingUndergraduate_ Final.pdf

Heywood, J. (2000) Assessment in higher education: Student learning, teaching, programmes and institutions. *Higher Educational Policy, Series 56.* Jessica Kingsley Publishers.

Hounsell, D. (2007) Towards more sustainable feedback to students, in D. Boud and N. Falchikov (eds) *Rethinking assessment in higher education: Learning for the longer term* (pp. 101–113). Oxon: Routledge.

Hounsell, D., Blair, S., Falchikov, N., Hounsell, J., Huxham, M., Klampfleitner, M. and Thomson, K. (2007) *Innovative assessment across the disciplines: An analytical review of the literature.* York: Higher Education Academy. [online]. Available: http://www.headacademy.ac.uk/ourwork/research/litreviews

Jones, A. (2009) Redisciplining generic attributes: The disciplinary context in focus. *Studies in Higher Education, 34*(1): 85–100.

Kinchin, I. M. and Hay, D. B. (2007) The myth of the research-led teacher. *Teachers and Teaching: Theory and Practice, 13*(1): 43–61.

Knight, P. (2002) The Achilles' Heel of quality: The assessment of student learning. *Quality in Higher Education, 8*(1): 107–115.

Medland E. (2010) Subjectivity as a tool for clarifying mismatches between markers. *The International Journal of Learning, 17*(7): 399–412.

National Committee of Inquiry into Higher Education (1997) *Higher education in the learning Society: The 'Dearing Report'.* Norwich: HMSO.

Nicol, D. (2010) From monologue to dialogue: Improving written feedback processes in mass higher education. *Assessment and Evaluation in Higher Education, 35*(5): 501–517.

Nightingale, P. (2000) Assessment matters in higher education. *Higher Education Research and Development, 19*: 177–189.

Nitko, A. J. and Brookhart, S. M. (2007) *Educational assessment of students* (5th ed.). New Jersey: Upper Saddle River, Pearson Prentice Hall.

National Union of Students [NUS] (2010) *Charter on Feedback and Assessment* [online]: Available: http://www.nusconnect.org.uk/asset/news/6010/Feedback-Charter-toview.pdf

O'Donovan, B., Price, M. and Rust, C. (2004) Know what I mean? Enhancing student understanding of assessment standards and criteria. *Teaching in Higher Education, 9*(3): 323–335.

Office of the Independent Adjudicator [OIA] (2009) Office of the independent adjudicator for students in higher education. *Annual Report 2009* [online]. Available: http://www.oiahe.org.uk/downloads/OIA-annual-report-2009.pdf

Price, M., Carroll, J., O'Donovan, B. and Rust, C. (2011) If I was going there I wouldn't start from here: A critical commentary on current assessment practice. *Assessment and Evaluation in Higher Education, 36*(4): 479–492.

Price, M., O'Donovan, B., Rust, C. and Carroll, J. (2008) Assessment standards: A manifesto for change. *Learning and Teaching, 2*(3) [online]. Available: http://bejlt.brookes.ac.uk/article/assessment_standards_a_manifesto_for_change/

Quality Assurance Agency [QAA] (2006) *Code of Practice for the Assurance of Academic Quality and Standards in Higher Education* (Section 6: assessment of students) [online]. Available: http://www.qaa.ac.uk/academicinfrastructure/codeOfPractice/sections6/COP_AOS.pdf

QAA (2003) *Learning from subject review, 1993–2001: Sharing good practice* [online]. Available: http://www.qaa.ac.uk/reviews/subjectReview/learningfromSubjectReview/learningFromSubjectReview.pdf

Ramsden, P. (2008) *The future of higher education teaching and the student experience* [online]. Available: http://www.bis.gov.uk/assets/BISCore/corporate/docs/H/he-debate-ramsden.pdf

Ramsden, P., Batchelor, D., Peacock, A., Temple, P. and Watson, D. (2010) *Enhancing and developing the National Student Survey*. Report to HEFCE by the Centre for Higher Education Studies at the Institute of Education [online]. Available: http://www.hefce.ac.uk/pubs/rdreports/2010/rd12_10/rd12_10a.pdf

Rust, C. (2007) Towards a scholarship of assessment. *Assessment and Evaluation in Higher Education, 32*(2): 229–237.

Sadler, D. R. (1989) Formative assessment and the design of instructional systems. *Instructional Science, 18*: 119–144.

Scriven, M. (1967) The methodology of evaluation, in: R. Tyler, R. Gagne, and M. Scriven (eds) *Perspectives of Curriculum Evaluation* (pp. 39–83). Chicago: Rand McNally and Company).

Sebatane, E. M. (1998) Assessment and classroom learning: A response to Black and Wiliam. *Assessment in Education, 5*(1): 123–130.

Surridge, P. (2008) *The National Student Survey 2005–7: Findings and trends* [online]. Available: http://www.hefcw.ac.uk/documents/council_and_committees/council_papers_andminutes/2008/TQI%2008%2079%20Annex%20A.pdf

Surridge, P. (2007) *The National Student Survey 2006: Summary report* [online]. Available: http://www.hefce.ac.uk/pubs/rdreports/2007/rd14_07/rd14_07sum.doc

Universities UK [UUK] (2007) *Beyond the honours degree classification: The Burgess Group final report*. London: Universities UK.

Watkins, D., Dahlin, B., and Ekholm, M. (2005) Awareness of the backwash effect of assessment: A phenomenographic study of the views of Hong Kong and Swedish lecturers. *Instructional Science, 33*: 283–309.

Williams, J. and Kane, D. (2008) *Exploring the National Student Survey – Assessment and Feedback issues*. York: Higher Education Academy.

Part 3

Enabling strategic change

Chapter 8

Change

Processes and resources

Paul Blackmore and Camille B. Kandiko

Change of any kind in an organisation is hard to accomplish. The major strategic curriculum changes that we are discussing are particularly challenging, and there is a great deal to be learnt both from existing research and from experiences within institutions. In this chapter we explore the nature of curriculum change in higher education, drawing on previous research, including in higher education. We use key ideas about organisations and change in order to illuminate some of the many curriculum initiatives that are being undertaken worldwide. We ask how the main issues arose in the institutions that we studied, how the institutions dealt with them, and what happened. We draw conclusions about what helps to make successful change possible and make recommendations. The question of what made successful change possible is difficult to answer simply. We begin with an exploration of some of the challenges.

Identifying successful change

All of the changes that we examined were proposed initially at an institutional level, and were the subject of a deliberate senior management initiative. This is not to say that all change is, or should be, of this kind, but that these are the kinds of change we explored. It is not easy to make overall evaluative comment about strategic curriculum changes because many of them have not been methodically evaluated even by the institution making the change. Elsewhere we explore issues in evaluation more fully. Here we note only some of the issues in evaluation, in order to set the scene for an exploration of some recent initiatives.

There are two obvious difficulties: having a yardstick against which to measure the extent of successful change, and knowing what actually happened. There are also challenges in attributing causes to the changes and, in some cases, failed changes that can be seen in universities. Drawing general conclusions from a range of initiatives may be equally difficult, because change is so influenced by context, and therefore what works in one place may not work in another. Understanding what works, therefore, is necessarily a tentative process that has to draw on an appreciation of the nature of organisations and those in them, in structural and cultural terms.

The nature of educational change

There is an extensive general literature on organisations and change, and a significant one on change in higher education institutions. Both the general and the specific literature note that organisational change can be viewed in a range of different ways. The levels at which change is initiated and takes place are also significant. If it is to be successful, change that is initially driven at an institutional level must in the end effect changes in practice in the academic department where teaching and research actually take place, between individual academic staff and students. The department is an important level for analysis and the relationship between the 'centre' and the department is therefore very significant. Universities tend increasingly to adopt a top-down approach to change, with strengthened central management implementing initiatives that are intended to work uniformly across the institution. However, academic departments have strong network characteristics internally, and the relationship between the centre of the university and the department may best be viewed as a network. The implementation of a major curriculum change is likely to be a complex and slow process. While there are clearly structural issues, much of the relevant literature concerns academic cultures, which are held to be highly significant in explaining why universities work as they do and why changes might be more or less successful. Each of these issues is considered here.

Categorising change

There have been a number of categorisations of change (Bush 1986). Writing on higher education, Trowler *et al.* (2002) propose five categories: technical–rational; resource allocation; diffusionist; Kai Zen or bricolage; and complexity. Underlying these categories are differing assumptions about: the nature of change and its objects; the degree of difficulty or ease; metaphors; the flow of power; typical change methods; conditions for successful change; and the identity and position of change champions. A technical–rational approach is positivist, assuming that change can be planned and implemented precisely through careful intervention. Power flows from the centre to the periphery or from the top downwards; the broad approach is managerialist-power-coercive and perhaps normative re-educative, making use of reasoned argument, and with the change likely to be led from a senior level. Such an approach to change can be found in many universities' curriculum initiatives, where a desire to alter an institution's position or offer is embodied in a detailed plan, led from the centre of the institution.

The limits of rational planning have long been noted (Mintzberg 1994). Organisations can be understood as political systems or organisms (Morgan 2006) or even as a 'garbage can' in which the coming together of a problem, a choice opportunity and a solution is a random occurrence which gives merely the appearance of rational choice (Cuthbert 2006). Active strategic management is in tension with the realities of organisational change and the limitations of rational planning.

There is an extensive literature on the increase in managerialism in universities. A theme of reduced academic influence through a process of centralisation and bureaucratisation can be found in recent times from Halsey (1992), and also in claims of proletarianisation (Hyland and Johnson 1998), casualisation (McInnis 2000) and McDonaldisation (Ritzer 2000). An accompanying technical–rational approach to change using corporate approaches (Dopson and McNay 1996) is seen to be a central part of a 'new managerialism' (Deem 1998; Deem *et al.* 2007). The incidence of management fads in higher education has been critiqued (Birnbaum 2001), with a staged process proposed of moving from fad creation, through to a claim that there is a crisis of some kind, to a final stage of explaining failure.

There has been criticism of the assumptions of the agents of institutional strategic change. It has been suggested that there is a privileging of the general knowledge of those promoting change over locally held knowledge, so that change has been seen to be a process of colonisation of people whose local knowledge is deficient (McWilliam 2002). It has been argued that a new development paradigm is needed in higher education, which takes account of complexity (Guest and Clinton 2007). Such evidence that change is difficult and often fails suggests there are strong arguments for pragmatism and compromise. However, there is also a strong risk that if an initiative lacks focus and does not have clear support, it is not likely to succeed.

The resource allocation approach assumes that decisions on resourcing will produce rational, predictable results as the institution responds like a market. There has to be a system of accountability, of incentives for desired behaviours and also penalties. Such a system may generate bottom-up change but it is principally led by those who allocate the resources. We have offered examples of institutions that have sought to encourage desired behaviour by managing the way resources are distributed. An obvious approach is to ensure that funding follows student enrolment in a modular system that encourages students to make choices. A diffusionist epidemiological approach is normative re-educative, working with early adopters, often with pilot projects, on the way to gathering broader support, perhaps through more direct pressure. Such an approach relies on effective information flow, so that examples of good practice and training are readily available. The majority of educational development initiatives in the UK in the last fifteen years have been of this kind, where funding has been made available for specific projects, the outcomes of which have then to be disseminated to or shared with others. The advantage is that fast progress may be made in a positive and well-resourced environment. However, the innovation may remain an isolated example of changed practice if dissemination is not successful.

A Kai Zen or continuous quality improvement approach makes use of the tendency for 'continuous tinkering' or bricolage in systems, empowering people to achieve better results. Small-scale, bottom-up changes are favoured, often as ways of solving a central problem. Change is therefore led by communities of practice. Such approaches sit comfortably in collegial environments and take account of the variation in the ways that teaching takes place. They also acknowledge the network nature of institutions, by encouraging all those who would like to make changes to do so, at whatever level of the organisation they are. However, pressures for uniformity in institutions are strong. The tendencies to be risk averse and to remove diversity are often reinforced strongly by quality assurance arrangements. Finally, models that use complexity work on the assumption that outcomes of change are unpredictable, so it is important to create the conditions under which beneficial change is likely to occur. Management is a matter of influence rather than control, in the expectation that small changes will together produce major change. The creation of affordances is an important aspect; change agents work organically and pragmatically. In universities where faculties and departments are strong and there is a tradition of autonomy, this may be the actual approach to change even where institutional rhetoric may be pitched in technical–rational terms. Certainly, those who undertake educational development activity are usually highly familiar with, and skilled in, working informally and collegially alongside mainstream academic colleagues. Again, an understanding of networks and how they operate can be immensely helpful when using such an approach.

Institutional culture

One key aspect is the culture of the institution. McNay (1995) has offered a series of cultures. A collegial culture, particularly strong in traditional universities, suggests that change must come about through consensus. A bureaucratic culture is typified by a close adherence to rules and procedures. An enterprise culture favours initiative, often in the pursuit of financial profit. A corporate culture emphasises the expectation that all in an institution will be focused on achieving corporate objectives. McNay points out that these cultures are not exclusive of one another and may exist simultaneously in an institution. While there is a strong belief from Halsey (1992) through to Deem (1998) and Deem *et al.* (2001) that academic influence and collegiality have been eroded in universities, they remain strong in the research-intensive, internationally connected universities that we studied. The change approach taken, then, was often a product of an initial top-down intention being enacted in an institutional environment where senior management freedom to act was constrained or influenced by cultural expectations.

The significance of the department

Universities remain, on the whole, loosely coupled organisations. Part of this may reflect collegial traditions, but in part also it has to do with the nature of academic work. The principal way in which academic work is organised is still around disciplines. These, for epistemological and sometimes quite practical reasons, tend to work in rather diverse ways. The more specialist expertise becomes, the harder it is to exercise external control over the expert (Friedson 1973). Further, it has been argued that academic life tends to attract those who have a strong preference for autonomy (Feldman and Paulsen 1999) and indeed that the interpersonal nature of teaching and learning requires a high level of professional responsibility, which implies, once again, a degree of autonomy. Trowler *et al.* (2002) have noted Stenhouse's (1975) claim, in relation to schools, that 'all curriculum change is teacher change' and suggested that it applies very much in higher education. Any change at an institutional level can only be enacted through the behaviours of those who teach and learn, mediated by the nature of the teacher and learner relationship.

It is not surprising therefore that the department has been identified by some as a critical level for understanding the social organisation of academic life, although earlier rather essentialist views of the dominance of epistemological difference (Becher 1989) have given way to more nuanced accounts (Becher and Trowler 2001). Knight and Trowler have explored leadership at a departmental level (2001). More recently, Gibbs *et al.* have explored the leadership practices of successful academic departments (2008). The departmental level is therefore necessarily influential in whether change is successful or not. However, it could be argued that even now, curriculum change initiatives risk neglecting this vital level. There tends to be a concentration on the institutional level, through strategic plans, and on the individual level, with the strong current emphasis in the UK on the student experience. This issue will be returned to in the next chapter.

Although the departmental level is significant, to see universities in terms of departmentally-based academics and central administrators is to ignore the ways in which roles have become increasingly blurred, with the growth of a 'third space' (Whitchurch 2006) of blended professionalism, in which are to be found hybrid roles that are essential for successful change. We return to this issue when we consider people and change.

Questions arising

A number of questions about the current trend in strategic curriculum change arise from the change literature. It is useful to know whether strategic curriculum change is always instigated and carried through by senior management, and whether institutions tend to adopt a managerial style, implementing initiatives in a top-down and technical–rational way, as recent critiques of leadership in universities might lead one to suppose. On the other hand, curriculum change is complex, for a number of reasons that are interesting to explore, and there must presumably be an accommodation between the realities of organisational life and the desire for rapid and uniform change. All institutional change involves a centre–department relationship, which can be managed in a number of ways and may be strongly related to institutional culture. Disciplinary differences may be a significant feature of organisational change. Organisational structures may promote or inhibit change and may need to be altered in pursuit of an initiative.

Finally, resourcing is an obvious way of encouraging change. Examining the experience of a number of institutions can help to illuminate these issues.

Management approach

Does practice bear out what is sometimes claimed about the dominance of managerialism and of a technical–rational approach to change? In general we found that the decision to embark on review leading to major curriculum change was almost always taken at a senior level, with the intention of institution-wide change. This perhaps suggests that a technical–rational path would be taken. If a major change is to be instituted across a whole institution in order to achieve specific outcomes that can readily be communicated to stakeholders and delivered reliably, there is a strong incentive to create an overarching strategic plan, with the expectation that the whole institution must change at roughly the same rate.

Certainly there was wide support for the view that curriculum change required effective management throughout. In particular, explicit senior leadership support was essential. Very frequently, heads of institutions are not closely involved in the change process, but they need to make clear that they are in full support. However, the change process itself is rarely handled in an entirely top-down way. A wide range of approaches from strongly top-down to bottom-up can be found, but most have tended to be a mixture of the two, often shifting over time as a pragmatic response to the level of success achieved by the initial approach. As has already been noted, such initiatives usually spring from a central decision to change, but sometimes the broad vision is interpreted at a local level.

There were numerous examples of elaborate consultation processes and a universal awareness among senior staff that change cannot simply be 'rolled out' across an institution. Even though there is clearly a stronger executive function in universities than was formerly the case, the degree of autonomy that individual academic staff, departments and faculties have traditionally had in research-intensive institutions would make such an approach very difficult.

Despite the concern for inclusiveness and consultation that is often shown by senior leaders, initiatives that are seen from the centre as being participative are sometimes viewed in academic departments as being top-down. Indeed, no matter how consultative and inclusive the approach used, all the changes we have reviewed have been difficult to achieve and involved convincing sceptical or opposed colleagues of the benefits of the proposed curriculum change.

Top-down approaches

Some top-down approaches have come from changes in the external environment. Clear examples of this are to be found in Hong Kong, where government remodelling of the entire education system has meant that universities were inevitably involved in major changes, including the move from a three-year to a four-year curriculum. In South Africa, the new demands placed on universities following the ending of apartheid meant that radical curriculum changes had to be considered. While such external reasons could be helpful, they were never sufficient to prevent resistance from some members of faculty, who were sometimes opposed precisely because the requirement for change was external to the university. It was sometimes argued that universities should not respond to such demands.

Sometimes a central initiative could be made acceptable if it was clearly academically managed. One university set up a steering committee with seven professorial staff and three students that developed a framework for programmes and then oversaw certification. Internal evaluation found the approach to have been successful.

Bottom-up approaches

As has already been noted, strategic change is almost always top-down initially, but there are examples of a bottom-up approach being taken when top-down efforts were ineffective. In one institution, within a broad general direction, faculty were invited to propose what would be implemented. This included being asked to develop three curriculum models, which were then debated, with elements incorporated into the final design.

Brown University has a tradition of curriculum review. Brown is known for its open curriculum, based on ideas of student-centredness and choice. As detailed in the case study in Chapter 3, the curriculum review at Brown began with a wide-ranging discussion about educational purposes that sought to draw in all staff and students. Massachusetts Institute of Technology (MIT) has also engaged in a major undergraduate curriculum review in recent years. The approval of a majority of members of faculty is required if the change is to be implemented. Another institution has deliberately aimed to develop a culture that values thinking about teaching, by setting up a series of events to offer an opportunity to discuss curriculum possibilities. Students have been strongly involved. A similar approach has been taken to drawing in interested parties beyond the university. At the heart of the initiative is the belief that change is not simply a management process, but requires that learning at both group and individual levels take place.

Change and complexity

The process and the outcomes of change are never as tidy as is generally set out in initial intentions. There are many reasons: the difficulty of achieving a shared sense of a rationale for change; the number of stakeholders involved and their varied interests; practical and bureaucratic limitations to the extent and speed of change; and difficulties in communication. All of these taken together mean that curriculum change is a slow process, and one that requires frequent compromise.

Change rationale

As mentioned, one aspect making change messy is its often diffuse rationale. Most change proposals rest on an analysis of forces in the world beyond the university. These commonly include government concerns for economic competitiveness and employability, but often also reach into claimed changes in the nature of knowledge and learning in the twenty-first century. This is frequently associated with claims that the role of the university is changing or should change. These are of course all issues that prompt debate, both within and beyond academia. The actual and desired condition of both the world and the graduate are areas where beliefs and values are strongly in play. The linked question of what should be the focus of a curriculum, whether on the learning of a discipline, on professional expertise or on individual growth, is answered differently across an institution, as has been touched on already. There are therefore ample opportunities for genuine and sincere disagreement both about the ends and the means of education. Thus it is always necessary to secure a broad sharing of perspectives about some of these issues – and perhaps also to accept the need to tolerate a legitimate diversity of views, as a basis for beginning a review.

Structures

Institutions are usually organised tightly along disciplinary lines. Institutions have highly developed structures and processes that help them to achieve particular tasks in teaching and research. For example, most research-intensive institutions in the UK are organised in strong academic departments, which enables them to deliver single-discipline undergraduate and postgraduate study and highly focused single-discipline research of the kind that continues to be rewarded by funding councils and national research assessment processes. Further, quality assurance requirements are now much stronger than was formerly the case, creating a culture in which risk tends to be minimised. This is reinforced in the UK by a National Student Survey (NSS) which, it has been argued, also discourages curriculum innovation that might, if unsuccessful, lead to low student satisfaction scores that could adversely affect the institution.

An extensive history of attempts in both the US and the UK to encourage interdisciplinarity shows that initiatives that go against the disciplinary grain of institutions are very hard to implement (Kandiko and Blackmore 2008). Even when this is achieved, often they will wither over time as the dominant structure of the institution reasserts itself. Some initiatives seek to work across a number of faculties or schools. Interdisciplinary provision, for example, requires a greater degree of collaboration across traditional disciplinary boundaries. There are examples of such changes that have found it hard to get established. Some institutions have found it most effective to work where there are natural links, such as in Biomedical Health Sciences or Business, Computer Science and Engineering – an example of the latter of these can be found at the University of the Witwatersrand – rather than to try to produce a uniform approach. Some institutions have attempted to make innovation easy. Most offer 'seedcorn' funding for innovation. Brown University has a practice of setting up pilot courses with minimal bureaucracy, so that ideas can quickly be tried out and either adopted or dropped. This encourages curriculum innovation.

Implementation

All major curriculum change takes a long time to implement. Not only does a reform of a three- or four-year undergraduate curriculum take that length of time to work through, there is always considerable time spent in gaining support and planning. In institutions with strong disciplines, a collegial culture and a devolved management approach, progress is likely to be slow. A number of such initiatives have taken around five years to get to the point of full implementation. For many of those introducing change, the time is well spent. Interviewees in the King's-Warwick study emphasised the importance of full and open consultation, including at departmental level. Even the clarification of curriculum aims could take up to two years. The University of Western Australia took five years to review its curriculum structures and implement changes and Harvard University took seven years to revise its undergraduate curriculum.

The complexity of an institution and the number and range of interest groups means that no change will be unopposed. Sometimes change required compromise, often an acceptance that an initiative could not be implemented fully across the institution as it had originally been envisaged. It was common for some disciplines to argue that an initiative would not work for them, and that they should be made an exception. In two universities, the Faculty of Medicine successfully argued that it should not be included. This could be portrayed as weakness on the part of senior management, but also perhaps as pragmatism and an ability to keep a bigger picture in view. The extent to which innovations were included in existing curricula was also often a place for negotiation. In some cases, initiatives were established outside the discipline-based curriculum so that progress could be made, rather than spending a long time in attempting to persuade colleagues to incorporate the innovation in their own programmes.

Centre–department relationship

In many universities, discussion about strategic curriculum change is largely confined to those in senior positions and to academic and educational developers charged with helping to implement the initiative. Discussion at faculty level and school level does not often include such institution-level initiatives. Attention tends to be focused much more locally. The tendency for educators to concentrate on events close to home has been extensively documented in relation to schools (Fullan 2001) and the reasons for this extensively examined (Huberman 1983).

At the University of Aberdeen, an ancient and very traditional institution, a central change initiative has taken place with implementation within each of the University's Colleges, and it is believed that this has contributed significantly to the success of the innovation to date. The University of Utrecht took a similar approach, adopting a broad framework that was then worked on at a local level. This is in keeping with the purpose of the Utrecht Model, which seeks to strengthen the connection between students and their learning through smaller-scale education, with more student choice and closer staff–student relationships through a mentoring system. Although there was local choice in implementation, all changes had to conform to the Utrecht Model and programme proposals were all checked to ensure this. At the University of Cape Town (UCT) strategic planning is devolved to schools that draw up their own strategic plans in the light of the institution's strategic goals. Schools in turn ask departments to plan for implementation, supported by a Vice-Chancellor's strategic fund.

Faculty also sometimes believe that curriculum changes are used as vehicles to strengthen the university centre at the expense of faculties and discipline-based departments. This suspicion arose most often where new and more interdisciplinary curriculum structures started to blur boundaries. In more than one case, senior staff agreed that such a change in the balance of power could be a helpful by-product, but it was never declared as a principal motivation.

Organisational structures and change

In the UK many institutions, for example Warwick, introduced 'skills' provision outside the formal curriculum, funded initially by additional short-term teaching enhancement funding from the Higher Education Funding Council for England (HEFCE). It was possible to set up the programmes quickly because it was not necessary to negotiate with academic departments. The provision quickly became popular with some students, particularly international students, but it was not easy to make such provision on a large scale. When external enhancement funding finished, and with reduced government core funding for teaching too, provision was reduced.

This neatly summarises the problem of locating change, both in terms of curriculum delivery and of its management. Institutions are generally funded only once for teaching, which suggests that innovation should take place within discipline-based curricula, which are already funded for teaching. Funding is usually distributed heavily to that level. Disciplines can also often offer a relevant context for learning. However, this almost inevitably means that change will be relatively slow, since it requires the willing cooperation of many members of academic staff, some of whose priorities may not be curriculum innovation. In its curriculum review, one Australian university declared that the slowest way of achieving change would be to leave it to faculties to propose and implement changes. Therefore many institutions have established parallel curricula that are often skills-based rather than discipline-based. This is politically simpler, and often faster progress can be made. However, it requires additional funding, the top-slicing of departmental budgets to fund such provision may not always be popular, and the level of funding may not be sustainable if provision is to be taken up by all students.

A focus for change

As research pressures increase, it becomes ever harder to ask departments in research-led institutions to give time and energy to teaching. It is tempting to allow much of the new curriculum opportunity to be made available outside academic departments. The disadvantage of this is that academic departments may increasingly withdraw from teaching, particularly undergraduate teaching. This damages a major market advantage that research-intensive institutions have in attracting the most academically-able students – and also detracts from their justification for charging higher fees.

Many institutions have established graduate schools as a means of sponsoring development across an institution when there has been felt to be too little focus on graduate education overall and sometimes also a concern that standards of provision were unacceptably varied. Undergraduate education however has largely remained entirely the responsibility of academic departments. There may be a case for establishing, at least in the short term, a head of undergraduate education in an institution, in order to provide a focus for an initiative. This may have the effect of further unhelpfully separating undergraduate and postgraduate provision.

Most major curricular initiatives involve the creation of new activities, such as the development and recognition of co-curricular engagement and the provision of interdisciplinary opportunities. While it could be claimed that the separation between academic and administrative staff is less marked, at least in UK universities, than used to be the case, with the growth of 'blended professionals' (Whitchurch 2006), there remain two distinct categories of staff, within which the management approaches, working conditions and expectations are rather different. UK universities still have both an academic and an administrative structure. Parallel provision has to be located in this landscape. Some institutions have established learning and language support and other curriculum enrichment provision within professional services. This has in some cases allowed fast progress, but may produce cultural and other difficulties.

In some institutions there has been concern that provision that is not academically based is not taken seriously by academic staff. Sometimes, where it can be taken and used as academic credit within an academic programme, participation is discouraged by academics, either because it is argued that it detracts from degree cohesion or because it effectively removes resources from a school if its students take choices from elsewhere. There may be difficulties in accrediting co-curricular activity outside academic structures. Institutions have found a variety of ways of dealing with this issue. However, the most successful institutions appear to find a way of ensuring that such provision is closely connected within the academy, even if formally it is located within the administration. Students may not know or care where their provision is based, provided it is available to them in a coherent way and is of a good standard. However, the implications for staff roles are considerable, an issue returned to in the next chapter.

Resourcing to support change

Curriculum change may be particularly slow if patterns of resourcing do not encourage change. Interdisciplinary initiatives have often faced difficulties because of uncertainties about how resources will be allocated to participating schools. Students may be discouraged from taking foreign language modules if by so doing they reduce the resource that they bring to the 'home' department. Many higher education systems are under major financial pressure at present, particularly in a number of European countries. At the same time, student expectations are rising steadily as the metaphor of the student as consumer becomes dominant. Recent moves in the UK to greatly increase the student cost of a higher education are bound to increase expectations further. Many institutions now view curriculum change as being very important as a means of marketing the institution, but have to make change with, at best, no additional resources. This requires universities to review how they are currently making use of funding and to find the most economical ways of delivering additional academic and support provision.

Portfolio review

Portfolio review offers institutions a way of systematically considering the cost-effectiveness of existing programmes. One institution, in reviewing its Master's provision, found that it had several hundred programmes that had five or fewer participants. Although programme leaders often claimed that by sharing modules with other programmes they could be cost-effective, 'drilling down' to module level revealed modules with extremely small numbers. Very often areas such as research methods are taught almost identically in various parts of the institution. While there may be other reasons for occasionally condoning small numbers, clearly there can be no more effective way of releasing resources for new provision than to look closely in this way at existing provision. At the start of its curriculum review process, the University of Manchester's proposal for change contained reference to the respective costs of running modules with ten students set against those modules with a hundred students.

One way of creating larger modules may be through encouraging faculty to work together, pooling their research expertise. The University of the Witwatersrand has done so, thus creating what they have termed 'intellectual efficiencies'. This has enabled the development of programmes such as Applied Computing, drawing on Software Engineering, Electrical and Engineering Science, and the School of Economic and Business Studies. Having such a programme has allowed for greater links with business and industry and the creation of job placements for students. As has already been noted, change within discipline-focused curricula may require fewer resources than new parallel provision, but the opportunity costs to academic departments of coping with new activities have to be taken into account, as does the management and other time that has to be committed to a programme of slow change, if an accurate comparison of costs is to be made.

Potential resources

Strategic restructuring and staffing provision can provide an opportunity for change without increased financial resourcing. Utrecht University chose to establish an elite college, University College Utrecht. This was largely funded through better student retention. The UCU completion rate of 99 per cent compares very well with the general Utrecht rate of 60 per cent. Some of the additional funding is used to support smaller classes, which it is believed contribute to the better completion rate.

Institutions have for many years used postgraduate students on an informal basis for teaching. Some universities have formalised this through Graduate Teaching Assistant (GTA) schemes, in which students engaged in postgraduate study are trained to teach and undertake a set number of hours' teaching and other student support. This may seem an attractive way of increasing the number of teaching hours very economically and it can be argued that well-prepared postgraduates teach effectively, since usually they have recently been undergraduates themselves. However, there are obvious dangers. The Boyer Commission Report, published in the US in 1998, castigated research-intensive institutions for promising students access to distinguished professors but not providing it: 'the research universities have often failed, and continue to fail, their undergraduate populations. Thousands of students graduate without seeing the world-famous professors or tasting genuine research' (1998: 5–6). Clearly, poor use of GTAs may detract from one of the marketing advantages that research-intensive institutions possess. However, some institutions have set up thorough training programmes for GTAs. The London School of Economics, in establishing its innovative LSE100 programme, has made highly organised use of a team of postgraduates to support lead lectures. All of them are trained to teach and are supported in their teaching.

Undergraduate students themselves may be useful resources in support of their own learning. The University of Warwick has an Undergraduate Research Scholarship Scheme (URSS) that offers students bursaries to take a role in live research projects led by academic staff. All parties benefit: staff have the support of a project worker; students receive some pre-specified preparation and subsequent recognition of their engagement. Sometimes existing resources and opportunities can be targeted to undergraduate students. Utrecht University enabled students to learn about research at the University when it created research gateways in the library system. Some students joined research projects, with benefits both to the projects and the students. The University of Chicago has a major Community Service Center that places 3,000 students a year in the public sector for work experience. The Center makes extensive use of undergraduates. Within their own work, students may also be encouraged to contribute, for example by self-assessing and peer-assessing. Third-year students in some universities are asked to mentor first-year students. Finally, most institutions invest their own funds in teaching innovation. Some institutions use the funding quite strategically, awarding it where they believe it will provide the most benefit and where it can sponsor change that can be self-sustaining in the longer term.

Resourcing for change

In some institutions, resources have been used quite strategically to drive change. At the University of Sydney, a particular kind of curriculum was envisaged, resting on a coherent set of beliefs about conditions that enabled successful learning. A student questionnaire was designed that would indicate the nature of students' experience. It was thus possible to measure departmental performance against desired outcomes (Prosser and Barrie 2003). A small proportion of teaching funding was top-sliced centrally and awarded to departments that achieved success in this way. It had the effect of concentrating attention on those aspects of curriculum delivery. Only a small percentage of funding needed to be allocated in order to strongly encourage change. In a further measure, a Scholarship Index was produced, showing the extent to which departments had engaged in desired activities, such as publishing on teaching and learning issues. Once again, additional funding went to those that performed well. Again, this was effective, although it is open to the objection that, as with many such systems, it gave additional money to those who had shown they could perform very well without it.

One institution found that establishing central provision that students could access for credit within their degree programme provided an incentive for schools to direct their students towards it. Otherwise they would be helping to fund provision that their school was not using. When programmes are opened up still further, so that there is a significant element of 'general education', it is possible to create a market for students. Schools will succeed to the extent that they provide modules that are attractive to students. This is open to a number of objections: it may be damaging to curriculum coherence; it may make 'hard' modules less appealing to students; and it could potentially create student flows that would be hard to manage. However, provided safeguards are built into a system, such an approach can be used successfully. Of course market approaches like this only work to the extent that schools wish to participate in the market. If undergraduate education is not seen as being central to a school's future, a poorly managed market might have the effect of encouraging schools to move away from teaching, if they are free to do so, when there are alternative sources of income. Some universities have chosen to alter the balance of resourcing across the undergraduate years. In Australian universities in particular there has been strong interest in the first year experience and, in some, a decision to increase funding at what is seen to be a vital time in establishing sound foundations for later study.

Conclusions

In conclusion, we note that major strategic curriculum change is usually an institutional initiative that relies heavily on local academic and administrative practice if it is to succeed. Therefore a central aspect of major institutional change, and one which determines whether the initiative will succeed or not, is the way in which institutional priorities relate to local action. There are a range of possible approaches, as the literature and our empirical work suggests. There is no wrong or right way; the culture of an institution will be highly influential in whether an approach works or not.

Effective learning, as has been noted, often depends heavily on the interaction of faculty and students. In the end, institutional strategy has to be effected at a very local level. This suggests that responsibility for change has to be widely distributed if it is really to make a difference. An institution that was seeking to develop a research culture for undergraduates found that what it was trying to encourage was largely a set of attitudes, including cooperativeness, goodwill and openness. In other words, it was a cultural change, which could not be made the responsibility of one individual to implement. The responsibility had to be 'owned' across the institution and could not be achieved by bureaucratic means. We note also the potential for untidiness in change: many initiatives fail and most will produce results that were not entirely anticipated in advance. Judgements about success require some criteria against which to make the judgement and also require that the institution undertakes a thorough evaluation of what it has done.

Once an initiative has become established, it is necessary to maintain momentum. This can be done in part through programme and course approval and review mechanisms, which have the advantage that in time all provision is reviewed. Thus it should be possible to promote evenness of treatment across the institution though an existing mechanism that may need only small adjustments to make it fit for the new purpose. Some institutions have continued to sponsor small-scale innovation by staff, often by providing 'seedcorn' funding for initiatives that are in due course expected to become self-sustaining.

One institution has developed a four-part approach to encouraging continuing development:

- using incentives and requirements by the centre to support change in the curriculum;
- developing partnerships with students, for example when establishing open and full reviews of the curriculum;
- identifying those champions or catalysts of change and development;
- providing resources for those interested in establishing creativity within the curriculum.

Drawing on the change literature above from Trowler *et al.* (2002), curriculum change involves several different approaches throughout an initiative. It often does not take senior managers long to realise that a technical–rational approach is incongruent with institutional cultures, structures and modes of working. However, through strategic resource allocation top-down approaches can lead to broader buy-in and cooperation. This idea links with the diffusionist approach, which by funding and directing change where it is most in line with current practice, can be a beacon for change across the institution. As noted, linking in with changes in the Medical curriculum eased wider curriculum change across institutions.

To a certain degree, all curriculum change has to involve continuous improvement, as there are always new students enrolling, changes in staff, new developments across fields and new external forces such as funding, policy and social changes. Some institutions, such as Brown University, have been successful in institutionalising and structuring continuous change efforts. However, overall, curriculum change is always a complex endeavour. Several institutions' change initiatives were derailed by new appointments in senior leadership, unpredicted external forces or unanticipated shifts in student demand and interest. This complexity makes the ability to control, manage and succeed in change efforts a challenge. As mentioned, the latter is often a moving target as well, although institutions with clear purposes and goals at the beginning have a greater ability to evaluate the initiative.

References

Becher, T. (1989) *Academic tribes and territories: Intellectual inquiry and the cultures of disciplines.* Buckingham: Society for Research into Higher Education and Open University Press.

Becher, T. and Trowler, P. (2001) *Academic tribes and territories: Intellectual inquiry and the cultures of disciplines* (2nd ed). Buckingham: Society for Research into Higher Education and Open University Press.

Birnbaum, R. (2001) *Management fads in higher education.* San Francisco: Jossey Bass.

Boyer Commission (1998) *Reinventing undergraduate education: A blueprint for America's research universities.* New York: Stony Brook.

Bush, T. (1986) *Theories of educational management.* London: Harper and Row.

Cuthbert, R. (2006) *Constructive alignment in the world of institutional management.* York: LTSN Generic Centre.

Deem, R. (1998) 'New Managerialism' and Higher Education: The management of performances and cultures in universities in the United Kingdom. *International Studies in Sociology of Education, 8*(1): 44–70.

Deem, R. (2001) Managing contemporary UK universities – Manager academics and new managerialism, *Academic Leadership, 1*: 1–18.

Deem, R., Hillyard, S. and Reed, M. (2007) *Knowledge, higher education, and the new managerialism.* Oxford: Oxford University Press.

Dopson, S. and McNay, I. (1996) Organisational culture, in D. Warner and D. Palfreyman (eds), *Higher Education Management* (16–32). Buckingham: Open University Press.

Feldman, K. A. and Paulsen, M. B. (1999). Faculty motivation: the role of a support-ive teaching culture. *New directions in teaching and learning, 78*: 71–78.

Friedson, E. (1973) *The professions and their prospects.* London: Sage.

Fullan, M. (2001) *The new meaning of educational change* (3rd ed). New York: Teach-ers' College Press.

Gibbs, G., Knapper, C. and Piccinin, S. (2008) Disciplinary and contextually appro-priate approaches to leadership of teaching in research-intensive academic depart-ments in Higher Education. *Higher Education Quarterly, 62*(4): 416–436.

Guest, D. and Clinton, M. (2007) *Human resource management and university per-formance.* London: Leadership Foundation for Higher Education.

Halsey, A. H. (1992) *The decline of donnish dominion: The British academic professions in the twentieth century.* Oxford: Clarendon Press.

Huberman, M. (1983) Recipes for busy kitchens: A situational analysis of routine knowl-edge use in schools. *Knowledge, Creation, Diffusion, Utilization, 4*(4): 478–510.

Hyland, T. and Johnson, S. (1998) Of cabbages and key skills: Exploding the myth of core transferable skills in post-school education. *Journal of Further and Higher Education, 22*(2): 163–172.

Kandiko, C. B. and Blackmore, P. (2008) Institutionalising interdisciplinary work in Australia and the UK. *Journal of Institutional Research, 14*(1): 87–95.

Knight, P. T. and Trowler, P. R. (2001) *Departmental leadership in higher education.* Buckingham: Society for Research in Higher Education and Open University Press.

McInnis, C. (2000) *The work roles of academics in Australian universities.* Canberra: Australian Government Department of Education, Employment and Workplace Relations.

McNay, I. (1995) From the collegial academy to corporate enterprise: the changing cultures of universities, in T.Schuller (ed.). *The changing university* (pp. 105–115). Buckingham: Open University Press.

McWilliam, E. (2002) Against professional development. *Educational Philosophy and Theory, 34*(3): 289–300.

Mintzberg, H. (1994) *The rise and fall of strategic planning.* New York: Free Press.

Morgan, G. (2006) *Images of organization* (updated ed.). Thousand Oaks: California: Sage Publications.

Prosser, M. and Barrie, S. (2003) Using a student-focused learning perspective to align academic development with institutional quality assurance in R. Blackwell, and P. Blackmore (eds), *Towards strategic staff development in higher education.* Buckingham: Society for Research into higher Education/Open University Press.

Ritzer, G. (2000) *The McDonaldisation of society.* Thousand Oaks: Pine Forge Press.

Trowler, P., Saunders, M. and Knight, P. (2002) *Change thinking, change practices: A guide to change for heads of department, subject centres and others who work middle-out.* Report for the Learning and Teaching Support Network, Generic Cen-tre. Available at: http://www.heacademy.ac.uk/assets/York/documents/ourwork/institutions/change_academy/id262_Change_Thinking_Change_Practices.pdf

Whitchurch, C. (2006) *Professional managers in UK Higher Education: Preparing for complex futures.* Interim report. London: Leadership Foundation for Higher Education.

Chapter 9

People and change

Academic work and leadership

Paul Blackmore and Camille B. Kandiko

Curriculum change is often dealt with from a relatively narrow perspective, asking what it is that students should know, understand and be able to do. This raises the question of what should be provided by the institution to ensure the best possible student learning experience. This is only a small part of the picture. As discussed in Chapter 2, as relationships between teachers, learners and what is to be learnt shift, new roles emerge and existing ones are adjusted for academic and support staff. A more student-centred approach may require academic staff to take greater account of individual students' interests. An emphasis on skills development, as noted in Chapter 4, may prompt the establishment of support posts with such a focus.

However, the current trend towards major curriculum review and change is part of a more fundamental shift in universities, and is taking place at a time when the nature and purpose of the university as well as of higher education are very much open to question. We have already noted trends towards mass higher education and its treatment as a commodity, the impact of globalisation and of growing pressures for research. This has significant implications for staff, their sense of identity and their roles, particularly for those in research-intensive institutions. The epistemological boundaries that are represented by academic disciplines may be breached by moves towards greater multidisciplinarity and interdisciplinarity. An increased emphasis on the economic usefulness of a graduate may be in tension with the idea of learning for its own sake. Prompted by the fundamental questioning of universities' purposes, the identities of those who undertake and support academic work are brought into question. Thus curriculum change is much more than a structural and technical activity, and involves a great deal more than the reorganisation of what students learn and how they are supported.

Therefore, we can see a very complex situation that has profound implications for those who work in higher education. Traditional, small-scale teaching based on an implicit set of assumed shared values is increasingly hard to sustain, challenged by what are often seen as externally imposed concerns about economic utility and employability. The ways in which academic staff have traditionally spent their time are increasingly in question and the pattern of staffing in academic work is much more complex. Who are the people who are being asked to deliver curriculum change, and how does their sense of who they are and what they value influence the nature of change and the likelihood of its success? An understanding of academic motivation is central in enabling successful change, particularly in institutions that recognise and reward their staff principally for research rather than teaching. All major curriculum changes have required effective leadership, but this begs the question of what it is to lead in an academic environment, especially where identities and interests are so much at issue. Who leads? How do they lead, on what do they focus and which behaviours are effective? This chapter explores how change is led and managed through networks of individuals, and how curriculum change affects the roles and identities of those involved.

Academic cultures and identities

Those who do academic work are under pressure to be increasingly productive. At the same time the nature of that work, and the relationships that academic staff have with students and others working in the institution, are in flux. Changing approaches to teaching require alterations in existing roles and the introduction of new roles. This is not simple to achieve, for a number of reasons. First, the culture within which academic work takes place has a significant influence on the ways in which people characteristically work. Second, and particularly in research-intensive institutions, academic staff remain strongly socialised into disciplinary and professional groupings. These affiliations not only influence how people see themselves but also the nature and extent of permissions that they perceive themselves to have. Third, it could be argued that in a situation where change depends on loose networks of largely autonomous academic and support staff, the reality of organisational life cannot readily be pinned down in conventional role descriptions. Change strategies have to take into account the culture in which they are working. Finally, and importantly, any proposed change must enlist the help of key staff and to do this it must appear to be in their interests or at least work to produce a change that key stakeholders can agree is desirable.

Organisational culture

There has been a clear tendency in recent years for institutions to develop an explicit view of the desired nature and purposes of teaching across an institution, expressed through mission statements and initiatives such as major curriculum reviews. It is one example of how universities are increasingly taking a strategic view of issues that were previously left implicit and considered to be the domain of the individual academic. Major change has a cultural component. It could be argued that such a change cannot come about unless there is a significant cultural shift. Organisational culture has been defined in many ways. Here we take Schein's broad definition of 'a pattern of basic assumptions that a given group has invented, discovered or developed in learning to cope with its problems of external adaptation and internal integration' (1985:9). The relationship between cultures and boundaries is usefully emphasised by Barnett, who defines organisational culture as: 'a taken-for granted way of life, in which there is a reasonably clear difference between those on the inside and those on the outside of the community' (1990:97).

There are several widely known models of academic cultures, all of which share the position that no institution has a single unified culture. McNay's (1995) influential four-part model consists of collegial, bureaucratic, enterprise and corporate approaches. However, as McNay points out, the model is not intended to imply a single uniform direction for an institution. At any time there may be differing dominant cultures in different parts of an institution. Berquist (1992), writing principally about the US system, offers four cultures, each of which has a distinctive way of finding meaning. A collegial culture is rooted in the disciplines, valuing academic research and scholarship. A managerial culture finds its meaning in the organisation, implementation and evaluation of work that is directed towards specified goals and purposes. A developmental culture is focused on furthering the personal and professional growth of all members of the university community. A negotiating culture recognises the need to distribute resources and opportunities equitably. Birnbaum (1988) also writes of the multiplicity of cultures in an institution.

A number of features of higher education appear to require a move towards more active management or, as some would claim, managerialism (Deem 2010). These include increasing student numbers; the need to contain costs; pressures for the maintenance, enhancement and demonstration of quality; and the sheer speed of externally imposed regulation, often aimed at changing the purposes as well as the practices of universities. McNay (1995) argues that a strongly collegial academic tradition has tended to give way in recent years to a more enterprising and corporate culture. In Berquist's (1992) terms too, the shift is towards a more managerial and less collegial culture, which will be accompanied to a greater or lesser extent by a developmental and a negotiating culture. Collegiality can be seen not only as having a concern for academic disciplines, but also a belief in a particular way of debating and arriving at decisions.

A more corporate approach, in McNay's (1995) terms, is strongly in tension with the allegiances that many academic staff hold. For example, it has been claimed that a first academic allegiance is to the discipline, then to the department and finally, perhaps, to the institution (Jenkins 1996). In visiting institutions we found that at a departmental level, academic staff spoke very little about the institution and its strategic intentions or major initiatives. Reference points were almost entirely to the discipline, the department and the programmes on offer. Analyses of academic staff orientations have suggested that there is a tendency to cosmopolitanism rather than localism (Merton 1968). It may be that many academic staff are orientated outward to the discipline, principally through engagement in research communities, and inward to the local, prompted by the day-to-day concerns of the department, but rarely to the institution as a whole.

Thus, although culture matters at an institutional level, it also has to be considered at faculty and departmental levels, where teaching is actually organised and delivered and where there may be marked differences among disciplines, an issue we turn to next.

Disciplinary and departmental cultures

Despite the growth of interdisciplinary research centres, most academic staff are strongly socialised into disciplines, with academic department boundaries following those of disciplines, especially in research-intensive institutions. Often analysis of the natures of disciplines has drawn on Biglan's matrix of four terms (1973a, b). Hard fields such as Physics and Mathematics have a strong theoretical structure and take a positivist position, while in 'soft' areas (Schon 1983), typically the social sciences and humanities, boundaries of knowledge are less clear and are open to interpretation. This marks the classic quantitative and qualitative divide in universities and also C. P. Snow's 'two cultures' (1961). Biglan also differentiates between pure and applied fields. Finally, less well used distinctions are proposed between urban and rural research (Becher 1989). The first of these refers to concentrations of research teams in a small knowledge area, contrasted with lone researchers scattered over a large intellectual terrain.

As noted earlier, there has been a tendency to move away from essentialist accounts of the power of disciplines. It might be argued that the culture of a discipline-based department may be markedly different from one institution to another; plainly other factors are at work too. However, disciplinary difference in academic leadership and management can be seen in a number of aspects (Blackmore 2007). It has been claimed that clear disciplinary differences can be found in relation to styles of leadership, patterns of interaction and decision-making, and conceptions of quality (Kekäle 2006). Other studies note academics' claims that they draw on their disciplinary knowledge when engaging in management activity (Deem *et al.* 2001). Significantly, in relation to change, conceptions of risk are claimed to vary among disciplines (Deem and Johnson 2000), with scientists, engineers, computer scientists and business school academics claimed to be more inclined to take economic risks although not necessarily cultural risks. A more nuanced view of departmental cultures and of their nature, questioning the strength of disciplinary influence, has been suggested by Lovitts (2001), who claims that departments have cultures that are not dependent on the parent discipline, consisting of patterns of norms that are passed down through written and informal rules, exemplified in practices and particular cultural forms that shape relationships in the department.

There are several implications for strategic curriculum change. The less permeable nature of some disciplinary boundaries may make interdisciplinary work harder to organise. If attitudes to change vary among disciplines, then it may be necessary to use different approaches according to the context. In practice, it was clear that some disciplines tended to be more resistant to change than others.

Often requirements from professional bodies were cited as constraints. However, it is interesting to note that some of the most radical curriculum changes have occurred in those disciplines and professions with a high level of regulation, such as Medicine. The medical curriculum has changed radically across the globe. There has been a general shift from two years of content followed by two years of practice to a much more integrated theme-based curriculum. Owing to these changes, the Medical faculty was often able to take a lead in university-wide curriculum change, as seen in the University of Utrecht and the University of the Witwatersrand. This shift has also been seen in many other health professions, leading to school and department reorganisations, such as the interdisciplinary approach taken in Health and Rehabilitation Sciences in the Faculty of Health at the University of Cape Town. In contrast, those disciplines that have least external control, such as in the humanities, are often less inclined to engage in major change. In the humanities, more incremental, local change (a bricolage approach) tends to be preferred.

Academic identity

An exploration of change at a departmental level can benefit greatly from an examination of the idea of academic identity. This includes the sense that individuals have of themselves, of their rights and responsibilities and of the affordances and constraints of their situation, all of which affect how change is viewed and whether and how it takes place. Broadly speaking, the department may be viewed as the most significant site for exploring academic identity because of the importance of disciplines, not only as epistemological entities with their own subject matter and truth practices that have to be mastered, but also as the principal way in which recognition and reward are gained. Further, identity is developed, sustained and revised through human interaction, and it is at the departmental level that close working relationships tend to reside.

Since identity sits at the intersection between the individual and the social, definitions tend to have a range of emphases. Giddens (1991) refers to the need to make personal sense of a life, describing self identity as 'a reflexively organized endeavour ... which consists in the sustaining of coherent, yet continuously revised, biographical narratives' (5). It is that need for coherence that is in question when radical change is proposed that is not consistent with existing self-identity. The social aspect of identity was strongly emphasised by Bourdieu (1988) who, in his explorations of academic life, introduced the concept of '*habitus*', which he described as 'a system of shared social dispositions and cognitive structures which generates perceptions, appreciations and actions' (279). In academic life, academic *habitus* is of course strongly linked with disciplines. The strength, separateness and potential power of a discipline is emphasised in Nissani's (1997) description of it as 'any comparatively self-contained and isolated domain of human experience which possesses its own community of experts' (203). Although disciplines have been claimed in some areas to be weakening in influence, they nevertheless are strongly formative in shaping academic *habitus*, providing 'the language in which individuals understand themselves and interpret their world' (Henkel 2000: 15).

Bourdieu (1988) also proposed that much of academic life could be understood in terms of the generation, valuing and exchange of a range of forms of capital. Alongside economic capital he cited cultural capital, which might consist of writing and other cultural artefacts, and social capital, referring to membership of networks and the possession of social standing. These can be very useful terms in examining what it is that is valued in academic life as a whole and by particular groups. However, Bourdieu has been criticised for omitting an account of pleasure that can be derived from discovery and from human interaction (Lamont 2009: 36).

Curriculum change requires not only changed practices but often changed values too. No matter how insistent those requesting change are, the motivation of academic staff is significant. This is a complex question. Attitudes to academic roles and therefore to change are likely to vary not only by discipline but also by career stage. It seems likely therefore that initiatives will find favour to the extent that they support rather than act against the preferred career paths of significant people who are affected by the change. Motivation may seem to be a phenomenon that is best understood at an individual level. However, recent research into the motivation of staff who do or do not engage in interdisciplinary work suggests that the dominant culture of the department is likely to be very significant (Blackmore and Kandiko 2011).

Networks and change

An awareness of networks is important in understanding the process of change. Universities contain many groups of people who function together as networks – and many disciplinary networks transcend the institution, as our earlier comment on cosmopolitanism acknowledges. Equally, there are many potential networks that might be brought into existence to facilitate change. As noted in the case studies, the curriculum committees that formed often functioned as networks leading change and innovation across the universities. In many institutions, there is no forum for staff undertaking similar roles, for example meetings of heads of departmental teaching committees. The deliberate encouragement of such networks can build into the institution a capacity to learn informally.

Changing ideas about the purposes of a higher education may be challenging to some academics' sense of identity. In particular Barnett *et al.* (2001) have pointed out the shift in curriculum from a concern for truth to one of usefulness, to 'doing, rather than knowing, and performance rather than understanding ... there is a mistrust of all things that cannot easily be quantified and measured' (436). The strong disciplinary focus of many academic staff may be challenged by conceptions of curriculum that are founded on different notions of coherence, that may be based on students making a programme that makes personal sense to them, or else a curriculum that is structured around the development of skills or capabilities rather than subject understanding. The relationship between teacher and learner is also a point of contention. Increasingly, students are seen as the consumers of an educational service. Inadequate and unhelpful though the metaphor might be, it is a powerful one, challenging the more traditional relationship between teacher and student. The development of a network of colleagues with a shared view of the purposes of a change can be a powerful way of enabling a change.

Academic roles

There has been a strong trend in recent years to define work roles formally in universities, partly through detailed job descriptions. Major strategic change in universities may involve the formal alteration of existing roles and the designation of new ones, whether permanently in the staffing structure or on a short-term basis. Additional or different expectations may be asked of those who are currently in posts. This normative view of role masks its interactionist nature. That is to say, roles are continually negotiated as part of a social process. Changes may be made in formal job descriptions and titles, which may seem to define roles, but there may be a considerable gap between formal and actual roles. The implication is that an organisation cannot fully control the ways in which roles are enacted in practice. In fact it may be much more deep-seated and enduring aspects of organisational life that influence how people see themselves, what they do and how they do it.

A change in identity is implied both by the way in which the teaching component of the academic role is seen and in its importance in relation to the whole. As curricula become more complex and based on other organising principles than the epistemology of a discipline, it becomes necessary for academic staff to develop a more sophisticated view of the curriculum. Knowledge of one's own subject and the ability to deliver a lecture and mark an examination script are no longer enough. Teaching has become a much more nuanced activity. This requires that greater attention be given to teaching and that a higher level of proficiency be achieved. In most institutions in the UK, this is marked by a requirement for probationary staff to undertake a formal certificated course in higher education pedagogy. There is now a significant literature discussing the extent to which pedagogy is, or should be thought to be, discipline specific. Academics in disciplines are likely to bring their own discipline-related perspectives to their consideration of teaching, and some disciplines are likely to be more attuned than others to the predominantly social science-based education literature. In some disciplines, the soft knowledge of education may struggle to be seen as having parity with the hard knowledge of other disciplines (Schon 1983).

How roles are changing

Some of the very practical changes in roles and relationships are explored here, in terms of the fundamental underlying issues that introduce tensions when change is contemplated. There is reference to the broad themes listed below, and a more extensive exploration of the specific changes that are currently observed in universities. While the 'traditional' route into academic life, via a PhD and postdoctoral appointment, remains a very common pattern in research-intensive institutions, particularly in the natural sciences, an increasing number of staff join the academy in mid-career, particularly in professional and vocational fields. This is likely to become more common with the continuing trend for universities to engage increasingly with 'mode 2' knowledge (Gibbons *et al.* 1994). It is necessary for universities to find ways of valuing expertise along with traditional disciplinary knowledge, as the boundaries of academic life become a great deal more permeable.

We have already noted the increased pressure on academic staff to be excellent in both research and teaching, and there is a consequent tendency towards an 'unbundling' of the traditional tripartite academic role. This can be seen in the number of teaching-only appointments that are made, including a growth in the number of graduate teaching assistants. We have also seen an increase in the number of support roles, usually on professional rather than academic contracts. In some cases, significant new professional groups have emerged, an obvious example being the learning technologists, whose expertise spans technology and pedagogy and should enable them to give useful advice and guidance to academic staff. This growth in hybrid roles has been noted as a widespread phenomenon (Whitchurch 2008, 2011).

Much of the growth in support staff has taken place in a relatively piecemeal way, with staff distributed widely across an institution, often poorly networked with one another. For example, it is common for universities to employ learning technologists centrally, at school and at departmental levels. Those in such posts may or may not be well networked with one another. It could be argued that career paths are a great deal less clear for such hybrid roles than is the case for either academic or mainstream administrative staff. The adoption of a new curriculum has been the trigger in some institutions for a review of the way in which support staff are organised, partly so that they can be managed more effectively against institutional objectives, and partly to provide a seamless service for students who might find it useful to access a range of forms of support from the same point.

Teaching is now far less often undertaken by an individual teacher in isolation. More teaching is done in teams, sometimes because of the need to deal with larger numbers of students and sometimes to provide the breadth of expertise that an interdisciplinary field might require. The increase in the use of learning technologies brings another group of support staff into the picture. Thus teaching requires engagement with a larger number of people, and institutions need to ensure that appropriate connections are made so that effective teamwork can take place. There may be tensions, in that some groups of staff may value some things more than do other groups. For example, the degree of commitment to the institution can differ between academic and support staff. The former may have a cosmopolitan orientation and the latter a more local one (Merton 1968). The frustration of support staff who perceive that academic colleagues are less committed than they themselves are to the institutional enterprise has been noted (McInnis 1998).

Communication across roles

A further factor in a change process is the extent to which various stakeholders are included. There are many stakeholder groups within and beyond the institution, with interests that may not coincide. Successful initiatives engage key stakeholders. Not surprisingly, there are usually strong efforts to engage academic staff in curriculum change. However, the extent to which students, employers and community representatives are included varies considerably. We noted that this appeared to make a considerable difference to the kind of change that was implemented and also to the process of change. Very often, where a stakeholder group is not consulted, there is an assumption made about their viewpoint that may then be cited as a reason for not proceeding.

The need to involve as many of the stakeholders as possible means that effective two-way communication is a vital part of a change process. One of the most important features was openness of process. Some universities went to great lengths to ensure that every aspect of discussion was recorded and made widely available. Staff in one university felt that the best advice they could offer others was to ensure that there was a 'paper trail' of decision-making. Another institution used a website as its central repository, recording information about over seventy public events and offering webcast meetings, newsletters and blogs. 'Roadshows' were a favoured way of taking ideas out into academic schools and departments. Even if they were not well attended, they provided an opportunity for discussion and tended to reduce dissent.

Some universities found that having information about other institutions' initiatives could be a useful lever, especially if it could be seen that a peer institution had decided to make a change. Opinions from stakeholder groups could also be powerful. Student opinion is hard to discount: a proposal that has strong student support is far harder to oppose publicly. Often it was suggested that a change would not be acceptable to bodies outside the university, such as employers and accrediting agencies. One institution found it useful to gather views in advance, so that supposed external opposition could be shown to be inaccurate supposition. It was common to see signs of 'us and them' attitudes developing in some institutions. This was most likely to happen when a change was thought not to have originated in the academy but from the administration. For such purposes, Vice-Chancellors and Pro-Vice-Chancellors count as administrators. Networks of academic supporters in key positions across the institution often helped to make change possible, highlighting the role of leadership, which we now turn to.

Leadership issues in curriculum change

We have noted that universities exist in an increasingly fast-moving and complex environment. Within institutions, individuals and groups experience rapid change. Existing roles are changing; new roles are coming into existence and through this existing identities are challenged. Curriculum change is thus a very complex issue. Its epistemological component reaches deeply into the nature of a university and the identities of those who work in them. Leading curriculum change is therefore a challenging activity.

Defining leadership

The term 'leadership' is a contested one with a variety of meanings that have been explored in a higher education context (Middlehurst 1993). Much current writing focuses on leadership as a practical activity. For example, Ramsden describes leadership as: 'a practical and everyday *process* of supporting, managing, developing and inspiring academic colleagues [that] ... can and should be exercised by everyone, from the vice-chancellor to the casual car parking attendant' (1998:5). In keeping with this, leadership is most usually seen as having a strong relationship with its context. In discussing departmental leadership, Knight and Trowler describe it as a socio-cultural phenomenon, embedded in a context so that leadership work is 'contingent ... it involves dealing with the specifics of a time, a place and a set of people' (2001:viii).

Levels of leadership

It may be useful to differentiate among levels of leadership, especially if it is viewed as being widely distributed. As the case studies in this book show, change requires strong and consistent senior leadership support for it to be successful. However, hyper-rational change processes that took no account of local context were likely to be ignored or explicitly resisted. We researched a number of institutions that attempted a major curriculum change and then had to abandon plans for change. It has been claimed that academic work cannot be heavily managed, partly because in the end its quality resides in the interchange between teacher and taught, partly because its technology is not widely understood (Cuthbert 2006) and also because its nature requires professional autonomy so that complex situations can be dealt with in appropriate ways. Thus, alongside the strong senior support, there is a need for a more distributed view (Cowan and Heywood 2001), which enlists a large number of academic and support staff in the change project, delegating responsibility to the greatest possible extent. However, there is an obvious danger of stasis in this approach. To make progress, major change requires action at all levels – the institutional, the departmental and the individual.

The quality of leadership at a departmental level has often been cited as a decisive factor in the provision of excellent university teaching (Martin *et al.* 2003). Clearly the role of Head of Department is a vital one. In many research-led institutions it is a role that is not sought by many staff, who may see it as an impediment to promotion. It may be taken on reluctantly as a part of good citizenship (Macfarlane 2007). Often it is still filled on a rotational basis, usually on a three-year basis (Bryman 2007) to limit the impact on research productivity. The extent to which role holders are offered induction varies considerably.

Another important level within the department is that of course or module leadership. Two studies in recent years have shown the importance of this level and that preparation for it is often informal or non-existent. Blackmore's study (2007) showed that although course and module leaders have responsibility for designing, managing and evaluating provision, they generally do not see themselves as having a leadership role in terms either of pedagogy or evolving content. The function is largely seen as administrative, simply a matter of making sure that teaching takes place and that essential requirements, such as those for quality assurance, are met. Another study by Johnston and Westwood (2007) of twenty UK universities came to similar conclusions about the lack of formal preparation and the reluctance of many to take on the role. The study recommended personal and professional development support for those coming into the post. Those who were driving change efforts often found themselves in the position of 'hero innovator'; Georgiades and Phillamore (1975) have argued that, for this reason, leadership development should be widely distributed. Research in both industry and education has shown that a dominant work culture was usually stronger than the effect of any training undertaken away from the workplace.

A study by Gibbs *et al.* (2008) of excellent teaching departments in eleven research-intensive universities has strong relevance to leaders promoting curriculum change. Gibbs was unable to find any standard pattern of approach to change: he found a complete diversity of approach from strong central action through to no apparent attempt at all to facilitate change. Departments studied had widely differing cultures and leadership, and change approaches were similarly diverse. Heads of Departments reported a range of ways of encouraging change, which they frequently blended, including using external consultants, student consultation, consensus building, making time available to innovators and attempting to neutralise those who would disagree and prevent change. That study did not attempt to link leadership style with academic discipline, but some have done so. The preferred styles and practices of leadership differ on a disciplinary basis. Adair (1998) suggests that leaders need the qualities that are expected of the group they lead – so a head of engineer should have the qualities of a good engineer if he is to command respect. His is an interesting claim, given that institutions are increasingly actively managed by staff who often have cross-institutional responsibilities and are therefore working beyond their original disciplinary remit. For all of these reasons, a distributed approach to leadership seems appropriate in the promotion of curriculum change. However, this does not remove the need for a strong change supporter at a senior level. This point is noted throughout the case studies in this book.

Practices in leading curriculum change

The situated and embedded nature of curriculum leadership makes it challenging to describe what it is that leaders do. Here we draw from two recent studies of leadership of this kind. A study of the leadership behaviour of academic staff at a

UK and an Australian university developing interdisciplinary approaches (Blackmore and Kandiko 2010) drew on Adair's three-part model of action-centred leadership, which consists of achieving the task, building and maintaining the team and developing the individual. Given the academic context, this was modified to a concern for learning, identity and discipline. In other words, to effect change interdisciplinary leaders needed to understand the academic content of the discipline, the way in which individuals and groups saw themselves, and the ways in which the capacity for changed behaviour could be brought about, through learning at both an individual and a group level. This is a challenging combination of abilities, suggesting that those who are not highly aware of academic identity and of disciplinary cultures are not likely to be successful, which points to insider-driven change. It also perhaps suggests that an understanding of individual and organisational learning cannot be taken for granted. Analysis of extensive interviews identified four principal areas of activity: identifying need and opportunity; working with motivation; co-ordinating and directing; and communicating (ibid). Perhaps the most significant conclusion of the study is that the term 'leadership' does not always sit comfortably in an academic environment, and yet at its heart academic work is an act of intellectual leadership.

A further study of a range of academic departments and research centres (Blackmore and Kandiko 2011) drew on the anthropological conception of a 'prestige economy' (Bascom 1948; Grinev 2005; Herskovits 1948) and Bourdieu's notions of *habitus* and capital to explore patterns of motivation at a departmental level. Most accounts of motivation refer to intrinsic and extrinsic motivation. However, the idea of a prestige economy adds the socio-cultural and political entity of the academic discipline and department. The study shows that the culture of a department places a stronger value on some activities than on others. Only those who are very secure in their position, usually through seniority, can afford to stand outside such a culture. One conclusion is that a thorough understanding of academic motivation at a local level is essential if change is to take place. Alongside this are institutional-level motivational aspects, such as the way in which probation and promotion and other forms of recognition are managed.

A study of attitudes to leadership development at two institutions was undertaken as part of our curriculum project (KLI 2010). Interviews suggested that a wide range of skills is needed, and also that staff tended to focus on some skills more than others. Programme directors felt that local institutional knowledge of aspects such as the decision-making structure of the institution was essential. Senior administrators were conscious of the value of the particular expertise that they could bring concerning, for example, course approval and review processes and university regulations. Perhaps unsurprisingly, senior staff tended to think in more strategic terms, and junior staff tended to think more operationally.

The interviews revealed a widespread awareness of the need to work within the constraints of a collegial academic setting. Senior staff spoke of taking a facilitative approach, of consultation and achieving consensus. There was a preference for a contingent leadership style that took account of individuals' motivations and

Case study: A failed interdisciplinary restructuring

Institutional initiatives may start with clear intentions and a carefully structured plan, but the reality of change is often messier and less coherent. University X attempted to develop interdisciplinarity in the undergraduate curriculum, by grouping together disciplines that were considered to be cognate and introducing programmes that drew on the grouped disciplines. The initiative encountered pedagogical, logistical and personal challenges. The groupings were opposed by academic staff across a range of disciplines. The change brought together staff who sometimes felt they had little in common with one another and who were not prepared to invest time and effort in learning to work productively together. The new arrangements were also seen as being too rigid. After the courses were launched, enrolment numbers fell and there was a high administrative load. Senior academics and administrators reviewed the curriculum and reverted back to the original disciplinary-based majors system. Several years after the start of the change, only one of the discipline groups remained. Although the change did not last long, the endeavour has had a long institutional impact. No major changes have been attempted since. Curriculum change is widely seen in the institution as being difficult, undesirable and to be resisted, as it immediately evokes memories of a very turbulent and unproductive experience.

The perspectives of a number of staff involved in the initiative help to illuminate some of the sources of difficulty. An academic in the humanities felt that interdisciplinarity was important to the new Vice-Chancellor. The new programmes were produced from 'bundles' of existing disciplines, and it was assumed that staff would find no difficulty in working across disciplines. One of the reasons for the failure of the programmes was believed to be that the programme convenors had no power, partly because resources had not been reallocated. This highlights the need for resourcing to follow strategic changes.

Another academic from Education spoke of 'adventures with programmes'. He believed that there was a lack of advice and support for students, who had been left to make sense of a fragmented experience. The disciplines – referred to as taproots for the university's work– were withering. Although the change was popular with some students, brighter students, he claimed, were not sufficiently grounded in a discipline and therefore lost out when they went on to postgraduate study.

From the view of an anthropologist, the programmes, which required faculty to teach outside of their disciplines, were too rigid and could turn off the 'high-flyers' who were disappointed by the loss of the creative options they previously could choose for themselves. Overall there was a sense that the programmes reduced opportunities for all students. Before (and after) the programmes initiative, in the humanities there was freedom for students to mix and match across disciplines, although no bridging or co-ordination had been built into the curriculum.

Similar problems were seen in the Sciences. From the perspective of a Chemistry professor, there had always been interdisciplinary opportunities, with extensive choice and variability. There was also a focus on research, generic skills and practical work, so in some ways it was business as usual. Overall there was disillusionment with the programmes, which were felt to be too complex to administer and for students to come to terms with, and the new programmes were scrapped.

ways of working. It was important to achieve a mix of skills within a team, with all members contributing their strength. One commented that it was not productive to attempt to require staff to take part in a curriculum change if they did not wish to. Colleagues' attitudes featured strongly. It was suggested that some were entrenched in disciplinary silos. A frequent lament was the perceived low status of teaching, set against research. Obvious and consistent senior support was felt to be vital, together with very public recognition of and reward for excellent teaching. There was widespread recognition that academic work was becoming faster and more complex, that leadership was required, and that the time has passed when a 'gentleman amateur' approach to leadership is acceptable. There was little support for formal taught leadership programmes, although those who had undertaken them said that they found them useful; learning from practical experience was valuable. There was a need for excellent role models and recognition of the value of coaching and mentoring. The need for leaders to attend to local cultures is shown in the case study on page 140.

Conclusions

Curriculum change in a research-intensive environment is challenging because changes in roles and relationships are involved, touching on issues of identity. Institutional change has to deal with the strong orientation that academic staff often have to their discipline or profession, which engages them with a network of colleagues beyond the university, and also to the immediate environment of the department. The institution, even though it is the employer, often has the weakest claim on staff loyalty. The pace of centrally mandated change may therefore be very slow. Simply getting agreement to make changes may take several years, and sometimes change initiatives may make no progress at all.

Yet individuals and groups in fact adjust to changing conditions and needs all the time and have the capacity to make significant improvements. In any research-intensive university, research groups and networks are established, initially often quite informally, taking advantage of immediate needs and opportunities. Course teams find pragmatic solutions to problems in the management of teaching. It therefore makes sense to encourage a climate in which at the lowest possible level, staff are encouraged to take responsibility for shaping change. This requires sympathetic HR approaches and a change strategy that favours local interpretation and recognises the value and importance of networks.

The discourse around change may also either help or hinder. In our study we found very wide agreement about the purposes of a higher education: that it has to do with developing autonomy, criticality, tolerance of others and a range of other attributes, alongside disciplinary knowledge. However, some of the ways in which that broader agenda for learning are approached did not find favour with many academic staff, often because it was seen to be framed in terms of a rather reductivist and decontextualised notion of 'skills', rather than rooted in the exploration of a discipline. A re-evaluation of what it means to lead in an academic environment would be timely. A flexible organisation that is able to change organically requires that leadership capacity be broadly distributed, and that the social aspects of leadership – the ability to inspire and enthuse colleagues working in a collegial environment – are centrally important.

References

Adair, J. (1998) *The skills of leadership*. Aldershot: Gower.

Barnett, R. (1990) *The idea of higher education*. Buckingham: Society for Research into Higher Education/Open University Press.

Barnett, R., Parry, G. and Coate, K. (2001) Conceptualising curriculum change. *Teaching in Higher Education*, 6(4): 435–449.

Bascom, W. R. (1948) Ponapean prestige economy. *Southwestern Journal of Anthropology 42*: 211–221.

Becher, T. (1989) *Academic tribes and territories: Intellectual inquiry and the cultures of disciplines*. Buckingham: Society for Research into Higher Education/Open University Press.

Berquist, W. H. (1992) *The four cultures of the academy*. San Francisco: Jossey Bass.

Biglan, A. (1973a) Relationships between subject matter characteristics and the structure and output of university departments. *Journal of Applied Psychology, 57*(3): 204–213.

Biglan, A. (1973b) The characteristics of subject matter in different academic areas. *Journal of Applied Psychology, 58*: 195–203.

Birnbaum, R. (1988) *How colleges work*. San Francisco: Jossey Bass.

Blackmore, P. (2007) Disciplinary difference in academic leadership and management and its development: a significant factor? *Research in Post-compulsory Education, 12*(2): 225–239.

Blackmore, P. and Kandiko, C. B. (2010) Interdisciplinary leadership and learning in Davies M., Devlin, M. and Tight, M. (eds) *Interdisciplinary higher education: International perspectives on higher education research* (Vol. 5) (pp. 55–74). Amsterdam: Emerald Group Publishing Ltd.; New York: JAI Elsevier Press.

Blackmore, P. and Kandiko, C. B. (2011) Interdisciplinarity within an academic career. *Research in Post-Compulsory Education, 16*(1): 123–134.

Bourdieu, P. (1988) *Homo academicus*. Cambridge: Polity Press.

Bryman, A. (2007) Effective leadership in higher education: A literature review. *Studies in Higher Education, 32*(6): 693–710.

Cowan, J. and Heywood, J. (2001) Curriculum renewal in an institution of higher education in Heywood, J., Sharp, J., and Hides, M. (eds) *Improving Teaching in Higher Education* (pp 7–18). Manchester, University of Salford.

Cuthbert, R. (2006) *Constructive alignment in the world of institutional management*. York: LTSN Generic Centre.

Deem, R. (2010) Herding the academic cats: The challenges of 'managing' academic research in the contemporary UK university. *Perspectives: Policy and Practice in Higher Education, 14*(2): 37–43.

Deem, R. and Johnson, R. (2000) Managerialism and University Managers: Building New Academic Communities or Dismantling Old Ones? in McNay, I. (ed.) *Higher Education and their Communities* (pp. 64–84). Buckingham: SRHE/Open University Press.

Deem, R. (2001) Managing contemporary UK universities – Manager academics and new managerialism. *Academic Leadership*, 1: 1–18.

Georgiades, N. and Phillimore, L. (1975) The myth of the hero-innovator and alternative strategies for organisational change in C. Kiernan and P. Woodford (eds) *Behaviour modification with the severely retarded* (pp. 313–320). Amsterdam: Associated Science Press.

Gibbons, M., Limoges, C., Nowotny, H., Schwartzman, S., Scott, P. and Trow, M. (1994) *The new production of knowledge: the dynamics of science and research in contemporary societies.* London: Sage.

Gibbs, G., Knapper, C., and Piccinin, S. (2008) Disciplinary and contextually appropriate approaches to leadership of teaching in research-intensive academic departments in Higher Education. *Higher Education Quarterly*, 62(4): 416–436.

Giddens, A. (1991) *Modernity and self-identity: Self and society in the late Modern Age.* Cambridge: Polity.

Grinev, A. V. (2005) *The Tlingit Indians in Russian America*, 1741–1867. Trans R. L. Bland and K. G. Solovjova. Lincoln: University of Nebraska Press.

Henkel, M. (2000) *Academic identities and policy change in higher education.* London: Jessica Kingsley.

Herskovits, M. J. (1948) *Man and his works: The science of cultural anthropology.* New York: A. A. Knopf.

Jenkins, A. (1996) Discipline-based educational development. *The International Journal for Academic Development*, 1(1): 50–62.

Johnston, V. and Westwood, J. (2007) *Academic leadership: Developing a framework for the professional development of programme leaders.* York: Higher Education Academy.

Kekäle, J. (2006) *Academic leadership in perspective.* New York: Nova Science Publishers.

KLI (2010) *Creating a 21st century curriculum: The King's-Warwick Project.* London: King's Learning Institute, King's College London.

Knight, P. and Trowler, P. (2001) *Departmental leadership in higher education.* Buckingham: Society for Research into Higher Education/Open University Press.

Lamont, M. (2009) *How professors think.* Cambridge, Mass: Harvard University Press.

Lovitts, B. E. (2001) *Leaving the ivory tower: The causes and consequences of departure from doctoral study.* Maryland: Rowman and Littlefield Publishers Inc.

Macfarlane, B. (2007) *The academic citizen: The virtue of service in university life.* Abingdon: Routledge.

Martin, E., Trigwell, K., Prosser, M. and Ramsden, P. (2003) Variation in the experience of leadership of teaching in higher education. *Studies in Higher Education*, 28(3): 247–259.

McInnis, C. (1998) Academics and administrators in Australian universities: dissolving boundaries and new tensions. *Higher Education Management*, 8(2): 161–173.

McNay, I. (1995) From the collegial academy to corporate enterprise: the changing cultures of universities, in T. Schuller (ed.) *The changing university?* (pp. 105–115). Buckingham: Society for Research into Higher Education /Open University Press.

Merton, R. K. (1968) *Social theory and social structure.* New York: The Free Press.

Middlehurst, R. (1993) *Leading academics.* Buckingham: Society for Research into Higher Education/Open University Press.

Nissani, M. (1997) Ten cheers for interdisciplinarity: The case for interdisciplinary knowledge and research. *The Social Science Journal*, 34(2), 201–216.

Ramsden, P. (1998) *Learning to lead in higher education.* London: Routledge.

Schein, E. (1985) *Organisational culture and leadership.* San Fransisco: Jossey-Bass.

Schon, D. (1983) *The reflective practitioner: How professionals think in action.* New York: Basic Books.

Snow, C. P. (1961) *The two cultures and the scientific revolution.* Cambridge: University Press.

Whitchurch, C. (2008) Shifting identities and blurring boundaries: The emergence of third space professionals in UK higher education. *Higher Education Quarterly,* *62*(4): 377–396.

Whitchurch, C. (2011) *The rise of 'third space' professionals.* London: Routledge.

Chapter 10

Case study

The whole-of-institution curriculum renewal undertaken by the University of Melbourne, 2005–2011

Richard James and Peter McPhee[1]

In 2005, the University of Melbourne embarked on an ambitious process of curriculum change that was unprecedented in Australian higher education. Under the leadership of a new Vice-Chancellor, Glyn Davis, and guided by a new strategic plan, *Growing Esteem*, the University sought to strengthen the quality of the University's research, learning and knowledge transfer. Curriculum renewal was to be the centerpiece. The 'Melbourne Model', as the new curriculum structure came to be dubbed, issued a challenging new vision for higher education in Australia. The philosophy, in essence, was to focus undergraduate education on developing graduates with broader skills through a small set of more general three-year degrees while shifting professional training almost entirely into graduate level programs. This degree structure has been referred to as '3+2' – three years of Bachelors level education and two years of professional training at Master's level – though this shorthand over-simplifies the new network of degree programs that provide numerous exit and entry points for students within an array of professional and research pathways and outcomes.

The chapter is an account of the Melbourne experience of curriculum renewal. Its focus is primarily with the execution of the process of change. While Melbourne's new curriculum structure is hardly novel in international terms, it represented at the time of its conception in the mid-2000s a significant change in higher education thinking in Australia. Melbourne's plan confronted the assumptions about higher education of prospective students and their parents, school communities, the professions and their associations, and, not least, the staff of the University itself. The University's intentions for a radical new degree structure also required public policy settings to be confronted head-on if the plan was to be financially feasible.

What is particularly significant from a higher education research perspective is the demanding process of change that was carried out to a pressing timeline. The chapter is an attempt to map this process, as objectively and critically as possible for authors who were participants in the renewal. We highlight the challenges associated with a radical restructuring of higher education and suggest a number of lessons that can be learned from the Melbourne experience. Finally, we outline the outcomes that have flowed from the curriculum reforms, insofar as such evidence was available at the time of writing.

The context and impetus for change

Melbourne's curriculum restructure was the product of an innovative and confident university. It emerged neither from a period of crisis nor degeneration, but from an era of comparative prosperity and optimism at the University and at the start of the term of a recently appointed Vice-Chancellor, Glyn Davis, who was full of vigour for reform.

In mid-2005, when plans for the curriculum renewal were first mooted, the University of Melbourne was arguably Australia's leading university, being ranked either first or second in the various international rankings schema, with a wide-ranging, comprehensive curriculum. If the University was already in a strong position, why embark on a major and potentially risky process of change? Melbourne's curriculum overhaul was designed to rebuild the University's educational programs around an explicit pedagogical philosophy and in doing so to dramatically re-position the institution nationally by introducing a curriculum model well understood overseas.

When the incoming Vice-Chancellor began consulting with the University community, a number of senior members expressed the view that the University should seek a unifying rationale for its course offerings. Decisions to offer new courses were rarely based on a deliberate vision for the institution. There was limited university-wide discussion of curriculum philosophy and practice and individual faculties tended to operate independently and to focus solely on their own courses and programs. Over its 150 year history, the University had steadily expanded its postgraduate and undergraduate offerings. Through slow accretion, the University had assembled an unwieldy number of undergraduate degrees – approximately 100 degrees in total. A high proportion of students, around one-quarter, were undertaking dual degrees. There were well over five hundred postgraduate coursework programs, most of them small and devoid of a sense of cohort. Consolidation was called for, both for educational and administrative reasons.

The direction to be followed emerged from consultation. Discussions with employers, with alumni and with recent graduates had shown the importance of developing graduates who have both discipline depth and the breadth to ensure they can cross discipline boundaries and communicate well in all cultural settings. This was viewed as necessary for lives and careers in which knowledge is rapidly renewed, knowledge boundaries are more permeable and professional practice often requires complex, multidisciplinary understandings.

Broadly, the University set out to respond to and align with global trends in education and employment, optimising career choice and preparation for careers in knowledge economies, while improving the Melbourne educational experience to encompass both broader and deeper educational outcomes. This was to be done by moving to broader, more generalist undergraduates programs and shifting professional training into graduate programs in the main part.

This new curriculum would defer students' final career choices until completion of their undergraduate education. The University faced the problem of students' career choices being heavily influenced by the tertiary entrance ranking system used for admissions in Australia. A student ranking based on school achievement is a primary tool of university selection in Australia and is the 'currency' for attaining a university place. Student demand for particular courses is reflected in the entrance score required to gain admission. To some extent demand drives prestige, which in turn further drives up demand. Many school-leavers make choices about the higher education on the prestige 'signals' conveyed by entrance requirements and the implicit or explicit pressure not to 'waste' their rank, rather than a considered sense of purpose for a future career. There were far too many examples of students committing themselves to career choices they later regretted.

The curriculum renewal would establish a distinctive niche for the University of Melbourne, a point of differentiation for the University in both the domestic and international markets. Prior to the Melbourne initiative, the Australian tertiary sector was characterised by little curriculum differentiation. Despite the fact that Commonwealth public policy settings seek to encourage curriculum and institutional diversity, Australian universities had – and continue to have – highly similar offerings at the undergraduate and postgraduate level. Melbourne's innovations in both undergraduate and graduate education enabled the University of Melbourne to distinguish itself from other Australian universities in terms of curriculum offerings and awards granted.

Curriculum distinctiveness and quality were highly important at a time when Australian universities were considering how to respond to the growth in undergraduate education in East Asian and South East Asian universities. Students from China, Hong Kong, Malaysia and Singapore, who were Australia's key source of international enrolments, were increasingly choosing to undertake undergraduate study in their home countries or to look elsewhere on the globe. A renewed focus on professional graduate course offerings in the proposed curriculum might assist the University of Melbourne to maintain its international student enrolments.

The financial implications of a restructured relationship between undergraduate and graduate education were a necessary consideration. The Australian policies for student tuition fees established tightly regulated pricing for undergraduate education and offered more flexibility in graduate education. The new curriculum with a stronger graduate orientation might, over time, be modestly financially favorable for the University as graduate students began to occupy a growing share of places and opportunities for pricing were opened up.

The model: A summary of the Melbourne degree structure and philosophy

Melbourne's curriculum is now based around the general structure of a potentially eight-year program for a student who goes on to complete a PhD: a three-year undergraduate degree in the humanities, social sciences and sciences characterised by both breadth and depth, followed by a professional or research Master's degree (where appropriate, of two years' duration) and the option of a PhD program. The curriculum structure draws on the 3+2+3 or three-cycle structure identified with the Bologna Process, the objectives of North American undergraduate 'liberal education' and related developments in Asia, but does so within the context of Australian higher education policy and history. The undergraduate degrees provide both depth and breadth, and clear pathways into graduate programs and research higher degrees through the Honours year and Master's. The graduate offerings seek to provide in-depth professional training to students with greater maturity and breadth of perspective.[2]

The educational objectives underpinning the new curriculum are captured in a set of highly aspirational statements that encapsulate the University's ambitions for a distinctive 'Melbourne Experience':

- distinctive undergraduate courses that offer pathways into professional graduate programs but which also stand alone as strong degrees;
- a sound discipline-based education, including an introduction to research as a foundation for research higher degrees;
- closer alignment of course structures with desired graduate attribute outcomes;
- 'deep generalist' graduates with the generic and interdisciplinary skills suitable for both postgraduate programs and diverse and changing workplaces;
- a stronger likelihood of well-rounded and motivated graduate students at both Master's and PhD level;
- more informed student choice about careers and graduate education;
- a stronger shared experience, engagement and sense of university community;
- enhanced opportunities for external experiences such as community work or international study;
- strengthened international recognition of degrees;
- broader access for students, especially those from disadvantaged backgrounds;
- greater opportunity for students (and staff) to experience interdisciplinary teaching and research collaborations across the University;
- an improved classroom experience, including smaller classes for courses which move to graduate entry.

The University consolidated its undergraduate offering into six degree programs, which became known as the 'New Generation' degrees:

- Bachelor of Arts
- Bachelor of Biomedical Science

- Bachelor of Commerce
- Bachelor of Environments
- Bachelor of Music
- Bachelor of Science

A focus on interdisciplinary or multidisciplinary study is one feature of the New Generation degrees. All students undertake 20–25 per cent of their studies in an area of knowledge outside of their core discipline or area of major. The aim of the breadth requirement is to expose students to a wide range of intellectual perspectives and to encourage interdisciplinary study as appropriate.

The New Generation undergraduate degrees were designed to provide disciplinary rigor and to operate as strong, stand-alone degrees in themselves – leading directly to employment if students wished – as well providing adequate preparation for selected graduate programs. A requirement of capstone study was introduced for all major strands of undergraduate degrees. A major must be characterised by intellectual development across a three-year program, culminating in a capstone subject in the third year.

Prior to 2008, the University offered professional qualifications at both the undergraduate and graduate level. Within the new curriculum, all professional training courses are offered exclusively at the graduate level in either Master's programs or Doctoral programs.[3] The Master's programs tend to be two-year qualifications and include, for example, the Master of Architecture, Master of Teaching and Master of Social Work. The Doctoral programs tend to be three or more years in length and include the Juris Doctor, Doctor of Medicine, Doctor of Dental Surgery, Doctor of Physiotherapy and the Doctor of Veterinary Medicine. The University also continues to offer the full range of postgraduate higher degree research and other courses it has always offered exclusively at the graduate level.

The mechanics of the change process

Governance

The architecture for the new Melbourne degree structure was created rapidly in roughly a seven-month process from February to September 2006, for it was realised that swift implementation would reduce community uncertainty. Following the Vice-Chancellor's release of the *Growing Esteem* strategy and his outline of the broad parameters of possible curriculum reforms the University's Academic Board agreed to create a committee – the Curriculum Commission – to investigate a radically new curriculum model.

The Curriculum Commission was responsible for debating and developing the precise nature of the reforms and their implementation. The Commission was chaired by the University's Deputy Vice-Chancellor (Academic) and was composed of the Associate Deans for Teaching and Learning, the staff within each faculty with curriculum responsibilities. Throughout 2006 the Commission met intensively with a schedule of weekly meetings for six months. The Associate Deans played a vital role in grounding the process of reform in the educational possibilities and issues rather than financial considerations. They reported the Commission's deliberations to their Deans, whose feedback would be fed back to the Curriculum Commission. The participation of Associate Deans was a deft mechanism for managing the debate constructively and harmoniously. The debate within the University was at times intense, for much was at stake.

The University's Academic Board played a central role in ensuring that there was a University-wide commitment to the quality and coherence of the new degrees. Ultimately, it was the Academic Board that approved the new curriculum structure. The new curriculum was in operation for the start of the academic year in March 2008. The pace of change was influenced by a number of factors. The higher education sector is a competitive environment and the University sought to remove any uncertainty for school students, families and schools about its new approach. In addition, the University was concerned to limit the number of undergraduate cohorts who entered the old degree structure – thus the 2007 first year cohort was the only one to enter the University prior to the introduction of the new degrees. Finally, the University's internal process of consultation and discussion had to be bounded if the reforms were ever to be realised. Key figures of the Curriculum Commission insisted that allowing an additional year to consider the changes would stifle the impetus for change.

The key points of deliberation for the Curriculum Commission

The Curriculum Commission began by confronting the central questions that would define the character of the new undergraduate offerings of the University. How many New Generation degrees should be offered? What length should they be and what should be their nomenclature? Should an Honours year be retained? How might a breadth requirement operate?

It was broadly agreed that the University needed to offer a sufficiently broad range of courses to enable undergraduate students to identify the focus and pathways of their preferred degree, but at the same time a restricted enough range to optimise intellectual coherence and a sense of 'learning community'. After lengthy discussion and negotiation, which began fleetingly with the idea of a single degree, styled perhaps as a Bachelor of Arts and Science, it was determined to offer six New Generation degrees (as listed in the previous section).

There were differing views within the University regarding the length of the degrees. Some academics maintained that the degrees should be three years in length, as were many of the existing degrees at the time; others insisted that the University should adopt the American model of four-year undergraduate degrees. The Curriculum Commission decided to retain the three-year model partly because of the desire to preserve a separate Honours year in undergraduate degrees (a decision in itself that was discussed intensively) and because of concerns about the nine-year length of a 4+2+3 model through to PhD.

The Curriculum Commission spent much time discussing broad curriculum content. There were difficulties encountered in establishing common ground on specific dimensions of the curriculum, revealing the significantly different 'world views' in different faculties and the differing epistemological perspectives of academics across the University. The discussions around curriculum structure and content often led to realisation of the good sense incrementally built into the previous curriculum over a long period of time.

Despite the differing world views, a consensus developed that the New Generation courses should offer both the discipline knowledge basis necessary for graduate programs or for employment and exposure to a range of disciplines from other programs. The New Generation courses should be strong 'stand alone' degrees in themselves, but their major internal sequences ('majors') should also make them preferred pathways for graduate programs. The tension between keeping students' options open as long as possible and providing the necessary disciplinary preparation for graduate study needed to be managed adroitly.

The breadth requirement

The Curriculum Commission was responsible for formulating a policy on the inclusion of the breadth requirement in the New Generation degrees. Breadth was initially described in terms of a 'general education' and other expressions and its precise formulation and nomenclature proved elusive for some time. In the end, 'breadth' seemed the best descriptor, for this captures the counterpoint to disciplinary depth.

Various options for breadth were considered, including compulsory core units for all students, but ultimately the decision was made to give students the option to choose their breadth studies from subjects outside of their home New Generation degree, with appropriate guidance and checks and balances with regard to prerequisites. The principal objective was to encourage students to undertake studies in a part of the disciplinary terrain as epistemologically different from their core studies as possible.

Faculty buy-in with the idea of breadth was a struggle throughout, not because the idea of a broader education was opposed but because breadth subjects took time from the core disciplinary curriculum. The Commission was conscious of the challenge of maintaining a sound discipline base while also creating opportunities for students to undertake or be introduced to research. There was also a desire to use the breadth of the new undergraduate degree structure to underpin a better understanding of the relevance of discipline studies in a wider context and of the value of interdisciplinary connections. Weighing up these goals, which in effect competed for time in a three-year degree program, was difficult and there was no logic that might prevail for determining the optimum extent and nature of breadth. Time has shown that students make a diverse range of breadth choices, an outcome with which the University is very comfortable.

The University also created a specialist group of breadth subjects dubbed 'University Breadth Subjects'. These subjects are interdisciplinary or multidisciplinary subjects that are taught by multiple faculties. All students are eligible to choose these subjects regardless of their new generation degree. A fascinating array of subjects are available, many focused on complex social, economic and ethical issues. The University Breadth Subjects in many ways epitomise the educational goals of the Melbourne curriculum.

Selection and admission

Having established the basic architecture of its educational model, the University needed to develop new processes for selection and admission to graduate courses. The Curriculum Commission worked in consultation with faculties to determine new selection and admission policies. Key to these policies was the 'provisional selection' policy for high-achieving school-leavers. This policy aimed to stem any loss of highly vocationally focused students to other universities by offering students who obtained a very high achievement in the secondary school certificate a guaranteed place in one of the University's graduate schools. These students were required to maintain a certain average throughout their undergraduate studies at the University. The policy for guaranteed pathways has evolved over time in response to patterns of student choice. At the same time, the shifting of selection into professional programs to graduate levels has facilitated the University's goal of opening up entry to undergraduate courses by simplifying prerequisites.

Finally, the University had to consider the distinction between professional and research higher degree pathways. There was much concern about the squeeze on preparedness for the PhD – for three-year undergraduate programs with a sizeable breadth component substantially reduced disciplinary specialisation. The challenge for the University's research higher degree programs was to combine features of both Bologna (eight years) and US (considerably longer) models to improve the quality of our degrees within a timeframe of eight years of Federal funding. The development of two-year Master's programs as a pathway to PhD study has provided an opportunity for more in-depth preparation than previously the case.

Implementation

Ultimately, the introduction of the Melbourne Model required the University to engage with difficult questions about curriculum design, the provision of student services and the nature of student policies and procedures. The scale of the task was massive. Every faculty, every department, had to work through the curriculum changes necessary to maximise the desired benefits of the proposed curriculum. No course remained untouched by the changes.

The University had to determine the nature and pace of change in the 'teaching out' of undergraduate professional degrees and the introduction of postgraduate professional degrees. All faculties had to continue to provide undergraduate courses to students who commenced their studies prior to 2008. In addition, some faculties began simultaneously offering postgraduate professional qualifications. The Melbourne Law School is a good example of the challenge: the first cohort of the new Juris Doctor commenced in 2008, while the final 2007 cohort of LLB students are not expected to complete their studies until 2012 to 2013. For other faculties, the resource demands of offering two courses simultaneously was believed to be too demanding and the introduction of new programs was delayed.

The restructuring of the University's degrees called for different and expanded course advising and student services. The features of the new undergraduate program – far fewer degrees, interdisciplinary, cross-faculty and generic in character – meant that course advice and planning, both in person and online, became even more important. The need for expert course advice, and for whole-of-university course planning, became more pronounced. A Science student, for example, would need advice each year on the specific subjects which will best prepare them for their preferred area of employment or for the postgraduate coursework or research field towards which their developing interests were leading. Crucially, they needed to be aware of very different graduate study options, such as in Teaching or Law.

The introduction of the new degree structure necessitated significant change to the University's suite of academic policies. A policy and procedures working group was established to undertake the gargantuan task of reviewing the plethora of different policies, including faculty policies, with the objective of formulating a single set of student policies to apply to all New Generation degree courses, as well as to the graduate courses to the greatest extent possible.

Pressure points and challenges

There were some tense discussions throughout the creation of the Melbourne Model. Not all staff of the University agreed with the need for change or with the broad direction proposed. Some staff did not agree philosophically with the idea of a broader curriculum in undergraduate education. Many staff expressed a commitment to breadth study in principle, but significant divisions arose when discussing the amount of curriculum time that should be devoted to breadth and defining the content of breadth study.

Some faculties were more concerned than others with the introduction of a new curriculum. These were primarily the areas of the University that were prospering under the existing structure and had sizeable international student intake. They feared changing the settings might risk upsetting good business models. A number of members of academic staff resisted 'giving up' certain subjects and courses that they had taught for a long period of time and some experienced the sense of loss that is commonplace in processes of organisational change.

There were various teething problems upon implementation as well, particularly with the interdisciplinary University Breadth Subjects. The curriculum design and teaching was more complex than had been anticipated—for example, a climate change subject introduced some high-level scientific material that students from non-science backgrounds found difficult to understand—and the coordination of subjects across multiple faculties was challenging. Some students were highly critical of these subjects in the early stages but the redesign of programs attempted to correct these impressions.

In terms of public relations, the University received ongoing unfavorable reporting around perceived problems with the Melbourne curriculum that was misleading or simply false. The conservatism of the mainstream media towards curriculum innovation was unexpected and surprising, as was the unwillingness of the media to embrace the value of curriculum innovation and diversification in Australian higher education overall. The continued use of tertiary data that do not reflect both undergraduate and postgraduate course applications has been a concern for the University. Mainstream media sources frequently cite data from the Victorian Tertiary Admissions Centre (VTAC) relating to students' first preferences for undergraduate study. Admissions Centre data presents only undergraduate student demand and fails to indicate the significant proportion of Melbourne students that now enter the University as graduates. For example, undergraduate applications to the University have fallen by around 25 per cent over the past six years – a direct result of professional degrees being moved into graduate schools – but some 3,000 graduate coursework students joined the University in 2011 but were not recorded in Admissions Centre data.

The University also learned how sensitively the 'teach out' programs, which became known as 'heritage' degrees, needed to be handled. The interests and concerns of the existing students needed special attention: Arts students, for example, were concerned about a reduction in subjects available to them; similarly, Law students were concerned about the limits on the timeframe for finishing their degrees and perceived differential treatment compared with the new Juris Doctor students. The management of two parallel degree structures created much complexity for the University, not least because the spotlight on the new courses and the media publicity and advertising campaigns around them inadvertently encouraged existing students to feel they were being forgotten. This was not the case, of course, but seemingly small issues often escalated during the period of transition.

Insights into the nature and effectiveness of reform processes

What conditions underpinned this successful curriculum reform process? We can identify some elements of the Melbourne experience that might be relevant to other institutions or contexts. First, the University of Melbourne was a high-morale, aspirational institution when it took this path, an institution with a widespread commitment among its staff to being a deeply international, highly ranked, world-class university. In 2006, the University of Melbourne was confident in its ability to innovate and create change. The Melbourne Model – with its emphasis on graduate education and redefining the goals of undergraduate education – spoke to many staff and their personal academic values.

Second, committed leadership and senior endorsement was vitally important of course. The University of Melbourne had a committed and energetic Vice-Chancellor who articulated a vision and advocated publicly and privately for its adoption. He could draw on effective leadership in many areas of the University. The process required tenacity and resilience in the face of the inevitable opposition and concerns that emerge with a change process of such far-reaching impact.

Third, the University had a reasonable resource base. Creating a new curriculum and radically restructuring the course structure places significant demands on staff time and requires high levels of commitment from professional and academic staff, as well as from leadership. The commitment of professional staff was especially crucial to successful implementation. The University was particularly careful to avoid any slide in its research performance while it engineered this significant curriculum change. The governing Council made a major commitment from budgetary reserves to enable the transition to occur without major disruption.

Fourth, external stakeholders were engaged every step of the way. The University was committed to consulting with key stakeholders at every stage of development and implementation and put considerable resources into market research, before, during and after the implementation of the new curriculum. It was particularly concerned to identify the implications that the new curriculum might have for school-leavers, careers advisors and the international market. The findings helped shape decision-making and informed the design of communication of the new curriculum structure and its underpinning rationale. The University allocated significant resources to conducting market research with prospective students and employers.

Fifth, the unwavering educational focus of the Curriculum Commission was paramount. As far as possible the University placed educational values and beliefs at the heart of its deliberations and factors such as financial considerations, market reactions and the like – important as they are – were given secondary attention. This does not imply debate was stifled – far from it, for there was open and robust debate and all proposed reforms were thoroughly examined before acceptance by the University community.

Curriculum design is in some ways the art of compromise – there are usually more good ideas than the time and resources with which to implement them. The initial articulation of a new structure for the Melbourne degrees swung on the Curriculum Commission being able to successfully weave a path through a suite of intersecting considerations on which there were often incommensurable views within the University community and among its external stakeholders. Front and centre were the beliefs about the nature of a higher education curriculum and what it is valuable for a university student to learn. The Curriculum Commission in effect sought to reach consensus around a shared set of educational values. This experience confirmed that academics hold quite different world views when it comes to the curriculum, views that are shaped in part by their disciplinary upbringings. The language of curriculum conversation with its abstract concepts of 'depth' and 'breadth' itself invites misunderstandings. Finding a shared, common logic for the curriculum in a comprehensive institution is fraught. The pedagogical dimension in the Curriculum Commission's deliberations was highly complex and it created tensions. The idea of a disciplinary breadth requirement that would take students beyond their major areas of study was broadly endorsed, but there was much devil in the detail on implementation, including the appropriate volume of breadth and way in which course advising might guide and regulate student choices to ensure their breadth components matched up to the University's aspirations for genuine exposure to areas of studying with 'different ways of knowing'.

But curriculum reshaping is rarely purely based on pedagogical grounds. The Curriculum Commission also grappled with the market implications. There is a market dimension to curriculum change of this magnitude that cannot be ignored, for it would be a brave university that introduced a curriculum that flew in the face of the values and expectations of students and their families. A particularly important issue for the University of Melbourne was the fact that one quarter of its students were international students and any alienation of these students would have been financially catastrophic. Equally, however, a leading institution has a social leadership role and obligation to do what in its judgment is best for its students and the communities it serves and to inform and educate accordingly. A university cannot, or should not, be entirely market-led and the University committed to reforms aware that there would be some bumps on the road ahead as it challenged prevailing norms.

There was also a political dimension, needless to say. The politics had both internal and external manifestations. Introducing far-reaching institutional reform will always involve internal institution politics as change affects resource flows and the business models of faculties and schools. The Melbourne restructure dramatically affected the patterns of student enrolments and thus funding allocations as well as confronting core beliefs. There were important external political contexts to be considered too. The University of Melbourne had to consider how the public policy settings would impinge on its capacity to offer the 3+2 sequence. In particular, the commonwealth policy at the time only offered public subsidies for tuition to undergraduate students. For equity, the University sought and was granted the allocation of publicly subsidised student places to its graduate courses needed for entry to professional practice. The transfer of commonwealth places to the graduate level enabled the University to use these places both as a form of scholarship, thereby addressing access and equity concerns, and as the basis of conditional offers to high-achieving school-leavers. This was crucial. The University also lobbied the Commonwealth Government to lift the caps on the national student loan scheme and to amend the Youth Allowance policy. Careful negotiation was also required with a range of professional associations, institutes and registration authorities and their endorsement of the new degrees was vital. The University allocated significant resources to consulting with professional bodies in Engineering, Medicine, Dentistry, Law and Architecture, some of whom were initially lukewarm in their reactions to the proposed curriculum model. The approval of professional bodies was an essential prerequisite to implementing the graduate model of professional education at the University.

Finally, there was the logistical dimension. A university has finite space, finite staff and finite time in which to deliver a curriculum. The decision to opt for three-year undergraduate degrees placed certain constraints on the curriculum structure and possibilities; similarly, practical considerations around campus spaces and delivery capacity were in the background during the formulation of the new curriculum structure.

The outcomes to date

The educational effects of curriculum change are notoriously difficult to evaluate due to the large number of variables and the lengthy timeframes before outcomes can be measured. At the time of writing those students from the first cohort to commence the new Melbourne undergraduate degrees who completed their undergraduate programs within the expected three years were in the first year of graduate education or their first year of employment. Thus it remains early days in terms of rigorous evaluation of the outcomes and the observations to follow are impressionistic rather than definitive.

To begin with, there have been major effects on the institutional culture. The process of curriculum renewal has given the University a new sense of identity, a renewed sense of optimism and new confidence for taking on change. The institution is more adaptive, more nimble and more flexible; there is a feeling of 'can do'. Part of this stems from successfully carrying off the most far-reaching reform attempted by an Australian higher education institution and in doing so establishing a truly distinctive curriculum – while at the same time maintaining the University's position as Australia's leading research university. The University has learnt that it can successfully undertake change on a major scale, establishing a platform for future change that includes building and enhancing the graduate character of the University over time to achieve a level of quality not previously available in the nation.

The Melbourne Model itself has been externally evaluated and praised in a series of reports. These include the Australian Universities Quality Agency audit of the new programs in the sciences, the Australian Council for Education Research evaluation of the Masters of Teaching, the Australian Medical Council report on the Medical Doctor program, and similar reports from accrediting bodies on the Master of Engineering and the Master of Architecture.

Student demand for the University of Melbourne has not significantly altered. Individual degree entry scores have remained high, despite taking many more students into fewer programs. The Bachelor of Arts remains the degree with the highest demand in the State of Victoria. The University continues to be the institution of choice for Australia's more able students. Having said this, the University accepted at the outset that it might no longer attract the students who are most focused on commencing professional studies immediately upon completion of schooling. National curriculum differentiation brings choice in the nature of the 'product', which is a good thing, and not all curricula will appeal to all students. Melbourne's curriculum has found an audience with students who like the idea of a broader undergraduate education, who welcome the opportunity to choose breadth subjects and who wish to delay career decisions. Against national trends, the logic of Melbourne's offerings has encouraged students towards study in arts and science – Melbourne has given science a particular shot in the arm in a national context in which enrolments have been dwindling. University Breadth Subjects have enabled students from different faculties to share courses in diverse interdisciplinary areas of world-wide importance, such as Ecological History, Human Rights and Global Health. More Melbourne undergraduates are studying languages (particularly as a breadth choice), volunteering for co-curricular activities, and taking study abroad activities.

An unexpected outcome perhaps has been a noticeable if modest improvement in the share of undergraduate places held by students from lower socio-economic status (SES) backgrounds. There is no direct evidence that the new degree structure lies behind this outcome, but it can be concluded that the new Melbourne degree structure has not adversely affected the participation of students from lower SES backgrounds, despite the opportunity costs of the extended number of years of study required for professional training and earnings foregone. The social composition of graduate cohorts will be the next test of the equity performance of the 3+2 structure.

The long-term educational and employment outcomes of the Melbourne curriculum are yet to be clear. The signs are very good, however. The University has received positive feedback from students about their experience of the new curriculum – with student satisfaction rates matching or surpassing those from the years immediately before the new curriculum was introduced – and continues to have the highest retention rates of any university in Australia. The student experience of breadth subjects has been varied. Some students would prefer to study solely within their disciplines. Most, however, have appreciated the opportunity to study in broader fields, and in some cases, interdisciplinary fields.

There is solid evidence that the two-stage, 3+2 vision is working well. Some 60 per cent of the 2008 commencing cohort applied for further study at the University in 2011, many choosing fields they first discovered as undergraduates. This pattern of choice confirms the University's rationale that undergraduate study provides experiences for informed, mature decisions about career directions. The initial premise, that graduate professional programs would prove attractive to overseas students more likely to undertake undergraduate education at home, is proving well-founded.

It is too early to assess the employment outcomes, as the first graduates with Bachelor degrees entered the workforce late in 2010 or in 2011. Employer feedback data and the findings from the Australian Graduate Destination Survey will follow shortly and will provide important comparative information. Informal advice from employers about interns and graduates suggests they are welcoming their greater breadth of knowledge and experience alongside strong disciplinary skills.

With the new generation undergraduate degrees successfully bedded down, the University's attention has turned to fine-tuning and extending its graduate programs. The Melbourne curriculum revolution has created an undergraduate and graduate educational platform that will serve its students and graduates well as Australia moves towards universal participation in higher education. The decision to undertake curriculum renewal and re-positioning on the Melbourne scale was courageous but highly strategic. We believe history will judge it favorably.

Notes

1 While Deputy Vice-Chancellor (Academic) of the University of Melbourne, Professor Peter McPhee led the Curriculum Commission that designed the new Melbourne degrees and then, as Provost, oversaw their introduction. Professor Richard James was also a member of the Curriculum Commission and is presently a Pro Vice-Chancellor of the University. Both authors are in the Centre for the Study of Higher Education. Lucy Maxwell provided excellent assistance in the preparation of this chapter.

2 http://www.learningandteaching.unimelb.edu.au/curriculum/melbourne_model

3 The University established fifteen graduate schools that are responsible for the provision of postgraduate education. These include: Graduate School of Business and Economics; Graduate School of Humanities and Social Sciences; Melbourne Graduate School of Education; Melbourne Graduate School of Science; Melbourne Law School; Melbourne School of Design; Melbourne School of Engineering; Melbourne School of Land and Environment; Medicine, Dentistry and Health Sciences; Veterinary Science; Graduate Studies at the VCA and Music; and Melbourne School of Graduate Research.

Part 4

The networked curriculum

Embedding and looking forward

Chapter 11

Supporting change through development and evaluation

Paul Blackmore and Camille B. Kandiko

Curriculum review is likely to benefit from effective development support. A range of provision has been introduced at institutional and national levels to enhance academic practice, including teaching and learning. The multiplicity of initiatives, the variety of organisational arrangements and their frequent restructuring suggests that development is a complex field in which there is no settled view of how it should be thought about and supported. In this chapter we offer a number of principles for effective practice, drawn partly from an analysis of the literature and of policy and practice in universities. An increasing amount of evaluative data is now being obtained. Although there are limits to the extent to which practice and its development can be fully evidence-informed, we suggest that the availability and interpretation of relevant data is immensely helpful in guiding curriculum reform initiatives.

The role of development

Strategic curriculum change usually involves a fundamental review of what is taught and learned and of how learning is enabled and supported. The process of review involves problematising many taken-for-granted issues, such as the purpose of a higher education and the content of a particular curriculum. The discussion benefits from an exploration of other possible ways of working, of why and how other systems and individual universities have changed. An effective review involves many people in all parts of the university, at all levels. It can be a valuable developmental process in itself for individuals, groups and the institution, especially if it is well supported.

Any comprehensive review results in a need for changed practices 'on the ground', particularly those of academic staff, and for these changed practices to become embedded in an institution. As noted in the previous two chapters and the case studies, major changes challenge existing beliefs and values. They often bring together members of staff who have not worked closely with one another before. For example, a new interdisciplinary structure may draw together staff whose ideas about what, and how, they should teach differ significantly. Many kinds of learning take place. Re-design may require a shift along the continuum between a discipline-centred view and a student-centred one (Ramsden 1992). It may involve critically applying ideas such as constructive alignment in curriculum design (Biggs 2003) or approaches to learning (Trigwell and Prosser 1991) to existing and planned curricula. As noted in Chapter 7, the role of assessment may change with, for example, differing emphases between formative and summative assessment. Innovative approaches to assessment may be needed. The growth of learning technologies makes it possible to offer students learning opportunities in different ways.

Offering high quality education in an efficient and effective way requires organisation and management approaches at all levels to be thought through carefully. At the same time, the individual and collective well-being of staff who are asked to deliver more, often without increased resources, needs to be taken into account. The process of change, with groups of individuals needing to become teams, taking responsibility for planning and making changes at their level, in itself may require support. In all of these areas, it cannot be assumed that staff are always sufficiently knowledgeable.

Most institutions make an investment in development support, usually by appointing expert staff members who have that particular responsibility. This raises questions about what kind of support is effective, how it should be provided and by whom. However, many other aspects of an organisation have the potential to be developmental, raising further questions about the ways in which organisational learning can be encouraged throughout the institution.

Approaches to development

We have already mentioned two principal ways in which change has been approached – through people and through the organisation of resources. We now take a broader look at development. Our starting assumptions here are that the environment for universities will continue to be highly complex, fast moving and in some respects unpredictable. A university-wide curriculum change is most likely to be successful if individuals, departments and the institution are flexible and self-motivated, with staff encouraged to take as much initiative as possible at all levels, while maintaining institutional coherence. This suggests that change is likely to be a continual process that must be accommodated as an integral part of the ongoing work of the university. This in turn raises the question of how this aspect of a university can best be supported.

Structural approaches

Many national governments have invested significantly in encouraging better teaching in higher education. At national level in the UK, the establishment of the Institute for Learning and Teaching (Bucklow and Clark 2003), followed by the Higher Education Academy, are two obvious examples. In Australia, the former Australian Learning and Teaching Council was a parallel development. The UK government encouraged all institutions to develop learning and teaching strategies in return for additional support funding, although little attention was paid by institutions to planning for evaluation of such programmes (Gibbs 2001:3). It is not easy to achieve change in a university from outside, although national level support for development can be helpful in the setting of standards for those who teach and, in the UK, the network of subject centres proved popular (Oakleigh Consulting Limited 2008).

Although development has always taken place in universities, in that practices have changed over time, historically development as an identified function in universities is a relatively recent creation, starting in the 1960s in the UK, US and Australia. When first established it had a low status and the head of a development unit was usually not in a senior position. Commonly, decisions would be taken at a senior level without their development implications being considered. Development was seen, when it was considered at all, to be a low-level skills training function. The increasing size of universities and the more demanding environment in which they now work has focused attention on the need to encourage and manage change and to use resources, both human and otherwise, effectively (Blackmore *et al.* 2010). All institutions invest in development centres or units, variously named and constituted (Gosling 2001), working alongside mainstream academic departments. This approach to development has been praised (Gosling and D'Andrea 2002), but also criticised as a form of colonialism, based on a deficiency model of academic staff (McWilliam 2002).

The range of terms in use helps to illustrate the different ways in which development and the organisation are viewed. Staff Development (SD) has traditionally been a Human Resources-based (HR) approach, dealing with all staff in the organisation. Educational Development (ED) focuses specifically on the support of student learning, but usually from a staff perspective. Increasingly, the terms 'student development' and 'learning development' are being used to describe an approach that focuses on students rather than on staff. Academic Development (AD) refers to the treatment of academic work as a whole. Organisational Development (OD) draws its ideas from the literature on learning at an organisational level. In the US, faculty development refers in the main to pre-tenure support for members of faculty. More than one of these approaches may be in use in an institution, reflecting the desire to tackle specific development needs in particular ways. In others it may perhaps show that provision in universities has sometimes come about largely through happenstance, with one externally prompted initiative overlain on another, rather than through coherent planning. A range of key decisions is taken in relation to the form, focus and function of differing forms of provision. Whether the decisions are made consciously and deliberately or not, they have real effects (Blackmore *et al.* 2008).

A recent review of approaches to development in thirty institutions in the UK that looked beyond the above labels yielded differences in relation to four key terms. While in some institutions provision was 'inclusive', in the sense that it dealt with all categories of staff, and was usually based in HR, other institutions tended to have specialist development functions, particularly for academic staff. For an increasing number of institutions, development is seen as making a significant contribution to the achievement of strategic goals, and therefore needs to be in close alignment with them. Others have retained a less closely aligned model. All institutions take an integrated approach to the recognition of academic work in their systems of probation and promotion. However, often the various components of academic roles are dealt with separately by the development provision in an institution. In other words, there are often centres or units that deal specifically with teaching and learning, or with research. Finally, development provision varies considerably in its scholarly component. Provision, particularly when related to teaching and learning, tends to emphasise and encourage the development of scholarship in the field, including taking a critical approach to practice. Other aspects of academic work tend to be dealt with through training-based approaches that do not require scholarship, either on the part of the members of faculty involved or those in development roles (Blackmore 2009).

As noted in Chapter 2, development can be an integral part of transformative change initiatives in universities. Global collaborations, such as the growth of the Scholarship of Teaching and Learning (SoTL) have worked to promote academics' own research into pedagogical practices (Kreber 2002), although it can be challenging to bring such work out of disciplinary silos. Despite the multiple approaches described above, development initiatives continue to face structural, resourcing and management challenges. However, many institutions have strongly embedded academic development programmes which, because they usually work across an entire institution, often operate in a network-like form and may also generate informal networks, because they bring staff who might otherwise never meet into contact with one another. Such initiatives can act as conduits for further curriculum developments.

Staff-focused approaches

The environment for development is becoming more complex, as new target groups are identified for development support. The support of teaching in many institutions has traditionally concentrated attention on full-time permanent staff, often requiring probationary academic staff to undertake a formal teaching qualification. However, this has always underplayed the contribution that other staff make to teaching delivery. The growth of support for teaching and learning has meant an increase in the numbers of staff who deal directly with what has traditionally been seen as academic work, but who are not necessarily academic staff. These have been termed 'blended' or 'third space' professionals (Whitchurch 2011). Given that universities have traditionally been organised into academic and administrative domains, and these posts span that boundary, there is a danger that third space professionals may not receive the level of support and consideration accorded to other staff, particularly in relation to development opportunities and promotion.

Many universities employ significant numbers of part-time staff. Much teaching provision, for example in health sciences, is delivered by clinical and professional staff who have not been trained to teach and whose teaching expertise has not been the concern of the university employing them. Measures of student satisfaction are now focusing attention on the perceived quality of teaching, irrespective of who is delivering it. Universities have to think more carefully about how they can support all of those who teach students. This presents a number of challenges. First, many of those who teach may not be directly employed by the university at all. Second, the sheer number of those who affect the student experience by, for example, engaging with them through placements or volunteering activities, means that the cost of such provision could be very high; an affordable delivery model is needed.

Graduate students have been used for many years to support teaching. Many universities have formalised such roles by establishing graduate teaching assistantships (GTAs), through which students who are registered for PhD study receive a stipend in exchange for a specified number of hours' teaching. This usually involves leading seminars and supervising laboratory sessions and tutorial classes. As has been suggested earlier, this offers universities the opportunity to increase the amount of support that students receive, much more economically than employing more members of faculty, but it does require that appropriate development support be made available. It also blurs the boundary between student-facing and staff-facing approaches to development, since GTAs are students who are acting in a staff capacity. A number of approaches to development can now be found in universities, all of which are relevant to the support of teaching and learning, and which we turn to in the following section.

Leadership and organisational development

A perceived need to work strategically has led to a growth of interest in leadership development. This recognises that although development can be supported by a specific unit, it is in fact generally undertaken by those who have leadership responsibilities for making decisions about general direction, staffing and resourcing. Traditionally, senior academic posts in universities have often been held on a short-term basis, with staff appointed to them as a result of academic success that might not require the same abilities or prepare them for such roles. Senior academic appointments are now much more commonly made on a permanent basis and many universities have instituted leadership development programmes, often dealing extensively with the management of change.

A valuable way of looking at the role of the leader is to see it as being principally about the enabling of learning (Blackmore and Kandiko 2011). This means being concerned with what is to be achieved and how in practical terms it is to happen. Attention to learning needs to occur, individually and collectively at various levels, if change is to take place successfully. Beyond that, a concern of those with leadership responsibilities is to foster the institution's general capacity to learn and grow so that change can happen in a more organic, responsive and networked manner.

In addition to research on network organisations discussed in Chapter 1, further literature on organisational learning supports this idea, referring to an institution's capacity to enable those within it to learn and grow and for the institution to be able to transform itself. A learning organisation has been claimed to have five characteristics: systems thinking, meaning a conception of the institution as an interconnected, bounded system; personal mastery, referring to development of the abilities of individuals; mental models, consisting of the assumptions that are held in common; shared vision and team learning (Senge 1990; Argyris 1999). These ideas have been applied to universities by Duke, who claims: 'To thrive in the knowledge economy under conditions of global competition universities must be vigorous organic learning communities, able to adapt to and proact organically in the fast-changing environment' (2002:4).

As mentioned above, OD (Thackwray *et al.* 2005) is now a significant feature of many universities. A number of systems-based approaches to development of the whole organisation are in use in the UK, including Investors in People, the European Framework of Quality Management (EFQM) and the 'Balanced Scorecard' approach. Such approaches draw attention to the importance of all the staff in a university and to the ways in which the institution is investing in its staff. There is a danger, however, that such approaches can be mechanistic and time-consuming unless implemented with a light touch and with sensitivity to local differences.

Human Resources and educational development approaches

The two most common organisational arrangements place support for teaching and learning either in its own specialist unit or else integrated with other development provision, usually under HR. In the UK, regular periodic surveys of educational development provision have been undertaken (Gosling 1996, 2001, 2008a, 2009a). A South African survey (Gosling 2009b) showed wide variety in the remit of academic development units, such as whether student-facing provision was included, and contestation over whether it had a strategic remit. Similar work has been undertaken in Australia (Gosling 2008b).

It can be argued that a specialist unit can pay particular attention to its remit. Its more academic orientation, both in terms of its perceived place within the university and its approach to its programmes, may enable such a unit to work effectively on academic issues and gain faculty support. The extent to which it is strategic is significantly influenced by the nature of the reporting line. In the UK such centres usually report to the Pro-Vice-Chancellor for Teaching and Learning, or the equivalent post. Related factors are the extent to which that role is an executive one and the relationship with the centre or unit. An alternative widely followed model in many UK research-intensive institutions situates educational development as part of the overall development provision within HR. This places it firmly in a non-academic location, with a reporting line through the Head of HR to the Registrar. There are some clear advantages in this arrangement, including the potential to emphasise the interconnectedness of academic and non-academic roles and to facilitate closer linkages with probationary and promotion arrangements, which are traditional HR functions, albeit academically led for academic staff. The main disadvantage of such a model is that provision may appear to be managerially driven and not to be located within the academy.

Attention over the last twenty years in universities in the UK, Australia and the US has largely been on development of the skills and capabilities of academic staff. Significant resourcing has been deployed in the establishment of postgraduate certificates in higher education, or the equivalent, which are now almost universally available in UK institutions and often compulsory for probationary staff.

Student learning and development

An interesting trend in recent years is towards provision that focuses on student development rather than that of staff. In many institutions this has long been present through the student tutorial system, supplemented more recently by skills-focused provision. This has encouraged the development of what have been variously termed transferable, key, core or employability skills, as discussed in Chapter 4. In the UK, much of this provision was established initially on 'soft' money supplied through a range of government initiatives and was set up within the administration of universities, usually in quite small units.

With increased attention being paid to the student experience, many institutions make the student experience the focal point and organising principle in their support for teaching and learning. This creates the necessity for new networks of contributors to the student experience who may previously not have been closely connected in institutions. These may include Estates, Student Finance, Registry, Library and Information Technology Services. It can be argued that if the quality of student experience is the principal driver in university teaching and learning, then those major contributors should be brought into a closer organisational alignment. There needs to be a sense of ownership and collective responsibility for the student experience. Because the focus of such provision is on students rather than on staff, there appears to be less tension around the question of whether it is academically led or not. Institutions need to support these functions, working together to enable coherence. Connections may be managed through physical reorganisation, or management or committee structures. Some institutions have worked at unity through communication technologies. Here the web is a very useful tool, which can enable all provision to be made available in one portal, even if it is provided from a number of places in the university.

Development through communication technologies

A new focus for approaches to development may be emerging, based on the possibilities for development that are offered by communication technologies. We focus on a number of these in the following chapter, but they are here drawn together to point up their interrelatedness. The growth of institutional research (IR) as a field of study and a practice in institutions shows the effect that the generation, sharing and interpretation of data has on organisations. An increasing number of statistical measures are published that compare aspects of performance at school, departmental, programme and module levels. The existence of this data can be extremely helpful for decision-making, and we consider this in greater detail. IR has emerged as standard practice in the US, and is developing in many other countries. As governments around the world increasingly require institutions to provide them with data, this field is gaining increased attention.

The availability of the web means that aspects of the university can be projected to specific audiences. This opens up possibilities for the building of communities that would otherwise be very difficult, for example among staff who may be working in overseas campuses, and among physically dispersed groups of students studying abroad. As already mentioned, the web offers a way for a range of services that are provided from a number of points in an organisation to be brought together. There is also the opportunity to offer these in a tailored form that is most helpful to the person wanting to access them. This is of particular benefit in student learning and development initiatives, where there is a need to communicate often quite complex provision directly to all students.

Development conclusions

The organisation of development support in institutions continues to vary considerably from one institution to another and is subject to frequent change. This is likely to continue as tensions between centralisation and local provision, integrated versus separate support, training and education and so on will never be entirely resolved. Government-level intervention is also likely to continue to shape institutional provision through development funding and the introduction of particular performance indicators.

Institutions rightly take decisions on support for development quite pragmatically, on the basis of what appears to work. However, this raises the problem of evaluation. Some institutional policy may reflect a lack of conviction that development makes an obviously valuable addition to the work of the institution. This may be a comment on the quality of development work but it is also likely that it relates to the difficulty in demonstrating payback from a university's investment in development support. There are so many factors in play that it is extremely hard to attribute gains to any particular intervention. Allied to this is the contestable nature of the changes that institutions often seek to bring about in the outcomes of the learning that their students undertake. Therefore we now turn to evaluation, which has the potential to make a major contribution to successful curriculum change initiatives.

The context for evaluation

The growth of evaluation practice has coincided with change in the management of higher education over the last thirty years at both national and institutional levels. During that time, public services as a whole have experienced much higher levels of intervention from central government and more intensive management – some would argue managerial – approaches. Evaluation has become important as a means of holding the public sector accountable, through the adoption of measures of efficiency and effectiveness that then become yardsticks for evaluation. This is significantly different from traditional practice in universities, in which change was left largely to professional discretion and ideas about quality were relatively implicit. There is therefore an obvious tension between two main approaches. On the one hand, evaluation may be conducted in a top-down way, usually with external scrutiny and standardised procedures based on explicit definitions of quality. On the other it may be bottom-up, adapted for local context and locally owned. Curriculum change evaluation will tend to take one or other of these broad approaches. Top-down initiatives may have significant benefits in driving change, but can be resented and if not done well, reveal very little or have unwanted side-effects.

External evaluation of the student experience has been a significant influence on how institutions organise their support for it. Student evaluation feeds directly into university league tables and is one of the factors that, in some ways, can be most readily influenced. In consequence league tables have become highly influential in guiding policy and practice within universities. At its worst, this leads universities into diverting their effort into exercises in performativity, seeking to produce improvements in nationally determined measures that are often not aligned with the institution's goals. However, at its best, evaluation measures focus attention on key aspects of what a university does, and ensure that the student experience is at the centre of its concerns. As the scope of major curriculum change is so encompassing, evaluation of any initiative is often done through existing institution-wide evaluation processes. The principles in the next section apply to evaluating the curriculum as well as to broader evaluative institutional practices.

Some principles for proceeding

Evaluation is a value-laden activity. What we choose to look at and how we do so says a great deal about our view of the world, of organisations and human relationships. It is not possible to take a neutral position on evaluation. Here we suggest some principles for proceeding that are inevitably values-based, drawn from the literature on evaluation and on observation of practice in many universities around the world.

First, we suggest that an institution should aim to adjust its own practices as part of its normal working over time, creating networks of evaluation practice. If it is to be self-sustaining and economical in its use of resources, this suggests that a 'culture of evaluation' is needed, one in which all staff feel they have a part to play. This requires local ownership, even if it is within an overall institutional framework.

Second, we suggest that evaluation should take account of the reality of how institutions work, and not assume a rational world in which mandated change can be pre-specified and 'rolled out' across an institution. The aims of any change are contestable. A change takes place in a dynamic environment, with myriad intersecting variables, and needs change over time, so no effort will fully achieve its intended outcomes. Therefore evaluation needs to be sensitive to both intended and unintended consequences and aware of opportunity cost. Third, we suggest that the principal purpose of evaluation is improvement. This implies a culture where it is acceptable to admit when something has not been successful, but also indicates a need to develop systems and processes that feed such information back into improvement so that the evaluation loop is completed.

Fourth, evaluation should focus on the aims and goals of an institution. There is plentiful evidence that evaluation systems can become cumbersome and focus too much on the maintenance of documentation and procedures, rather than on student learning, the student experience, or the improvement of practice. In the UK, the distinction is often drawn between quality assurance (QA) and quality enhancement (QE). We note that in a low-trust culture of inspection, QA tends to drive out QE. Lastly, evaluation practice should be based on best practice. Institutions need to gather and interpret multiple sources of data in appropriate ways to come to justifiable conclusions for action.

Four domains of evaluation

Evaluation practice can be analysed in four domains: national/systemic, institutional, programme and self (Saunders *et al.* 2011). All are relevant to thinking about major curriculum change. It is helpful to consider each of them separately as a means of structuring discussion, and avoiding the diffuseness that can come with such a varied and widespread practice. The national/systemic approach operates through a higher education system's quality assurance processes, such as audits of institutional provision. It sets the climate for evaluation and makes it hard for an institution to take action that appears to work against the national system. An institution's approach to evaluation is expressed through its quality assurance and enhancement arrangements, which may vary in relation to national level arrangements. This often depends on the degree of centralisation in the national system. Institution-level evaluation is also found in staff recognition and reward processes. Programme evaluation is usually focused around a particular initiative, which may be at national, institutional, subject or theme level, and is often undertaken as an external consultancy arrangement. Finally, at an individual level, it can be argued that the most valuable, context-sensitive and economical evaluation is that which is done by an individual member of staff, thinking through and seeking to improve their own practice.

National/systemic

For those attempting strategic curriculum change, the national level system of evaluation may be a significant driver, especially when particular aspects of student experience and learning outcomes are highlighted. Single institutions have little power or control over this environment. As with the US News & World Report rankings in America, the National Student Survey (NSS) is now a very influential driver for universities in the UK. Universities' performance in most league tables is heavily influenced by NSS results. The NSS covers particular aspects of support for teaching and learning and focuses on student satisfaction. It necessarily contains implicit assumptions about what good teaching provision looks like.

There are inevitably disadvantages in any methodology, and there is now an extensive literature critiquing NSS and other similar approaches (Hanbury 2007; Harvey 2008; Wiers-Jenssen et al. 2002; Williams and Cappuccini-Ansfield 2007); and moreover the NSS has faced strong opposition by several of the research-intensive Russell Group Student Unions in the UK. Some have argued that the consumer theory basis of satisfaction surveys places the student in the role of customer and that the responsibilities and contribution of the student-as-learner are not represented. It has also been argued that it does not help institutions improve teaching provision (Harvey 2003). Furthermore, while the breadth of NSS allows for comparisons across institutions, it provides little detail for institutions to improve internally. NSS may discourage behaviours that would be beneficial to students. It is often believed that greater emphasis on the first year experience, including transfer of resources from other years to support students in their first year, would be desirable. However, since NSS measures student satisfaction at the end of the final year, there is a disincentive for institutions to follow this path even though it could be educationally beneficial.

The NSS originated in work undertaken in Australia (Ramsden 1991). However, internationally, the National Survey of Student Engagement (NSSE) has been widely adopted in the United States, Canada, South Africa and Australia to provide data on students' university experiences and engagement. While retaining a focus on aspects that are likely to lead to effective student learning, NSSE reflects a move away from student satisfaction. NSSE asks about student behaviours; institutional actions and requirements; reactions to the institution; and student background information, providing a system of student evaluation and feedback that allows for local customisation, in keeping with the particular mission of the institution. NSSE focuses on the time and effort students devote to educationally purposeful activities and on students' perceptions of the quality of other aspects of their university experience. The data allows institutions to identify areas of the student experience, inside and outside of the classroom, which can be improved. Overall, the survey is designed to help institutions evaluate indicators of the conditions of learning, and work to make improvements in the institutional environment to enhance the student experience.

There is an argument for instituting a system of student evaluation that is more closely linked with the intentions of any local curriculum change. However, there are obvious dangers in survey fatigue and as long as NSS is the survey used by league tables, other metrics may have limited impact. This suggests that it may be in the interests of UK institutions to work together to devise and adopt an alternative system and to argue for amendments to the methodology of the existing NSS approach.

Institutional

Although institutional and programme evaluation are treated separately here, one important lesson in curriculum change is that for a change to be sustained, it has to become embedded in an institution. While a discrete change initiative may be needed to kick-start a major change, as soon as possible its work should be subsumed into the overall working of the institution. For example, one institution evaluated some new aspects of a change initiative (e.g. enhanced transcripts and community engagement efforts), but most of the evaluation was done as part of routine evaluation procedures.

At the heart of curriculum change is the commitment to ensure that students have the opportunity to experience the features of the designed curriculum and that they benefit through enhanced learning outcomes. As discussed in Chapter 4, institutions often specify a number of attributes, which they envisage that students will develop. To enable this to happen, it is necessary to: ensure that institutional structures and processes are congruent with the direction of the change; develop close collaborative quality assurance and enhancement working at all levels; and develop a research and evaluation capacity to inform decision-making in relation to the capabilities at all levels.

One of the key decisions that a university has to take is to decide whether to use existing metrics or to invest time in establishing its own. Few institutions develop new metrics to evaluate curriculum change at the student level. Most institutions already have course and programme-based student evaluation surveys but these are rarely put into the 'evaluation loop'. Whichever path is taken, the use of data about students' experience and a range of other teaching-related matters is potentially a very powerful aspect of development provision in a university. Several institutions have greatly benefited from creating networks through which data is routinely collected, analysed and fed into development programmes and evaluation schemes.

Programme

It is important to identify the changes that key programme participants are seeking to bring about in their students, in the systems for teaching and learning that form the focus for the programme, and in the desired student learning experience. These can then be translated into impact indicators for the programme.

A baseline impact evaluation would be required at the outset, against which later change could be evaluated. Building in the capacity for formative evaluation helps to inform decision-making in relation to the capabilities at all levels. Finally, a summative evaluation draws out key lessons from the programme and indicates the scope for further development.

Appropriate evidence-gathering instruments can be devised in consultation with the key players identified above to: enable teaching staff to record their views on changes in the teaching and learning system and of their own roles; encourage students to comment on changes at key points in their courses; engage a sample of students in structured focus groups at significant points in their courses to reflect on the changes that they are experiencing; and encourage teaching staff to introduce other methods of systematic reflection, such as the use of concept maps to track changes in perception of their own learning, at various points on their learning journeys. The aim should be to capture teaching staff and student perceptions at the inception of the programmes, at later points which should feed into the decision-making processes (i.e. using an action research model of evaluation) and at the conclusion of the programme. An ideal evaluation framework offers evidence on all of the above, and is unobtrusive and economical to undertake. It also makes effective use of existing data and of educational and institutional processes, including the assessment of student learning and institutional quality assurance.

Evaluation can focus on a variety of activities. For example, changes in student achievement can be evaluated through the inbuilt systematic assessment of students and review of courses. An alternative or additional focus could be on changes in teaching and learning systems, including support systems, and consideration of their appropriateness for provision of the desired curriculum characteristics and support of the development of student attributes. Much of the evidence of change would be derived from the inbuilt student assessment and course review activities, but it is also important to focus on the course teachers' perceptions of changes in the teaching and learning system and of their own roles. To this end, participants engaged in delivering the programme can be encouraged to record their views on the effects of the programme at key points along the way. Finally, changes in the overall student learning experience might be an appropriate focus of evaluation, achieved in part through existing student surveys, such as the NSS, and augmented where necessary, as discussed further in this chapter. Students can be encouraged to record their views on their evolving learning experience and a sample of students can be asked to reflect on their learning experiences in a more structured manner at various points in the programme.

The importance of bringing students into the curriculum change process was iterated at several institutions, and this sometimes extended to evaluation of aspects of curriculum change. However, one institution noted that it was difficult to obtain student opinions of curriculum change because students experience only one curriculum and therefore it can be difficult to make comparisons between the 'old' and the 'new' curriculum.

One of the challenges of a programme-based evaluation is that its starting point is usually the aims of the project. This can provide a helpful focus, but it can also blind the evaluator to other relevant ways of working. Some evaluators would argue that it is not important to see whether specific intended outcomes have been achieved and it is better to understand the actual experience of those involved in the change. An evaluation that was targeted closely on student learning gains and the student experience might miss out altogether on the broader staff experience. Trajectory studies, which plot the path of an initiative and its consequences for those involved, whether positive or negative, can be used to capture desirable and undesirable outcomes differentiated by stakeholders including 'intended, unintended and unanticipated outcomes' (Saunders *et al.* 2011: 10). Studies of this kind can help to identify features of the environment that impede or assist progress.

A further difficulty of programme evaluation can occur when a pilot programme is evaluated. Commonly, the pilot for an initiative is well resourced and may also begin with the most enthusiastic supporters of the change. Conclusions drawn from such a situation may not be relevant when an initiative is extended. Broader initiatives may have a less favourable funding base and involve others who feel little ownership of the programme as it is rolled out. If it is to be useful for the future, evaluation needs to pay attention to the problem of scaling up.

Individual

Chapter 9 dealt with the desirability of encouraging staff to develop the capacity to work in an evidence-informed way. Developing networks for this is a strategic way of increasing the institution's general capacity to improve as a learning organisation. Individual staff need assistance to develop the ability to gather, interpret and act upon data, but there is also a need for a culture of improvement stretching beyond the individual. Development support and recognition and reward are not issues solely for academic staff.

Curriculum change evaluation conclusions

Curriculum change can be very expensive for an institution. The time spent by staff in planning for change is a significant investment and there is an opportunity cost in that other uses might have been found for that time. Therefore it makes sense to evaluate an initiative thoroughly. Certainly staff in many institutions that were visited as part of the KLI survey noted the importance of evaluating a curriculum change. However, despite this, few institutions had undertaken an evaluation. It was frequently reported that making the change was in itself so difficult that implementing it was often seen as success enough. At several institutions the change had been so arduous that there was little energy to spare for evaluation.

Inevitably a great deal of political capital is invested in strategic curriculum change by its proponents. It is perhaps unrealistic to expect that a full and objective evaluation would be sponsored by the institution. Nevertheless it was easy to gather evaluative comments about a change and interesting to review the basis on which it was made. Staff tended to make judgements about success based on whether the change that was proposed had actually taken place, rather than on the basis of any improvement of students' learning and experience. It was also clear that the position of the person in the university made a considerable difference to how the change was viewed. Those with a cross-university brief tended to adopt a broad perspective and to link it with institutional mission and strategic objectives; those based within schools tended to judge it in relation to its effect on their programmes and students.

We would argue therefore, notwithstanding the limits of evaluation that we have discussed, that careful attention be paid to evaluation, from the beginning of an initiative, and that flexible and practical evaluation approaches should be built in throughout, at all levels, to maximise the possibilities that learning will take place speedily within the organisation as a result of experience.

References

Argyris, C. (1999) *On organizational learning* (2nd ed). Oxford: Blackwell Publishing.

Biggs, J. (2003) *Teaching for quality learning at university*. Maidenhead: Open University Press.

Blackmore, P. and Kandiko, C. B. (2011) Interdisciplinarity within an academic career, *Research in Post-Compulsory Education*, 16(1): 123–134.

Blackmore, P., Dales, R., Law, S. and Yates, P. (2008) *Investigating the capabilities of course and module leaders in departments*. York: Higher Education Academy.

Blackmore, P., Chambers, C., Huxley, L. and Thackwray, B. (2010) Tribalism and territoriality in the development world. *Journal of Further and Higher Education*, 34(1): 105–117.

Bucklow, C. and Clark, P. (2003) A new approach to professionalizing teaching and accredited training: The Institute for Learning and Teaching in Higher Education in P. Blackwell and P. Blackmore (eds) *Towards Strategic Staff Development in Higher Education* (pp. 79–90). Buckingham: SRHE/Open University Press.

Duke, C. (2002) *Managing the learning university*. Buckingham: Society for Research in Higher Education and Open University Press.

Gibbs, G. (2001) *Analysis of strategies for learning and teaching: A research report*. Bristol: Higher Education Funding Council for England.

Gosling, D. (1996) What do UK educational development units do? *International Journal for Academic Development*, 1(1): 75–83.

Gosling, D. (2001) Educational development units in the UK – what are they doing five years on? *International Journal for Academic Development*, 6(1): 74–90.

Gosling, D. (2008a) *Educational development in the UK*. London: Heads of Educational Development Group.

Gosling, D. (2008b) Survey of directors of academic development in Australian Universities in *Development of Academics and Higher Education Futures*, in P. Ling (ed.) (Vol 2: pp. 5–33). Sydney: Australian Learning and Teaching Council.

Gosling, D. (2009a) Educational development in the UK: A complex and contradictory reality. *International Journal for Academic Development*, *14*(1): 5–18.

Gosling, D. (2009b) *Report on the survey of Directors of academic development in South African universities.* Higher Education Learning and Teaching Association of South Africa (HELTASA) Accessed 6 August, 2011. http://stbweb02.stb.sun.ac.za/sol/documents/Report%20on%20Survey.pdf

Gosling, D. and D'Andrea, V. (2002) How educational development/learning and teaching centres help HEIs manage change. *Educational Developments*, *I*(2), 1–3.

Hanbury, A. (2007) *Comparative review of national surveys of undergraduate students.* The Higher Education Academy. Available at: http://www.heacademy.ac.uk/resources/detail/ourwork/nss/NSS_comparative_review_resource

Harvey, L. (2003) Scrap that student survey now. *Times Higher Educational Supplement* (*THES*), 12 December. Available online at: www.thes.co.uk/search/story.aspx?story_id=2008131

Harvey, L. (2008) Jumping through hoops on a white elephant: A survey signifying nothing. *Times Higher Educational Supplement* (*THES*), 12 June. Available online at: http://www.timeshighereducation.co.uk/story.asp?storyCode=402335&sectioncode=26

Kreber, C. (2002) Teaching excellence, teaching expertise, and the scholarship of teaching. *Innovative Higher Education*, *27*: 5–23.

McWilliam, E. (2002) Against professional development. *Educational Philosophy and Theory*, *34*(3): 289–300.

Oakleigh Consulting Limited (2008) *Interim evaluation of the Higher Education Academy.* Bristol: Higher Education Funding Council for England.

Ramsden, P. (1991) A performance indicator of teaching quality in higher education: The Course Experience Questionnaire. *Studies in Higher Education*, *16*(2): 129–150.

Ramsden, P. (1992) *Learning to teach in higher education.* New York: Routledge.

Saunders, M., Trowler, P. and Bamber, V. (eds) (2011) *Reconceptualising Evaluative Practices in Higher Education: The practice turn.* London: Open University Press.

Senge, P. M. (1990) *The fifth discipline.* London: Century Business.

Trigwell, K. and Prosser. M. (1991) Improving the quality of students' learning: The influence of learning context and student approaches to learning on learning outcomes. *Higher Education*, *22*: 251–266.

Wiers-Jenssen, J., Stensaker, B. and Grøgaard, J. B. (2002) Student satisfaction: towards an empirical deconstruction of the concept. *Quality in Higher Education*, *8*: 183–195.

Williams, J. and Cappuccini-Ansfield, G. (2007) Fitness for purpose? National and institutional approaches to publicising the student voice. *Quality in Higher Education*, *13*(2): 159–172.

Chapter 12

The physical and virtual environment for learning

Paul Blackmore and Camille B. Kandiko

Curriculum change inevitably raises questions about what is to be learned and how it is to be learned. The second question, in particular, leads us to consider the physical and virtual environment for learning. There are many surface signs of change over the last decade. Almost all students now have access to their own PC or laptop and most universities offer a virtual learning environment hosting support material for courses. The efficiency and effectiveness of face-to-face lecturing in universities is increasingly questioned.

However, these are just fragments of a much larger picture. Rapid technological change raises questions about the traditional purposes and boundaries of universities. There are increased possibilities of universities moving beyond their dominant transmission function of inculcating a set body of information into the minds of students, and becoming places for more stimulating and educational uses of time. Virtual worlds need to be as educative as possible and not simply viewed as a way of replicating existing approaches to teaching and learning or saving on costs. They need to exploit potential advantages and deal honestly with disadvantages in comparison with face-to-face learning.

A university's physical location will be much less significant for some students, such as students abroad. For these and other students, such as those whose learning is most effectively done elsewhere, perhaps in the workplace, their link may be largely virtual. By these means universities can in part deal with external requirements that they recruit students in an inclusive way (BECTA 2008).

Despite these changes, campuses are not likely to disappear, which raises the question of why students attend a physical location, what they gain from it and how the university should be organised in order to maximise the benefit of both the physical and virtual environments. Virtual and physical learning are not entirely separable; indeed blended learning, in which physical attendance is augmented both on-site and off-site by virtual opportunities, is increasing. This is reflected in new terminology including the advocacy of 'e-learning' and endorsement of 'appropriate technology' (Higher Education Funding Council for England [HEFCE] 2009: 1).

The support of teaching in such an environment is an increasingly complex activity. Developments in the design of physical space, together with the need to manage and make the best use of the virtual space that is opened up by learning technologies, have drawn renewed attention to the environment for learning. This brings to the foreground the role of support services and their relationship with the academic endeavour. There is major growth in student-facing support services and a concern that they be readily accessible for students; library and information services are a vital component. In a mass system there is awareness of the cost in scarce staff time of personal tutorial support and growing concern that it be retained in a sustainable form.

In this context, this chapter examines four main issues. The first is the impact of communication technologies and the second is the opportunities for learning that research-intensive institutions across the world claim to offer. Third is the idea of the 'learning space', both physical and virtual, its value in enabling learning and how the nature of spaces in the university has changed and may change in the future. Finally we consider the institutional support that is necessary to provide learning space. Many of the challenges of aligning support with the curriculum are created by divisions within institutions, which are often archaic structures that have not been updated with changes in universities. Yet as the roles of physical, virtual and electronic spaces become blended, these aspects need to be integrated in practice, particularly from the students' perspective. There is a clear need for blended and networked support functions, both physical and virtual, to be led and managed in a coherent fashion.

The impact of communication technologies

Communication technologies have changed many of the ways in which we search for information, buy products and interact with others. Communication technologies have had a transformative effect on the entire world, enabling many of the professional roles that have previously been undertaken on a small-scale or local basis to be exported anywhere in the world (Friedman 2005).

Technological changes also have the potential to radically change the pattern of provision of higher education. The large increases in the international flows of students and staff that have been experienced in countries such as the US, UK and Australia are evidence that higher education is highly prized and that more people are prepared to travel to access it. While many students will continue to study overseas for the experience and opportunities this provides, there may be less reason for some students to leave their home country if communication technologies allow them to participate in a higher education experience that originates elsewhere. This is not new; in the UK, the Open University has provided mass distance learning for over fifty years and there are many examples worldwide of institutions working in this way. However, despite technological developments, face-to-face learning has grown too; the high cost of distance learning provision requires a significant level of initial investment and discourages small-scale initiatives. What may now be different is that cheap, flexible and reliable communication, and the availability of information via the internet makes distance education cheaper and easier. At the same time it reduces the cost of providing some forms of educational support. Add to this the increasing marketisation of higher education, in which institutions are competing more with one another, including in the market for overseas students, and the environment for higher education is increasingly volatile and unpredictable.

Despite this potential for change in curriculum design and in the mode and methods of delivery, our survey found that major research universities are engaging in incremental rather than radical change. There is considerable inbuilt stability, possibly owing to the high costs of entry into the education market for providers and the access to social and cultural capital that universities offer, particularly highly ranked research-intensive ones. The nature and extent of learning technologies adoption in universities varies, which may well reflect legitimate institutional positioning (Browne *et al.* 2010). While there has been very substantial investment in learning technologies in universities and both staff and students are in constant contact with communication technologies in their daily lives, the impact on teaching approaches has been less marked than might have been expected. Most teaching still takes place face-to-face and a relatively small number of programmes are delivered entirely online. A blended approach is much more common, but it often simply provides the same information in both physical and virtual environments. Particularly in higher education, technology often seems to be 'a solution looking for a problem'; yet, in times of increasing expansion and decreasing budgets, technology certainly has a role to play.

The challenges for universities

The future for technology in higher education is far too difficult to predict. There are, however, two interlinked issues that face all universities now. First, institutions need to know how communication technologies can be harnessed to do things that are educationally useful. There are many uses of technology in support of learning; a recent study of curriculum innovation listed 'teaching, learning support, advice and guidance, coaching, mentorship, peer and collaborative learning, feedback and assessment, personal development planning and tutoring, skills development and practice and access to curriculum resources' (McGill 2011:3). In the UK it has been suggested that what is needed is: 'a more general problem-based approach to institutional change ('how can technology help to address my current challenges?') as opposed to a technologically determined approach ('what can I use technology for?')' (HEFCE 2008:2).

The KWP study of research-intensive institutions found little evidence that learning technologies were either a stated reason for change or even a principal vehicle for change. Most institutions were quite conservative in their institutional approach. Indeed it tends to be teaching-led institutions that are more innovative and have adopted institution-wide policy and practice, such as a universal virtual learning environment. The research-intensive institutions we visited had also invested in virtual learning environments, but were less prescriptive about the nature and extent of their use.

Technology must also be affordable. In times of economic constraint, institutions want to see definite benefits emerging from an investment in learning technologies, which may move us even more into a pragmatic approach (HEFCE 2009). It is vital to get learning technology decisions right because they are so expensive. There is evidence in highly competitive markets, such as the US, that technology is one of the areas in which institutions invest in order to gain an advantage over others (Archibald and Feldman 2011). It seems likely that this will become more marked in the UK too, as the impact of greatly increased tuition fees is felt. Even before this happens, one of the main drivers for investment is a perceived need to meet student expectations (Browne *et al.* 2010). There remains a need for institutions to 'move beyond pockets of innovative practice carried out by enthusiasts', as the Higher Education Funding Council for England commented in reviewing its own approach to support the uptake of learning technologies (2009:6). However, success in doing so has major costs associated with it, immediately raising the question of the 'scalable and sustainable use of technology in institutional contexts' (HEFCE 2008:4).

Beyond universities, a technology is adopted because it serves a need. For example, most people in developed countries now own a mobile phone, which they have paid for because they found it useful to own one. The risk in bringing the product to market was borne by the provider of the product. A university has to take very costly decisions about the kind of virtual environment that it provides for its students. In a sense, the university takes the risk of investing in technologies that may or may not be educationally beneficial. Cost is a major concern. It may be wise to adopt low-tech solutions or to explore further uses of current technologies.

Access to communication technology is now ubiquitous, although not universal. Most students equip themselves, willingly and at their own cost, with laptops and mobile phones. Learners expect to be able to use their own laptops and other devices within institutions (HEFCE 2009). This brings challenges and associated costs. University facilities have to be flexible both in the provision of physical space and in web and tools availability. Universities also face the practical technical challenge of connecting and supporting them within the university system (HEFCE). However, students' personal access to technologies provides opportunities too. The devices most students now have are not exploited to their full educational potential. Institutions are challenged by the range of devices that students have and the need for universal use and availability of applications used in formal learning environments.

Technology and learning

Universities are changing their approaches to the use of physical space, largely in response to technological change. However, that discussion needs to be grounded in the relationship between technology and learning. A recent report describes three levels of benefit to be gained from technology use in learning: more efficient processes; enhancement of processes; and transformation of processes or introduction of new processes (HEFCE 2009). The first two are common activities throughout most institutions. However, transformation is a higher and much more challenging aim. It may be that learning technologies can enable a quality of student experience that cannot be achieved by any other means. Beetham and Sharpe (2007) offer a helpful multi-level model of transformation, suggesting that it occurs at three levels: personal transformation through learning; curriculum change; and institutional change. The levels inform one another, institutional change enabling curriculum change and thus individual change, while the outcomes of personal learning can influence curriculum and institution (McGill 2011).

A fundamental question for institutions, then, is what is to be transformed? Some institutions, by remodelling their undergraduate curricula, introducing interdisciplinary options and developing students' digital literacies, are attempting to be transformative. However, often learning technologies are introduced to assist with existing curricula and methods of delivery, and are employed as a supplement without any serious consideration of the transformational opportunities they may offer. For example, a virtual learning environment can be introduced that provides only a syllabus, reading materials and lecture notes in another format, or such an environment can be made universal across an institution. Such changes are not transformative in their intention or effect, although they may be a useful first stage of a process aimed at developing engagement with learning technologies.

Transformation may be more likely in universities developing a distinctive curriculum and student experience, with the role of technology being to support these aims and goals. In previous chapters we outlined the direction of much strategic curriculum change in research-intensive institutions. Learning technologies are useful insofar as they enable institutions to make available these kinds of experiences and lead to the development of desired graduate attributes.

To do so it is essential to move beyond the rather transactional uses of learning technologies that are very often the focus of institutional development initiatives. An example of these lower aims would be the widespread insistence that all staff should post their lecture notes on the web in a virtual learning environment. Looking beyond this, higher education entails the development of capacity for intellectual autonomy, 'making' rather than 'taking' meaning (Blackmore et al. 2002). Technology offers learners vast amounts of data and the opportunity to communicate in complex ways with others. Learning technologies also open up possibilities for students to work independently of academic staff, alone, or in student groups. However, the very openness of this freedom and accompanying responsibility can cause anxiety (McGill 2011). It cannot be assumed that students will immediately engage with, or be capable of taking full advantage of the learning opportunities that are available; they may require higher levels of feedback to confirm or amend their approach (McGill). Along with the opportunities for autonomy comes the need to offer support in the use of the facilities and tools that are available. Studies of students' approaches to search tools suggests that many lack the ability to analyse the information that they find and tend to browse quickly, usually not reading in depth. However, this is claimed to be true of all those who use the internet; searching techniques for all ages have become broader and shallower (University College London [UCL] 2008).

Most research-intensive universities are seeking to differentiate themselves through enhancement of the link between research and teaching. This, as has been discussed, can come about in a number of ways. A 'product link', for example, can improve access to the outcomes of research. Web technology has made such knowledge potentially more widely and readily available than ever before. A 'process link' enables students to work in a more research-like way. This can be done through access to powerful research tools, data sets and other researchable materials. The social and cultural aspects of research can be developed through social media, which allows learners to work collaboratively and to engage with experts.

As well as making connections within an institution, many curricular and co-curricular developments focus on making links beyond the university, with the local community and the wider world. The availability of vast amounts of searchable information on the web has opened the outside world up to learners, including researchers. Again, social media may be very helpful in bringing groups together from both within and beyond the university.

Technology-enhanced learning has been used to enhance students' employability skills and competences in a number of ways. Real-world problems presented in the form of simulation exercises enable students to develop problem-solving abilities through proposing solutions and receiving feedback on the results of their actions. Some universities make use of e-portfolios as a way of enabling students to show their achievement. They can also be used for self-assessment and reflection in general. These can be portable, so that they are available after the student has left the institution. In addition to e-portfolios, e-assessment attracts increasing interest. While much of its use has been summative, there is a shift towards more formative uses of assessment, in the belief that 'well-designed and well-deployed diagnostic and formative e-assessments can foster more effective learning' (HEFCE 2009:9).

Computer-mediated communication tools, such as video, audio and text-based conferencing can encourage a higher level of student engagement, including peer collaboration and review. Students often spend considerable time using virtual spaces through social media, blogs and wikis, which provide opportunities for collaboration and also for personal expression. It may be possible to use these tools for educational purposes to harness that enthusiasm. However, students may not necessarily want to have those 'personal' spaces populated by others who are connected with formal studies.

Uptake of learning technologies

In the UK, research-intensive institutions are distinctive in some aspects of their uptake of learning technologies. A recent survey shows that in 26 per cent of institutions, strategies have no effect on implementation and nearly half of the surveyed institutions contained departments that host virtual learning environments in addition to the centrally provided one (Browne *et al.* 2010). Some subject areas make more use of learning technologies than others. In research-intensive institutions, Management, Computing, Medicine, Nursing and Health make the most extensive use of learning technologies and Art, Music and Drama the least (ibid).

Staff may feel considerably challenged by the need to be proficient in using technological tools and in adjusting to the major changes that communication technologies have brought to their roles and identities. The traditional role of academic staff is questioned by more research-like and interdisciplinary approaches to learning and an increasing concentration on complex 'real world' issues. Staff often find it hard to leave their area of expertise, but it is increasingly important to make connections across a range of knowledge and disciplinary approaches. This requires a meta-knowledge of structures, perspectives and their limitations, and how to navigate around an increasingly uncertain knowledge environment. As learning crosses disciplinary boundaries, new sets of abilities are required to understand and work with other disciplines' traditions and practices. Universities engage increasingly with 'mode 2' knowledge – that which informs practice in the world, rather than traditional propositional knowledge (Barnett 2000). Once again, boundaries are breached as technology provides broad access to knowledge and supports networks that generate and share knowledge quickly and flexibly.

Given such challenges, it is no surprise that not all staff engage actively in developing the uses of learning technologies. A survey of research-intensive institutions in the UK showed lack of time and money, and lack of academic staff knowledge and recognition to be the four most often cited barriers discouraging staff from engaging in technology-enhanced learning development (UCL 2008). At an institutional level, well-organised support services can assist by reducing the time academic staff have to spend using technology by ensuring that resources are deployed to the best effect and that staff have appropriate ways to develop their learning and skills.

A central problem for those advocating the use of learning technologies is that often the costs of an innovation appear to outweigh the benefits. In the 'real' world, a technological tool that meets a real need efficiently and effectively will be taken up with extraordinary speed, as can be seen with the growth in mobile phones and in websites such as Google and YouTube, which have become universally known and used within the last ten years. In comparison, much development activity in universities that aims to increase the use of learning technologies has struggled to make progress, and this may simply be because the claimed benefits are exaggerated or illusory. It is easy to devise tools and processes, such as software that enables students to assemble multimedia portfolios of their work, but neglect to understand that many students do not feel that this is useful or wish to do it. Staff may also not wish to do it, or have the time or skills to assess work in such a format.

Using evidence that an innovation actually works is one way forward. However, the extent to which curriculum change is evaluated in institutions, and the ways in which evaluation of technology takes place, appears to vary in relation to the scale of intervention. Small-scale innovation is often evaluated in detail and hard data can be gained. Institution-wide initiatives are inevitably more difficult to measure, far more politically sensitive and there is usually less hard data gathered about students' learning (McGill 2011). In the UK there have been calls for clear and unambiguous research-based evidence of the benefits of using technology, with examples of good practice from a representative range of institutions and subject areas and the need for measures of success and of a baseline or benchmark (HEFCE 2008, 2009). Adopting new learning technologies involves both physical and virtual environments in universities.

Teaching and learning spaces

Major curriculum change can lead to transformations in how learning occurs, through technology networks, as discussed, and of learning spaces, both physical and virtual. A study in the UK investigated the impact of good building design on institutional performance, concluding that quality has a significant impact on the recruitment of staff and students, particularly postgraduate students (CABE 2005). The main effects for students were: 'helping to motivate students in their work', 'facilitating inspiration amongst students' and 'providing key facilities critical to the course content' (8). Staff and students also commented on social factors, such as the level of inclusion and participation that building design affords.

Some of the best contemporary university design reflects an active concern for the experience of those who learn and teach. However, such aspects are slow to change. The lecture has been criticised for as long as it has been existence (Bligh 1998), and yet it continues to be a dominant means of teaching in universities worldwide. Lecturing is relatively cheap; one lecture may be given to a thousand students, and is a visible activity that can be timetabled for both staff and students. Much technological development has simply made the traditional lecture widely available through live streaming and video recordings. This offers obvious advantages in terms of access, but many of the inherent pedagogical limitations remain.

The majority of university teaching remains relatively traditional, with a strong element of lecture-transmitted content, usually linked with work in smaller groups through seminars, laboratories and tutorials. This reflects a very hierarchical and teacher-centred approach (Ramsden 1992). In lectures, the emphasis is on an individual learning in isolation from other students, rather than on working in groups; the social aspects of learning and the capacities that are developed though interaction with others is therefore neglected. A lecture also tends to emphasise the cognitive rather than the affective aspects of learning.

There have, however, been many examples of universities taking an imaginative pedagogical approach to the provision of space, such as flexible teaching spaces that can be configured in a number of ways and open, social spaces for independent study. In the former case, room occupancy in universities is relatively low (CABE 2005), creating an opportunity for more strategic uses of physical space.

There is a tension between pressures to provide specialist accommodation and to increase occupancy and use. In line with the specialisation of knowledge, there is a tendency for space to become more specialised in universities. It is increasingly common for research facilities to be built without regard to their potential uses for teaching. A more strategic view of the uses of buildings might lead not only to greater efficiency in their use but a closer integration of research and teaching.

Study space is in short supply in universities, yet its availability is vital in enabling both independent study and peer-to-peer interaction. The efficient management of public space can create a surprising level of difficulty in a university, much of which may come about because space tends to be used for a single purpose. For example, students frequently wish to study in places that have been set up for catering. This raises questions about the management of the space, since a catering department will not usually have a remit to enhance students' learning and, in a closely managed institution, will be trying to maximise its revenue from the sale of food and drink, in ways that will produce the highest possible throughput of students. Students who linger over books or who meet for extensive informal project discussion are poor customers. Imaginative use of space creates opportunities, such as the changes made by institutions that have opened cafes in library spaces.

New buildings are often insufficiently planned for future users, whether staff or students, and there is often little evaluation of actual use. Establishing systems to monitor levels of use can allow institutions to make evidence-informed decisions. However, it is important to choose the right measure rather than simply accept one that is easy to calculate. For example, if study accommodation is made available for students and it is rapidly filled, that may appear to be proof of success. However, simply measuring room or seat occupancy is not enough to capture data about transformational change in approaches to learning. More detailed evaluation of the ways in which space is being used and the impact on students' learning is necessary.

Supporting the curriculum

The provision of high-quality teaching and learning is dependent on professional support: the academic and administrative parts of the institution need to work together effectively. This requires, according to Melville-Ross (2010): commitment to the vision, values and organisational culture of the institution; effective communication; a clear strategic plan; quality in academic and service provision; the assessment of risk; and the support of innovation.

Heads of support services who were interviewed as part of the KWP project all stressed the major impact that curriculum change made on their service provision and the substantial contribution that they could make to ensure its success. However, they felt they were not always kept fully informed and that they were often brought in too late in the planning process. Heads of estates in particular have to plan for the long term. Heads of libraries and information services have to make major investment decisions. The rising costs of journals and information technology makes it essential to plan strategically. Heads of various units believed that the delivery of strategic curriculum change required them to work far more closely together than previously. As discussed above, the efficient and effective use of space was one issue that particularly required fresh thinking so that limited space could be put to multiple uses.

The strategic direction of support services is aided when data is available on which to make judgements. It is easy for institutions to capture data about library usage or for IT Services to monitor web use through automatically generated web statistics. However, if support services are to focus on their impact on curriculum change, evidence gathering needs to move beyond the level of use and general student satisfaction and to evaluate the extent to which innovation has led to improved student learning, as discussed in the previous chapter.

Support services can provide much of the information to justify and evaluate curriculum change. As noted previously, most curriculum change involves increased student choice and increased student flows across school and departmental boundaries. To provide incentive for such an innovation, resources can follow students. Robust systems are needed to deal with more complex patterns of assessment and of recording achievement beyond examination success. Staff workload models have to innovate as well. For example, a staffing model that recognises only face-to-face teaching in a classroom can actively discourage distance learning, where a very large tutorial commitment may not be recognised. Again, if the currency of teaching is the lecture hour, there is little incentive to do anything other than lecture.

Whitchurch (2008) describes the ways in which professional staff can support institutional change and development, within and beyond the institution. One major function is to cross boundaries. Academic work is still, in the main, organised in disciplinary silos. Whitchurch notes that these boundaries can make change very difficult to achieve. Professional services can bring a valuable cross-institutional perspective and help to break down unhelpful divisions, while respecting legitimate differences in practices and perspectives. Many institutions developed robust institutional research practices to gather standard information from across the university and feed into decision making.

Organisation of support services

Sources of support for student learning are often widely distributed in a university, and may have come about as a result of many unconnected decisions over many years. There are many student-facing services making a contribution to the support of students' experience, including study skills centres, language centres, student placement offices, international offices, library and IT services, open access facilities and so on. Other departments make a contribution but are not directly student-facing, such as staff and educational development units and centres. There is always a tension between centralisation and localisation, both within each aspect of provision and across student-facing provision as a whole.

Centralised support departments may be more capable of making a strategic intervention through close linkage with the centre and having critical mass to make a difference. They can be more efficient and fair in their ability to guarantee equity of access to all students. Similarly, they can be more satisfactory for the staff working within them, who gain from being part of a community of like-minded colleagues. However, dispersed student support services may be more in tune with local needs and more responsive to local curriculum issues.

There is a trend to bring student-facing support together, through physical co-location with 'one-stop-shops' for students or through common line management, retaining separate points for students to access services. However, whether provision is centralised, local or a combination of the two, there needs to be a close link between local and institutional levels. The internet offers an opportunity to provide a single access point for services to students, even if the providers remain rather separate in the organisational structure. It is important to manage an appropriate balance of roles and responsibilities among central support, academic staff and student associations in such matrix model approaches. Some institutions have paid particular attention to the connection with students, offering a contract identifying the level of service that a student can reasonably expect; others prefer the concept of partnership.

Many centres or units exist to promote and support curriculum innovation across an institution, working with staff and students. Examples include interdisciplinary programmes at the University of Hong Kong; writing support at Queen Mary, University of London; research-honours provision at the University of Western Australia and academic skills development at the London School of Economics. Some institutions have attempted to encourage innovative practice by improving the overall standard of teaching facilities, often working to a minimum classroom specification. Others have developed staff-facing and student-facing areas in which innovative ideas are piloted. These include developing quality teaching facilities to demonstrate new approaches and open access or bookable individual and small group learning facilities, such as the Learning Grid at the University of Warwick. Some centres work directly with students to provide a particular type of provision. Examples include University College Utrecht's college model and the Community Service Center at the University of Chicago. Technology can also be used in administration and support functions. More work can be done on the enhancement of continuing professional development initiatives through developing links with Library 2.0 and institutions' information systems, so that technology-enhanced learning interfaces with other initiatives, such as the Connected Campus at King's College London.

Conclusions

In an era of competition, the physical and virtual environment for learning is more important than ever before, both as a means of attracting students and of providing them with the best possible learning experience. Communication technologies, irrespective of the actions of universities, alter the ways in which students and staff gain access to information, share it with others and use it to produce their own outcomes. The challenge for universities is to decide what provision adds value to what is already available. This requires paying attention to what the university is attempting to achieve, knowing how students actually interact with technologies, both within and beyond the formal curriculum, making interventions that encourage beneficial behaviours and being able to evaluate the effects of those changes. Throughout it is necessary to be realistic about the actual and espoused benefits of learning technologies.

There is danger in the separate consideration of physical and virtual space, as most learning in universities is blended in some form. The pursuit of technology use as an end in itself, separate from the broad context of support for learning, cannot be justified or afforded. The provision of physical space is driven increasingly by the need for its efficient and effective use. Multiple uses of space provide a strategic way forward to increase flexibility and the level of occupancy. However, the level of use is not the only criterion: the nature of the student learning experience also has to be taken into account, which suggests a further role for evaluation.

Curriculum change has major implications for the support services of a university. The survey found a number of examples of change initiatives that were derailed because administrative structures and processes made it too difficult to work in these flexible ways. These structures can be key conduits in networks and should therefore be fully involved in all stages of the initiative. They are essential for communication throughout a change initiative. This notion needs to be considered at a number of levels: within support services; between support services and academic staff; and with senior management and students.

References

Archibald, R. and Feldman, D. (2011) *Why does college cost so much?* New York: Oxford University Press.

Barnett, R. (2000) *Realizing the university in an age of supercomplexity.* Buckingham: Society for Research into Higher Education and Open University Press.

BECTA (2008) *Harnessing technology: Next generation learning 2008–14.* Coventry: BECTA. Accessed 23rd May 2011 at http://webarchive.nationalarchives.gov.uk/20101102103654/publications.becta.org.uk//display.cfm?resID=37348

Beetham, H. and Sharpe, S. (2007) *Rethinking pedagogy for a digital age.* Abingdon: Routledge.

Blackmore, P., Roach, M. and Dempster, J. (2002) The use of ICT in education for research and development, in S. Fallows and R. Bhanot (eds). *Educational development through information and communications technologies* (pp. 133–140). London: Kogan Page.

Bligh, D. (1998) *What's the use of lectures?* Exeter: Intellect.

Browne, T., Hewitt, R., Jenkins, M., Voce, J., Walker, R. and Yip, H. (2010) *2010 survey of technology enhanced learning for higher education in the UK.* Oxford: UCISA.

CABE (2005) *Design with distinction: The value of good building design in higher education*. Bristol: Higher Education Funding Council for England.

Friedman, T. L. (2005) *The world is flat: A brief history of the twenty-first century*. New York: Farrar, Straus & Giroux.

Higher Education Funding Council for England [HEFCE] (2008) *Review of the 2005 HEFCE Strategy for e-Learning*. Bristol: Higher Education Funding Council for England.

HEFCE (2009) *Enhancing learning and teaching through the use of technology: A revised approach to HEFCE's strategy for e-learning*. Bristol: Higher Education Funding Council for England.

McGill, L. (2011) Curriculum innovation: Pragmatic approaches to transforming learning and teaching through technologies. *Transforming Curriculum Delivery through Technology Programme Synthesis Report*. London: JISC.

Melville-Ross, T. (2010) Leadership, governance and management: Challenges for the future of higher education. *Perspectives: Policy and Practice in Higher Education*, *14*(1): 3–6.

Ramsden, P. (1992) *Learning to teach in higher education*. London: Routledge.

University College London (UCL) (2008) CIBER group. *Information behaviour of the researcher of the future*. London: University College London. *CIBER Briefing paper*, 9.

Whitchurch, C. (2008) Shifting identities, blurring boundaries: The changing roles of professional managers in higher education. *Higher Education Quarterly*, *62*(4): 377–384.

Chapter 13

Case study

Curriculum structure as a key variable affecting performance in higher education: The case of South Africa

Ian Scott

This chapter presents a case, based on performance patterns in South Africa, for recognising that the fundamental framework of an undergraduate curriculum – including its structural parameters and underlying assumptions about prior learning – is an element of curriculum design that critically affects who benefits from higher education. In a range of systems, these curriculum 'fundamentals' are seldom seen as a variable in the educational process, yet can have a major impact on access and success for different student groups. This applies particularly in contexts of high levels of educational disadvantage and inequality. While the case study focuses on South Africa, it is argued that the challenge of responding systemically to a very diverse student intake, as is urgently required for development, will rapidly spread to other developing countries as well.

Key challenges for higher education in sub-Saharan Africa

Since the curriculum embodies everything that we want to achieve in the educational role of higher education, the issue of the nature and purposes of curricula is bound to be complex and contested. As manifested in this book and internationally – particularly in the developed world – the focus is on the character, quality and 'relevance' of the learning that is aimed at. The contestation is primarily about issues such as canon, selection of content, orientation (for example, the competing claims of traditional academic approaches and others, such as inquiry-based or problem-based learning), and whether the explicit development of graduate attributes such as employability, values and critical citizenship has a place in the curriculum. Where the expression 'transformation' in higher education is used, it commonly refers to these matters.

The question of what kind of learning should be achieved through higher education is at least as significant in South Africa and other African countries as in the first world, given the need for different forms of high-level expertise to address their pressing developmental needs and the growing North–South divide. Consider, for example, the tension in health education between the demand for primary health care and advanced medical science, in contexts of scarce resources.

A key distinction, however, is that in African and many other developing countries, 'quantity' – i.e. the numbers of graduates produced – is as important as the nature of the outcomes. This is because of severe shortages in the knowledge and skills needed for addressing development. The South African government, for example, has identified such skills shortages as the major impediment to development (AsgiSA 2007). The great majority of countries in sub-Saharan Africa (SSA) face the same challenge. According to a recent World Economic Forum report:

> the stock of human capital with tertiary education in Africa continues to be very low compared with other regions of the world. While the proportion of the adult population (25 years and older) who have completed tertiary education averaged 3.94 percent in the world in 2010, the average for sub-Saharan Africa in that year was 0.78 percent.
>
> (Gyimah-Brempong and Ondiege 2011:39)

The low levels of access to higher education in Africa are manifested in participation rates. On UNESCO's Gross Enrolment Ratio (GER) measure, the average SSA higher education participation rate is 6 per cent, against 70 per cent in North America and Western Europe (2010:379). South Africa's GER of about 16 per cent is the highest in SSA. The relationship between education levels and development is complex. One indication of this is the coexistence of graduate unemployment and skills shortages in various African countries, including South Africa. This highlights the significance of the quality and 'relevance' of graduate outcomes.

In addition to the quantity and quality challenges, representivity is a key issue in many African and other developing countries. Social class is a pervasive factor underlying most forms of exclusion, but there are a variety of manifestations such as the urban–rural divide, caste in India, regional inequalities in Mozambique, and ethnicity in Malaysia. In South Africa, because of its history, the issue of racial inequality continues to be dominant. In terms of access, the effects of its low overall participation rate of 16 per cent are exacerbated by large racial disparities: the GER for the black and 'coloured' groups is 13 per cent against 56 per cent for whites, and fewer than 10 per cent of black youth are entering any form of higher education[1] (Fisher and Scott 2011).

Lack of inclusiveness is an issue in many parts of the developed and developing world but in Africa it represents an acute problem, with two main dimensions. First, it means that the potential of large sections of the population is not being realised, in contexts where high-level capability is urgently needed for all forms of development. Second, continued exclusion from higher education of historically under-represented (and usually disadvantaged) groups acts against social cohesion and is a latent cause of unrest, particularly in South Africa where sensitivity about the persisting effects of apartheid runs high. Alongside quality and quantity, equity – of access and of outcomes – is thus the third key challenge.

It is for these reasons that the term 'transformation' in higher education has different dimensions of meaning in South Africa. It is commonly used narrowly to refer to the transfer of leadership to the black majority, and to racial representivity in the composition of the staff and students in historically white institutions. However, to be fully meaningful it must stand for inclusiveness in who *benefits* from higher education, both directly and indirectly. In so far as development depends on realising the potential in all communities, transformation in this broad sense is an essential condition for progress in any society with widespread poverty and disadvantage (including most African countries), and encompasses the challenges of quantity, quality and equity.

Therefore, while widening participation may be taking a back seat in a number of developed countries because of economic recession, in SSA it is a *sine qua non* for societal advancement. This chapter examines the importance of curriculum – particularly the structures and parameters that govern it – as a key factor affecting widening *successful* participation in higher education. It argues that it is essential to analyse not only the conventionally recognised aspects of curriculum but also embedded and virtually 'invisible' characteristics that influence its effectiveness. The primary reference is to South Africa, but it is argued that there are implications for other African countries as well.

A case for systemic change in higher education in South Africa

Since the structure of a curriculum sets a framework for the whole educational process, it powerfully influences what can be achieved in formal teaching and learning, as well as (albeit less directly) in the co-curriculum. The curriculum structure is therefore enabling or constraining. Its critical parameters include: the academic level of the starting point of the curriculum; the assumptions about students' prior learning on which the curriculum is based; the required pace of progress; the degree of flexibility in entry level, pace and volume of work; subject choice (breadth and depth) and modularity; and exit standards. As will be discussed, some of these parameters are more 'visible' and consciously considered than others.

Particularly in contexts where widening access or improving performance is critical, it is necessary to analyse the extent to which the curriculum, including its basic parameters, is enabling or constraining growth, quality and transformation. Using South Africa as the example, this section briefly examines undergraduate performance patterns as indicators of the effectiveness of the formal curriculum structure, and some implications that arise.[2]

Apart from some areas of high or good quality, the performance of South Africa's higher education system is very poor, and greatly exacerbates the effects of its low participation rates on the availability of high-level skills in the country. The following are some of the key indicators:

- Only 30 per cent of all first-time-entering students graduate within five years. If allowance is made for students taking more than five years to graduate or returning after dropping out, still only about 45 per cent will ever graduate.

- In the best-performing sub-sector, the 'contact' university programmes (that is, excluding distance education), only 50 per cent graduate in five years. The five-year graduation rate for contact vocational diplomas is as low as 32 per cent.
- Racial disparities remain severe. In the main contact university programmes, the black graduation rate is under half the white rate, with the result that, while black people make up some 80 per cent of the population and two-thirds of higher education enrolment, there are still fewer black than white graduates in many key degree programmes.
- Despite the low black participation rate – which indicates that the black intake is highly selected and has strong potential – the majority of this intake is being lost to the system. The net effect is that fewer than five per cent of the black youth are succeeding in any form of higher education.

This situation has major implications for South Africa's development. First, it is clear that the pressing need for advanced knowledge and skills is not being met, and if so much potential continues to go unrealised, it will not be met in future. Second, it is the needs of the majority that are least well met by the present system. Since (as the figures show) substantial growth in graduates can only come from the black population – which is subject to the greatest inequities in both access and outcomes – the prospects of overall improvement are minimal without changing the status quo. As the figures also show, simply increasing access is the most wasteful and costly way to increase graduate output, since, if the performance patterns do not change, failure and attrition will grow, or standards will fall, or both. In summary, the only effective way of substantially improving quantity, quality and equity in the graduating class is to improve the performance of the historically disadvantaged black majority. Yet the current system is least successful in accommodating black students, most of whom are underprepared for South Africa's traditional forms of higher education.

There is no dispute that South Africa's very poor and unequal school system, together with pervasive poverty and socio-economic disparities, is the primary cause of underperformance in higher education. Many in the academic community take the view that higher education cannot be expected to adjust to deficiencies in schooling, and that doing so would compromise the academic project. There are two counter-arguments.

First, virtually all current analyses of the school system agree that the fundamental challenges it faces – particularly the apartheid legacy of human and material resource constraints and the need to massify in order to achieve universal education even at primary level – effectively preclude substantial improvement in quality of the order needed to provide higher education with enough well-prepared candidates. Therefore, if higher education does not respond, the poor performance patterns will persist.

In considering whether the deficiencies in schooling are a temporary aberration, it is necessary to acknowledge that the school system is affected not only by the apartheid legacy but also by the realities of a developing country. These constraints will persist for the foreseeable future, and schooling cannot be expected to return to the privileged conditions that characterised the middle-class white sector of the last century, on which the parameters of the current higher education system were based. It is therefore important for higher education to come to terms with its changed context, and to adapt its structures and practices to the actual profile of a larger, more representative and educationally very diverse student intake.

Second, in addition to this pragmatic case for adapting the educational process in higher education, there is a principled argument. In SSA and many other developing countries, only a thin layer of the population has access to good schooling. This means that achieving graduate growth and inclusiveness inevitably requires successfully accommodating large numbers of students from disadvantaged backgrounds, who will constitute the majority of the intake. There thus appears to be a valid argument that higher education is obliged by societal needs and social justice to play its full role in transformation by being willing to do things differently, provided that this does not compromise the academic project.

In these circumstances, higher education faces a clear choice: to continue business as usual and accept the status quo, or to be prepared to adapt policies, structures and practices that are within its control. Analysis and the experience of educational development over the last twenty-five years indicate that the latter choice is feasible. The following sections examine the role of structural curriculum reform in improving both graduate output and outcomes through responsibly facilitating inclusiveness.

The relationship between curriculum structure and widening successful participation

As the international literature has documented, a wide range of factors affect student performance and retention in higher education. Some of these are wholly or largely within the sector's control, such as teaching approaches, academic and affective student support, and institutional climate. However, a number of the key factors – particularly those related to international academic culture and reward systems – are notoriously resistant to change and subject to powerful competing demands on academics' time and attention. This chapter focuses on the structure and parameters of the undergraduate curriculum as one of the key factors that, contrary to common perceptions, may represent one of the most practicable, affordable and effective areas of educational development for improving higher education performance in such conditions as those that prevail in South Africa.

In South Africa, educational disadvantage and consequent underperformance in higher education are not a minority problem. The scale of underperformance, in combination with the implications of the low participation rate, indicates that the underlying causes are systemic – not attributable to student deficits or even just 'poor teaching' – and hence call for systemic solutions. Research and analysis in South Africa point to key faults relating to curriculum structure.

Most prominent among these faults is the lack of continuity between schooling and the entry point of South Africa's standard undergraduate curricula, for all but a very small minority of school-leavers. This systemic mismatch, long known as the 'articulation gap' in South Africa (DoE 1997), has rapidly increased in significance with the growth in access that has occurred since the political transition in 1994, with the consequences of students' lack of sound educational foundations affecting their whole academic careers. As acknowledged earlier, its root cause is the poor school system, but it has been exacerbated by the higher education sector's lack of adaptation to the growing diversity of educational and linguistic backgrounds in the student body. The effects of the articulation gap are exacerbated by the rigid, one-size-fits-all parameters of South African curricula, which make no allowance for the major differentials in talented students' prior learning that arise from social inequality. Moreover, South African curricula (in comparison with, say, US liberal arts curricula) require very early specialisation which, superimposed on poor schooling, means that many students are forced to make life-determining subject choices with minimal knowledge of the nature of the disciplines or of their true interests and capacity.

To return to the question of whether South Africa's curriculum structures enable or constrain growth and transformation, a comprehensive analysis of their effects on the performance patterns outlined earlier is beyond the scope of this chapter, but the following manifestations offer evidence.

- There is a chronic shortage of candidates who meet the traditional entry requirements for key programmes in Science, Engineering and Technology (SET), Health Sciences, other professionally orientated fields, and Economics and Management, all of which are critical scarce-skills areas directly affecting development. This cannot be a true reflection of the country's potential, nor does it represent a lack of aspirations since there are large numbers of applicants for these high-status fields. The problem is again due primarily to poor schooling in core subjects, but is exacerbated by the shortage of provision in higher education for identifying and realising the potential of talented-but-disadvantaged students – that is, for addressing the articulation gap.
- High first-year attrition is a common phenomenon internationally, but in a low-participation system like South Africa's, it is both highly wasteful of talent and indicative of undue adjustment problems arising particularly from the articulation gap. Overall first-year attrition is about 30 per cent (Letseka and Maile 2008), with one in five contact-degree students being lost at that point. Failure in first-year modules affects the majority of first-time-entering students (Scott *et al.* 2007).
- Most tellingly, only a small minority of students graduate in the formally expected time. In key subject areas, well under 30 per cent of all 'contact' students graduate in the regulation time. The rates are lower in vocational programmes – a key growth area – than in general academic degrees. Again, there are strong racial differentials: the rate is under 15 per cent for black students,

where most future graduate growth must come from. The graduation rate even after four years is as low as 36 per cent for degree programmes and 26 per cent for vocational programmes, showing the length of time that even successful students need in order to overcome the systemic obstacles (Scott *et al.* 2007). The implications of this are far-reaching. The great majority of students never follow the curriculum as it has been planned, with the result that they are exposed to lack of coherence and to step-changes in difficulty and volume. Apart from contributing to failure, this means that many of the students who finally graduate obtain only marginal passes and never master their disciplines. This helps to explain the shortage of candidates, particularly black candidates, who qualify for postgraduate study.

- Evidence that curriculum structure is a major factor in underperformance also comes from the 'extended curriculum' initiative that has been developing in South Africa since the 1980s. Extended curriculum programmes increase the duration of regular degrees and diplomas by a year in order to allow for different entry levels and the integration of substantial developmental provision, with the purpose of enabling talented but disadvantaged students to establish a firm conceptual foundation for advanced studies. Extended programmes are thus designed as a systemic response to the articulation gap.

- While implementation has been patchy and funding has allowed for only a small minority of the intake (under 15 per cent) to access them, a number of extended programmes – especially in SET and other scarce skills areas – have been encouragingly successful, both in enabling responsible widening of access and in improving graduate output in disadvantaged student groups. There are a range of cases, covering all the university categories, of extended programme students outperforming their mainstream peers, despite most of them not having qualified for regular university entrance (Garraway 2009).

In summary, analysis and experience point to the significance of curriculum structure as a critical element of the teaching and learning process, particularly in contexts of widespread disadvantage and inequalities. In South Africa, it is evident from the performance patterns that the traditional three-year structure is *de facto* not the standard, and is no longer beneficial or viable for the majority of the intake, especially the under-represented groups from which future growth must come.

It is not only academic factors that result in poor performance. Material and affective factors play a significant part, and it is notable that, in the developed world, a number of retention studies attribute attrition primarily to such factors. However, apart from the intractability of socio-economic and related affective problems in developing countries, analysis of drop-out and academic exclusion patterns in some South African institutions suggests that academic obstacles *per se* (of the kind that arise from the articulation gap) are a powerful contributor, possibly the dominant one, to attrition across the board[3] (Fisher and Scott 2011). This again points to the importance of systemic educational development.

The rigidity of the curriculum and qualifications structure also has major implications for the roles and academic standards of South Africa's diverse higher education institutions, and hence for productive institutional differentiation. The twenty-three current institutions cover a very wide range of histories, student profiles, and human and material resource bases. In particular, differences between historically black and white institutions within the formal categories are at least as big as the differences between the categories. Given such differentials in capacity and student preparedness, it is not feasible for a historically disadvantaged rural university to achieve the same exit standards and outcomes as a well established and endowed research university within the same time frame and curriculum parameters. However, this is what is formally expected by the one-size-fits-all qualifications framework. There is little chance for a historically disadvantaged institution to achieve strong graduate outcomes or comparable standards without a flexible curriculum framework that allows for the curriculum space that is needed. This is of special importance in the South African context where the great majority of talented but disadvantaged students are in historically disadvantaged institutions, from which much of the necessary growth in graduate output must come.

A related matter is that a common first-world approach to addressing diversity in student background – namely categorising higher education institutions in an academic hierarchy, the best-known example of which is the American three-tier system of research universities, state colleges and community colleges – has periodically been propounded in South Africa as a solution to student underpreparedness and the articulation gap. This is a complex topic, detailed consideration of which is beyond the scope of this case study, but it may be noted here that the appropriateness of the institutional stratification model for the African context needs to be critically examined – particularly if it is seen as an alternative to university reform – because of the inherent risk of entrenching social stratification that it carries.

Last but not least, the rigid framework greatly constrains key forms of curriculum enhancement that are now increasingly regarded as essential for graduate outcomes that suit the contemporary world. While some important graduate attributes can be successfully facilitated through curriculum reorientation (as chapters in this book have shown), others need curriculum space for meaningful realisation. In the South African context, for example, critical 'new literacies' – especially quantitative and language-related academic literacies that are both learning tools and key graduate outcomes – cannot be effectively integrated into the current crowded programmes without serious risk to the core knowledge base (Muller 2009). Similarly, in a multicultural country with eleven official languages and a history of enforced segregation, learning an additional language is not only a career asset but a means of advancing cross-cultural understanding and social cohesion. Yet, as evidenced by the poor performance patterns, the formally stipulated curriculum time is wholly inadequate for effective learning even in the core disciplines. The formal framework is therefore an obstacle to the quality and breadth of graduate outcomes as well as to graduate output.

In short, there is considerable evidence that the appropriateness of the curriculum framework for its particular context is a major variable affecting success rates in higher education, and thus who succeeds and fails. In the South African context, since the performance patterns are so clearly indicative of dysfunction, one must ask who is benefiting from the status quo, and what justification there can be for retaining it. In the face of the dysfunction in the system, these questions are legitimate and important, yet are getting very little attention and no decisive action from the leadership of the higher education sector, in government or the institutions. Why this might be the case is discussed in the following section.

'Invisible' aspects of curriculum

As discussed earlier, the higher education sector can point to factors external to itself – particularly poverty and dysfunctional schooling – as primary causes of poor higher education performance, and argue that the sector should not be expected to address them. A counter-argument is the pragmatic one: that since these external factors will remain largely intractable for the foreseeable future, there is an obligation on higher education to do whatever it reasonably can to adjust to these realities.

There is also a principled argument, relating to the wider goals of transformation: that the universities should be willing to review their traditional structures and pedagogies in the spirit of extending the benefits of higher education to historically excluded students and communities. This argument does not contemplate any lowering of the value, standards or expectations of higher education – it would in fact be a bitter irony if, just as higher education became more accessible to the formerly excluded majority, the currency were to be devalued – but rather a preparedness to consider alternative means of achieving the desired ends.

Curriculum structure and assumptions can be taken as an example. South Africa's basic curriculum framework was adopted from the Scottish system in the colonial era, almost a century ago[4], and was normed on a small, privileged and largely homogeneous student body. Despite the great changes that have taken place in society, powerfully affecting the nature of the student body, the basic framework, together with the assumptions about student background and prior learning that necessarily accompany it, has not been adapted, at least not in any systemic way.

Even if the school system were not so poor, such major shifts in 'input' could be expected to prompt an examination of the effectiveness of existing approaches, as would be likely to happen in most enterprises. The widespread acknowledgement of the articulation gap should reinforce this. In the face of this *prima facie* case for reviewing traditional teaching and learning structures and processes, it is puzzling that the state and the higher education sector have not undertaken such examination. There are no doubt a variety of reasons, which justify investigation. The following are some possibilities.

First, it may be that such fundamental elements of curriculum as its underlying parameters and assumptions are so embedded in the system that they are virtually invisible. In the absence of a major policy initiative such as Bologna, this may be the case in many countries. An indicator of it in Africa is that, even though many academics are aware that different systems have very different undergraduate curriculum structures (for example, the American, English and German systems), the fundamentals of the frameworks are seldom problematised, in the literature or in institutional discourse. Even where qualifications frameworks have been foregrounded (as in South Africa and Mozambique, for example), the effort that goes into developing level-descriptors for qualification types is not matched by rigorous consideration of the entry-level assumptions about knowledge and capabilities that curricula are founded on. If these fundamentals are so taken for granted that they remain below the surface, there is no chance of their being recognised as a variable in the educational process that – as argued – can strongly affect responsible access policy and the widening of successful participation.

Second, on the infrequent occasions when the parameters of the curriculum are discussed, they are commonly seen as immutable. This perception may be founded on the belief that the starting level of higher education is universal. That this is a myth is shown by the significant differentials in entry level (and consequently the time required to get a comparable degree) between England and Scotland, where the school-leaving levels are a year apart. The differentials are greater in parts of Africa: in Southern Africa Botswana's secondary schooling ends at O-level, which is a year behind South Africa's Senior Certificate, which is in turn a year behind Zimbabwe's A-level. Since sound articulation in any particular system depends on higher education starting where the top end of secondary leaves off, there are (or need to be) significant differences in entry levels and curriculum assumptions between systems. A consequence of insufficient articulation is that, to be efficient, higher education has to remain extremely selective and exclusive, as has been the case in many SSA countries for decades.

Third, a closely related matter is that maintaining the traditional curriculum parameters is equated by many academics with maintaining academic standards. For example, in South Africa there has been considerable resistance to widening the use of extended programmes (as outlined earlier), even in institutions where the great majority of students come from severely disadvantaged educational backgrounds. Because of the isolation of the latter apartheid era, South African universities have only relatively recently been exposed to forces such as marketisation, 'massification' and financial accountability that have swept through higher education sectors across the developed world since the 1980s. Many academics have consequently seen traditional academic values and practices as being under threat. This has reinforced academic conservatism in areas over which the academic community has control, with traditional approaches regarded as essential for ensuring the desired outcomes and standards.

This situation is of course not without some justification and is not unique to South Africa. However, in contexts characterised by high levels of educational disadvantage and inequalities, academic conservatism can have particularly counter-productive effects in blocking reforms that are critical for realising the potential of the majority of the intake. In such circumstances, it can fairly be said that, if widening successful participation is accepted as essential, the only way to maintain standards is in fact to acknowledge the mismatches that have arisen, and to develop fresh educational structures and approaches that better respond to social and educational realities.

Finally, one reason why the academic community does not see curriculum fundamentals as warranting critical review is that a proportion of the student body continues to do well in the traditional framework. Focusing primarily on the top students (which in the African context usually means the best-prepared students rather than all who have strong aptitude or potential) commonly leads to underplaying the systemic teaching and learning causes of poor performance, overemphasising non-academic factors, or seeing solutions as lying outside higher education.

Apart from improving schooling, the most commonly propounded solution is to develop an intermediate college and sub-degree system that will take responsibility for preparing disadvantaged students for higher education proper. The US community college system is often referred to as a model. As noted earlier, this complex topic cannot be addressed here except to argue that, while a well-functioning college system would no doubt add value to South African education, seeing it as the central means of enabling the universities to avoid change is problematic, for pragmatic and principled reasons.

The central pragmatic reason is that, as is the case in most SSA countries, the intermediate or further education (FE) college sector is very poorly developed, and is likely to take a decade or more to make a significant contribution to fulfilling its primary mandate of providing intermediate technical and vocational education and training. Given the shortages of qualified academic staff, plant and resources that already impact severely on the universities, it does not seem feasible that the FE sector can be developed and equipped to successfully take on the task of offering sub-degree qualifications, or even of preparing disadvantaged candidates for higher education on the scale needed to absolve universities of a role in this responsibility.

The principled reason relates again to transformation as well as the internal efficiency of the education system. If direct entry from school to university is to be restricted to those who are sufficiently prepared to do well in the traditional curricula, the numbers will be a fraction of what they are now. If doing well means graduating in the regulation time, the direct-entry intake will be under a third of its current size, and under 15 per cent for black students. If doing well means not just marginally passing but mastering a discipline in a good-quality degree, the proportion will be even smaller. Direct access from school will thus revert to being limited mainly to the white middle-class community, and will be closed to virtually all township and rural students, irrespective of their potential. It would seem both inequitable and inefficient to require a talented rural student, in the top decile of her demographic group, to have to pursue university access via a college – with the additional selection hurdles that accompany this route – because the higher education sector is not prepared to respond to her learning needs.

In short, the central challenge and obligation for higher education in South Africa and other SSA countries is not just to maintain academic standards in providing for the thin layer of the population that has access to good schooling. Rather, it is to ensure that effective and good-quality provision is extended to as many as possible of the large numbers of people, especially of the youth, whose potential to succeed has been masked by their socio-economic and educational backgrounds. The developmental significance of this challenge calls for the higher education sector to be willing to consider all factors with a significant bearing on student success, including the fundamentals of the curriculum framework.

In conclusion: Implications for policy in African countries

In South Africa, disquiet about the higher education performance patterns and their effects on development is growing in areas of the state and the academic community. Local initiatives around curriculum restructuring are emerging, particularly in undergraduate Science, Engineering and Technology, and there are signs that curriculum reform is entering the national policy debate. In these circumstances, it is important that bodies concerned with higher education development should work rigorously through the issues and policy alternatives, and devise theorised exemplars of curriculum design that suit the context, in order to be well prepared to grasp opportunities to help shape national and institutional policy.

Members of the educational development community in South Africa have for a long time argued that one-size-fits-all curricula cannot accommodate the diversity in educational background that unavoidably characterises the undergraduate intake. There is increasing support for the view that what is called for instead is a flexible curriculum framework that will allow for a challenging but realistic entry level (and pace of progress) that suits the majority of the student body, while at the same time providing for the minority group of traditionally well-prepared students to follow an accelerated route. This is seen as a necessary condition for provision of the teaching and learning approaches that can realise the students' potential. While it is the institutions that must be responsible for enacting the curriculum, it is only government that can establish the qualifications and funding frameworks that the context requires.

As far as the rest of the region is concerned, participation rates show that universities in most SSA countries have historically been the preserve of a select few, but higher education is growing more rapidly in this region than in any other in the world (Africa Higher Education 2011). Given the levels of poverty, inequality and educational disadvantage in Africa, it is most likely that diversity challenges similar to those in South Africa will soon manifest themselves in a range of countries, with substantial implications for their higher education policy.

For example, the proliferation of new higher education institutions, public and especially private, is already making substantial regulatory demands, given the need to protect a vulnerable, opportunity-starved public. Allowing access to grow unchecked, without ensuring the effectiveness of provision for growing numbers of disadvantaged and underprepared students, will inevitably result in high failure rates, lowering of standards, or both. Similarly, as noted earlier, adopting American-style institutional stratification may have highly counter-productive consequences such as entrenching social and ethnic stratification and hence obstructing educational advancement for the groups who most need opportunities to develop their potential.

In the interests of their own development, SSA countries need to be willing to review the appropriateness of their higher education provision, including the structural fundamentals, if they are going to be able to reach the desired outcomes with significantly increased numbers of graduates. This includes systematically analysing the effectiveness of their traditional curriculum parameters for the realities of the context and the student body, and not uncritically accepting structures that have been inherited from colonial systems or are based on untested assumptions. The South African evidence suggests that translating such analysis into a qualifications framework where standards and outcomes are internationally benchmarked, but where the pathways to attaining these are well adapted to the context, is a necessary condition for sound higher education development and growth.

Notes

1   The 'race' or 'population group' categories referred to in this chapter are those used by Statistics South Africa with the term 'black' referring to 'African Black'.
2   To understand the performance patterns, it should be noted that South Africa's higher education qualifications framework is based on three-year 'general academic' degrees and vocational diplomas. (A one-year specialised 'Honours' degree follows the general academic degrees as a bridge into postgraduate studies proper.) There are also 'professional' first degrees, such as in Engineering, Law and Business Science, which are generally designed as four-year qualifications. The programmes are modular, being made up of full-year, semester or sometimes shorter examinable units. The performance patterns here are derived from cohort studies that track first-time-entering undergraduates until they graduate or drop out from their original institution, for up to five years. The main study used (Scott *et al.* 2007) is of the 2000 entry cohort, the latest for which comprehensive data are available. The patterns are believed to be persistent.
3   The inter-relationship between academic, affective and material factors in influencing academic performance and persistence is under-researched in South Africa. Student surveys that depend on self-reported data may have substantial shortcomings as a guide to development and policy.
4   The Scottish rather than the English model was used because the South African school system culminated in a 'matriculation' examination that was at a level similar to the Scottish 'Highers', and did not extend to the English A-level, a year higher.

References

Africa Higher Education (2011) *Higher education in sub-Saharan Africa*. http://www. arp.harvard.edu/AfricaHigherEducation/Factoids.html (accessed 16 September 2011).

AsgiSA (2007) *Accelerated and shared growth initiative for South Africa*. http:// www.info.gov.za/asgisa/asgisa.htm (accessed 16 September 2011).

DoE (Department of Education, South Africa) (1997) *A programme for the transformation of higher education. Education*. White Paper 3. Pretoria: Government Gazette No. 18207, 15 August 1997.

Fisher, G. and Scott, I. (2011, in press) Closing the skills gap in South Africa: The role of higher education. Unpublished report commissioned by the World Bank.

Garraway, J. (2009) *Success stories in Foundation/Extended Programmes*. Cape Town: Higher Education Learning and Teaching Association of Southern Africa.

Gyimah-Brempong, K. and Ondiege, P. (2011) Reforming higher education: Access, equity, and financing in Botswana, Ethiopia, Kenya, South Africa and Tunisia. In *The Africa Competitiveness Report 2011*. Geneva: World Economic Forum.

Letseka, M. and Maile, S. (2008) *High university drop-out rates: A threat to South Africa's future*. Pretoria: Human Sciences Research Council.

Muller, J. (2009) Forms of knowledge and curriculum coherence. *Journal of Education and Work*, 22(3): 205–226.

Scott, I., Yeld, N. and Hendry, J. (2007) *A case for improving teaching and learning in South African higher education*. Higher Education Monitor No. 6. Pretoria: Council on Higher Education. http://www.che.ac.za/documents/d000155/index.php (accessed 16 September 2011).

UNESCO 2010. *Education for all: Global monitoring report 2010*. Paris: UNESCO.

Chapter 14

Towards more successful curriculum change

Camille B. Kandiko and Paul Blackmore

> The best-laid schemes o' mice an' men
> Gang aft agley
> An' lea'e us nought but grief an' pain
> For promis'd joy!
>
> Robert Burns (1785)

The question of what is to be taught and learnt in universities will always be highly contentious. Answering it requires us to take a position on the kind of society we want, how we believe individuals can and should relate to others, the kinds of knowledge that we value and how we believe that people learn most effectively.

The values and practices that inform universities have traditionally been quite implicit; it has been possible for quite diverse views to co-exist in universities, usually within an overall broad shared sense of a university's purposes. That position has been challenged by many forces external to the university, which fundamentally question what a university is for. It is hardly surprising then that curriculum change can generate immensely heated debate and that it is often not successful. Such projects define, explicitly or by implication, what it means to be educated, across a hugely diverse and complex institution. Changes are usually centrally driven, implemented unevenly and rarely evaluated; none of this is unexpected. Achieving change in a university is difficult, owing to organisational complexity, strongly held and diverse values and the power of vested interests. A strong, centrally managed and uniform approach may seem the only way to produce the planned change. However, an alternative view is that curriculum change can create an environment that promotes the mission, values and goals of the institution. Curriculum reform can be an opportunity to build strategic networks, bringing together people, places and information, within and beyond an institution.

In reviewing strategic initiatives in universities across the world, we have seen the massive effort that has gone into planning and making changes. The impact on staff time is immense; there are opportunity costs in concentrating so much energy on a curriculum change. Therefore, it is vital to have a good reason for making a change and equally important to take an approach to change that is likely to be successful. We argue that an organic approach to strategic curriculum change is likely to be more productive and less damaging. Universities can deliberately support the conditions that foster it, partly through the management of incentives. This often takes a cultural shift, and minimally a renewal of values and principles. We advocate a number of positions that respond to the legitimate diversity and uncertainty that is part of all organisations, and particularly of university life.

A clear sense of purpose

Successful initiatives have been those with a clear message that is communicated effectively. A curriculum change effort competes for attention and resources with many other activities that are taking place at the same time. In addition to difficult structural and administrative hurdles, innovative curricula often increase the workload of both staff and students, particularly when they require interdisciplinary provision and engagement beyond the university. This was mentioned in the Hong Kong case study in Chapter 5 and was reported at a number of other institutions. Part of the leadership role is to provide a convincing justification for an initiative that, initially at least, entails more work for everyone involved. Curriculum change is often justified in terms of market advantage or as a response to external threats. These are negative reasons that rarely resonate with academic staff based in strong disciplines, who may feel loosely connected to the parent institution. Arguments about providing a better education are much more persuasive, especially when supported by comment from students.

Strong leadership and bold ideas can lead to significant change, even in mature, research-intensive institutions where such action would seem very difficult to achieve. The case studies in this book were chosen with this in mind. At Brown University, the statement that there are goals students 'will' embrace signifies the strength of the institution's curriculum aims. The Brown case study highlights the importance of students' responsibilities within the curriculum, albeit sufficiently supported by the institution. There was a strong drive to make connections across disciplines. As a result, students make and reflect upon intentional educational choices that draw on knowledge across disciplines, facilitated by staff. Interconnections across knowledge and practice were highlighted in the Hong Kong case study, with its focus on common experiences across human societies. This was also seen in the Melbourne case study (Chapter 10), which described how breadth in the new undergraduate degree structure could underpin a better understanding of the relevance of discipline studies in a wider context and of the value of interdisciplinary connections. The South African case study (Chapter 13) reminds us that the curriculum is more than a sequenced set of modules. There is a great opportunity for the curriculum to reflect the values and aims not only of the institution but of society.

Universities as networks

Universities are, on the whole, loosely coupled institutions that are resistant to attempts at strong, top-down control. Although they are organised into faculties or schools and into departments, in many respects they do not function in that way, and are better understood as collections of relatively non-hierarchical networks. As described throughout the book, these networks can occur:

- among people, notably staff, students and administrators;
- among bodies of knowledge and methodological approaches (interdisciplinary), driven through networks of people and disciplines;
- across the teaching and research domains of the institution (research-intensive environment);
- between the university and the local community (community engagement);
- between the institution, staff, students knowledge and the wider world (global connectedness);
- in the development of shared understandings about academic work (academic literacy).

Strategic curriculum change can acknowledge and make use of these networks and devise new ones that are beneficial, but may not have occurred 'naturally'. Such networks are founded on notions of people, socially-situated, engaging in their university environment. This means that change should promote greater social engagement. It means encouraging students to commit to their own learning and taking an active, not consumerist, role; academics committing to the sharing of knowledge, with students, colleagues, and the outside world, and not only to the generation of knowledge; and administrators working to support and show an understanding of such networks and relationships. The networked curriculum approach we argue for works to break down barriers and open up new pathways and connections. This increased flexibility in structures allows for more faculty autonomy and student choice, but at the same time more responsibility. When offering more choice and openness, institutions need to put sufficient advice and mentoring in place for students, as seen in the Brown case study. There needs to be parallel support for staff through development offerings, mentoring, coaching and leadership training.

The goal of such a networked curriculum approach is for students to learn from the processes and structure of their education and to be able to make connections, draw out themes, and integrate multiple perspectives as they carry on with their education and their professional and personal lives. Similar goals exist for faculty, for whom network approaches can bridge gaps and address societal problems, broaden their research, and increase the impact of their teaching, research and service. There are numerous ways that curriculum change efforts need to be supported throughout an institution. Rather than acting as a constraint, technology can offer ways of supporting networks. The same can be said of learning spaces, both physical and particularly virtual ones.

Large-scale changes may look transformative on websites, but often it is 'business as usual' on the ground, where top-down approaches can easily lose impetus. Effective strategic curriculum change initiatives will provide a stimulus to change social practices in the institution. Some of the more successful initiatives work by guiding change on a local level, through developing networks that promote the ideas of a curriculum change. They do not necessarily require a radical change of behaviour. A network approach does however mean that connections are not likely to be neat and consistent across an institution, and neither are the outcomes of change.

We believe a university based on creating, developing, supporting and sustaining such networks is stronger, more ethical, and more educationally sound. The current alternative, of corporate managerial models, is deeply uninviting and ultimately likely to be ineffective. At their best, universities have traditionally provided environments that foster many of the most meaningful connections of people's lives, generating and sharing knowledge in an open and collegial way. We have seen the most successful businesses adopt more university-like ways of working, with great success. It is vital that attempts to be more explicit about curriculum outcomes and to provide an educational 'product' do not result in the adoption of outmoded leadership and management practices in universities, based on wrong implicit assumptions about how effective organisational and individual learning actually happens.

Acknowledging diversity

Centrally led change often promotes a single view of a curriculum innovation, which is to be implemented uniformly across an institution. It can be argued that such an approach makes it more likely that something will change. However, universities are complex and diverse. Disciplines and professional groups have their own ways of knowing and being that are not readily reducible to a common formula. Many staff and students relate more to their discipline than they do to the institution. Indeed, in our survey, we found that most staff had a hazy idea of institutional priorities. Messages from the central management team were often felt to be at odds with the reality of teaching and researching within a discipline. Although a clear message is necessary at an institutional level, some of the most effective changes, such as at the University of Utrecht, encouraged interpretation of a broad framework at a local level, which provided a sense of ownership and flexibility for the change to fit the particular context. Networks in institutions take many forms. The case studies in this book describe distinctive approaches that institutions took to working with their mission and history, the national conditions, the local environment, the student population and the academic environment created by staff.

Promoting unbounded learning

Universities have historically assessed and recognised only formal, discipline-based study, while offering a much broader experience. In order to differentiate themselves in a competitive market and also to show that they are 'delivering' extensive benefits to students, many universities now attempt to be explicit about matters that were previously implicit. Many curriculum changes prescribe specific learning outcomes and introduce them into the formally taught curricula and into co-curricular activities too. This may allow a wider range of opportunities to be made available efficiently and effectively to all students. However, the manner in which such developments are implemented can be unproductive. Often, paradoxically, quite liberal curriculum intentions are presented in the form of tightly defined statements about what the person should know or be able to do. Thus the 'competence movement' that caused such controversy in the early 1990s in the UK re-presents itself in another guise. Such an approach also fails to acknowledge that much that is learnt is not formally taught. Many highly beneficial outcomes of a university experience are gained through serendipity rather than planning, and the gain may be very personal to the individual and related to his or her own life course. Therefore, we argue for providing an intellectual and social climate which fosters learning and does not attempt to prescribe what that learning should be.

Networks offer a powerful way of developing connections and pathways that can be used repeatedly by students and staff, promoting the sharing and creation of new knowledge. These networks will always be dynamic, and the institution needs to operate on that fundamental principle, that the outcomes of learning are not fully predictable; the process of teaching, learning and research is not linear. In creating such an environment, a university can offer students the most important education of all: the skills, abilities, attributes, and training to make connections with people, knowledge and the world beyond academia. This can be facilitated through the promotion of curriculum characteristics, which can function as networks or network pathways through institutional structures and may lead to developments in other areas, thus showing how networks can facilitate learning. By emphasising characteristics at a university-wide level, institutions can offer them status and legitimacy, covering gaps in provision through building on best practice. This was seen during the site visits where academics across institutions mentioned specific departments or academics that were leading on curricular innovations, such as interdisciplinary pedagogy, experiential-based learning and academic literacy.

Organisational climate

Throughout the book, we have analysed curriculum change initiatives in practice. This socially situated approach highlights the need to integrate pedagogical decisions with structures, institutional practices and people, including building leadership capabilities, academic development opportunities, and staff support.

Centrally mandated, uniform approaches to curriculum change are often not appropriate and often do not succeed throughout an institution. We have argued for the recognition of the networked nature of institutions, and the innate capacity that those networks have to learn and adapt. However, an institution has to retain responsibility for creating a climate in which such behaviour is allowed to take place. We found many examples where changes did not take root because the systems that were needed to support them were not in place. For example, interdisciplinary initiatives that require students to take modules in more than one school or faculty are likely to fail if the internal financial system does not allow money to follow students. If research-intensive institutions want staff to take teaching more seriously, then they have to align recognition and reward systems to ensure this. More radically, if an institution wants to heal the unhelpful divide between research and teaching, then the university's management structures should not be formed in a way that institutionalises that divide, with research and teaching functions each led by competing senior staff through research and teaching committees with no common membership.

It can be argued that an institution's need to conduct a major curriculum review is evidence that it is not a learning organisation. Some aspects have become static for so long that there is now a major problem to be addressed. An essential part of a learning organisational climate is the encouragement of review and adjustment at all levels of the institution as a normal part of the way the institution works. Strategically aligning an institution's assets can be an efficient and effective way of building an institution that supports learning and innovation. Many institutions restructured the curriculum to create a long-term sustainable learning environment, which can offer a cost-conscious dynamic structure that can evolve and change over time without needing major, time-intensive, expensive overhaul.

Safeguarding the university

The emphasis on student experience is very strong in higher education literature and system-level and institutional practice. This is a healthy corrective to a traditional situation where students had little influence over the curriculum. However, less attention is paid to the academic staff experience. Along with efficiency and effectiveness of change must come attention to the institutional culture. Changes that are implemented without concern for the additional burdens placed on staff are costly in terms of goodwill and the individual and collective sense of well-being.

A university is more than the sum of those who currently work in it. It exists as an idea, as an institution with traditions. Some institutions are of such antiquity and are perhaps so secure in their identity and role, that they feel they can resist calls for change, although in fact even the most traditional change over time in response to new circumstances. Resistance to change may be both good and undesirable. In many universities, rapid staff turnover and frequent government intervention can weaken the sense of identity at an institutional level. When a university is regarded simply as a unit for producing research and teaching, a great deal has been lost. Some of the more effective curriculum renewals, particularly in the US, occur when an institution has a clear sense of what it aspires to be and adjusts its provision to ensure that it is keeping abreast of contemporary needs, but without losing sight of its own institutional traditions.

Ideally, academic and staff development creates processes that support the educational values of an institution and conveys them to incoming staff, reiterating them for established staff. It can do so by supporting teaching, the primary connection that links academics and students in the university. Evaluation can assist by tracking progress, measuring success and creating opportunities for improvement.

Researching curriculum change

Members of institutions very often visit other universities that have engaged in curriculum change to learn from their experiences. However, our impression is that even among the institutions we visited, which were all from higher education systems that are relatively closely linked, knowledge of the global picture was patchy. One of the most striking findings of our survey was that very little research of any kind is undertaken in conjunction with strategic curriculum initiatives. Review groups quite frequently seek the opinions of a number of stakeholders, but rarely seem to sponsor any serious conceptual clarification or detailed exploration of the complex issues with which they are dealing, either at an organisational level or in relation to the educational questions that arise, particularly around the processes of teaching and assessment. While we acknowledge the dangers of 'paralysis by analysis' and the tension between the pace of much research and the need for institutions to move swiftly, the lack of research seems quite surprising. We found very few instances, for example, of an institution's education department having a role in curriculum change.

Evaluation offers a means of tracking progress, measuring success and creating opportunities for improvement but few initiatives have had a robust evaluation strategy. We have not found examples of universities undertaking a baseline study at the commencement of a change in order to measure the effects of the change. Although changes are often introduced in order to improve specific aspects of the students' experience and with the intention of improving learning outcomes, it is unusual for any institution to examine systematically whether any of the desired improvements have taken place. Some evaluation activity can be found, but the political cost of an innovation being judged not to have worked means that most institutions avoid such scrutiny. Therefore we argue for universities to use their own research capacity to help them undertake better curriculum change.

Closing comment

For many, globalisation and rapid economic and social change appear to threaten the traditional role of universities. However, it can equally be argued that this is a time of unparalleled opportunity for higher education, with a global recognition of its central importance and in most countries an increasing willingness to invest in it. Now more than ever, institutions need to be clear about what they are offering to their students, and should do so in ways that reflect what we know about how universities actually work.

Index